Social Capital

Social Capital

*Critical Perspectives on Community
and "Bowling Alone"*

EDITED BY

*Scott L. McLean, David A. Schultz,
and Manfred B. Steger*

New York University Press

NEW YORK AND LONDON

NEW YORK UNIVERSITY PRESS
New York and London

Library of Congress Cataloging-in-Publication Data
Social capital : critical perspectives on community and "Bowling alone" /
edited by Scott L. McLean, David A. Schultz, and Manfred B. Steger.
p. cm.
Includes bibliographical references.
ISBN 0-8147-9813-6 (cloth : alk. paper) — ISBN 0-8147-9814-4 (pbk. : alk. paper)
1. United States—Social conditions—1945–   2. Social capital (Sociology)—United States.
3. Social change—United States—History—20th century.
4. Putnam, Robert D. Bowling Alone.   I. McLean, Scott L.
II. Schultz, David A. (David Andrew), 1958–   III. Steger, Manfred B., 1961–
HN65 .S567   2002
306'.0973—dc21   2002008212

New York University Press books are printed on acid-free paper,
and their binding materials are chosen for strength and durability.

Manufactured in the United States of America
10 9 8 7 6 5 4 3 2 1

*To Carey McWilliams, teacher, colleague, friend.
You taught us more about democracy and civic engagement
than we could ever have imagined.*

As soon as public service ceases to be the main concern of the citizens and they come to prefer to serve the state with their purse rather than their person, the state is already close to ruin.

—Jean-Jacques Rousseau, *The Social Contract*

Contents

Foreword

Douglas Rae

Ideas become important not because scholars and intellectuals invent them, but because, once invented, they happen to answer to the pressing demands of a historical period. Most ideas emanating from the academy never become important, because they answer to nothing more forceful than the isolated nattering of a specialty journal. Some other notions— peace, freedom, justice—have answered the call in so many periods that they seem ahistorical, worn smooth like pebbles after a billion turns in the surf. Social capital is very different, a jagged stone hewn from its cliff only yesterday in historical time. As far as we know, the idea was chipped from the earth by one Lyda J. Hanifan in a piece published during World War I:

> In the use of the phrase *social capital* I make no reference to the usual [understanding] of the term *capital*, except in a figurative sense. I do not refer to real estate, or to personal property or to cold cash, but rather to that in life which tends to make these tangible substances count for most in the daily lives of people, namely goodwill, fellowship, mutual sympathy and social intercourse. . . . (Hanifan 1916)

Hanifan's notion of social capital is, as she makes obvious, built on the metaphor of economic capital. She was, after all, writing at just the time when capital*ism* was reaching its maturity in the vertically integrated joint stock corporation (Chandler 1962)—and at a time when that same system of capitalist production heaped up greater and greater concentrations of plant, housing, and work force in its signature creation, the industrial city. For more conventional observers, the industrial city was a social pox—a magnet for the unwashed, a clattering disturbance of nature's slow rhythms, a profit-turning evil from which the bourgeoisie should take the money and run (Fishman 1987). For all its smoke and noise, the industrial city was a dynamo for the production of capital—most obviously economic capital, but also *social* capital. Several others, including urbanist Jane Jacobs, have since independently discovered this idea, and Robert Putnam has made it part of the ordinary language with his *Bowling Alone.* But the importance of this idea owes a great deal to its historical origin, so it is worth taking the time to situate this book of critical interpretation in relation to the historical moment that provoked Hanifan's spark of insight.

When she wrote her essay, Hanifan was State Supervisor of Rural Schools for the very rural state of West Virginia. Like Putnam eight decades later, she looked at her human environment through the lens of social capital and saw *its absence*: "That there is today almost a total lack of such social capital in rural districts throughout the country need not be retold. . . . Everybody who has made either a careful study or close observations of country life conditions knows that to be true" (Hanifan 1916, 131). Hanifan's task was defined by the question, "How could these conditions be made better?"[1] Her guiding metaphor was very specifically the joint stock corporation:

> In community building as in business organization and expansion there must be an accumulation of capital before constructive work can be done. In building up a large business enterprise of modern proportions, there must first be an accumulation of capital from a large number of individuals. When the financial resources . . . have been brought together . . . they take the form of a business corporation whose purpose is to produce an article of consumption—steel, copper, bread, clothing—or to provide personal conveniences—transportation, electricity, thoroughfares. The people benefit by having such products and conveniences available for their daily needs, while the capitalists benefit from the profits reserved to themselves. . . . Now we may easily pass from the business corporation over to the social corporation, the community, and find many points of similarity. The individual is helpless socially if left entirely to himself. Even the association of members of one's own family fails to satisfy. . . . If he may come into contact with his neighbors, and they with other neighbors, there will be an accumulation of social capital, which may immediately satisfy his social needs and which may bear a social potentiality sufficient to substantial improvement of living conditions for the whole community. The community as a whole will benefit by the cooperation of all its parts, while the individual will find in his associations the advantages of the help, the sympathy, and the fellowship of his neighbors. (131)

Hanifan's explicit model is the joint stock corporation, and her implicit trope is, of all things, the dense neighborhood of the industrial city—dense in people, dense in social connections, dense in civic associations, dense in retail proprietorship, dense in ward politics. Unlike the patchwork isolation of the countryside, where neighbors are too distant for neighborliness, and where lives are lived so diffusely that trust is limited to family, the city is a great factory for social capital. Hanifan sees the absence of dense connectivity as a great disadvantage for rural places—and, by implication, a great advantage of urban places. To borrow language from this book's introduction, urban density of the sort which prevailed in Hanifan's day generates and sustains "networks that bind and lubricate interactions" (McLean, Schultz, and Steger, this volume).

Hanifan saw the absence of social capital in cross-section, looking from the countryside into the city; Putnam saw it in historical perspective, looking backward at the twentieth century. They were both seeing the same story, which consists in the process by which capitalism first built the socially dense city and then dismantled it. The first phase seems to have begun, roughly speaking, in the 1840s with the appearance of immense energy and shipping advantages for steam-based industrial production at rail-head and harbor-based lowland cities (Nye 1998). By the World War I era, these cities were at their midsummer's day with immense economic energy and exceedingly dense patterns of social interaction. New Haven in that period may serve as an illustration, with:

- Workers and bourgeoisie alike living, in the main, less than a half-hour walk from their place of employment.
- Retail density in the neighborhoods so great that more than 600 groceries served a city of about 160,000, one store for every 270 people or about 90 households.
- A "civic fauna" of fraternal and sororal associations, athletic teams, churches, temples, and neighborhood associations roughly ten times denser than what exists today.
- A political process, with parties and ward committees so fine-grained, and so absorbent, as to integrate thousands of persons into the government of the city.
- A poverty of indirect, electronic communication, encouraging close face-to-face interaction.
- The near-total absence of broadcast media.

All this depended on an historical accident, a concatenation of technological, institutional, and cultural forces that had begun to unravel even before Hanifan's writing. Once George Westinghouse's alternating current system of electrical transmission had vanquished Edison's direct current system, the energy advantage of central place location was all but erased—for manufacturing, for commerce, and, most consequential of all, for residential life. And once Henry Ford's Model T had come down in price to about $300 in the early 1920s, so that he could dispose of close to 100,000 per month nationally, the armory for the destruction of urban density was irresistible (Biggs 1996). With a great deal of encouragement—prodding, manipulation, even bribery—from capitalist enterprise, the great majority of American households have rejected the dense urban neighborhood, with all of its challenges. In our millions, we have moved away from urban density toward the suburban cul de sac, away from the club hall to the living room, away from the local athletic team and its besplintered bleachers to the safe and comfortable isolation of the TV and upholstered chair. The transformations are many, but a few stand out:

- Where we once lived close to work, and close to others very different from ourselves, we now live far from work, and close only to others similar to ourselves (Sennett 1970).
- Where neighborhoods once included all manner of activity, single-use zoning now dominates (Jacobs 1961).
- Where once retailing was very local, and closely integrated with place, it is now dominated by large outlets, owned by distant multinationals.[2]
- Religious congregations to one side, the civic fauna of many cities has all but collapsed (Hall 1999).
- Political participation in local politics, to say nothing of national, has fallen steadily (Putnam 2000).
- Face-to-face communications have been supplanted in many cases by indirect, unidirectional, and asynchronous media such as the telephone, broadcast media, and the Web.

Taken together, these changes are the mainspring of change in the twentieth century, and the idea of social capital is important because it responds to them.

It is beyond question that these changes are real, that they are of immense importance in everyday life, and that they leave us as a nation with no direct model of the sort which Lyda Hanifan saw in urban life at its peak. We have lost that model, and in its place we have an idea. And an idea of this kind is no small resource. Attempts in the late twentieth century to deal with the loss of community, the passing of the industrial city, the withering of old neighborhoods have been at once superficial and expensive. Dollars are easier to find than ideas in coping with our cities and their regions in the early years of a new century. In the hands of scholars like Putnam, and the hands of his critics—including those assembled in this volume, the idea of social capital will be refined, and may very well become a critical element of the way we seek our future as a society in coming generations.

Notes

1. Hanifan's actual strategy was to deploy school teachers as organizers or social workers, bringing rural families together for "sociables," for debates and lectures, for the formation of athletic teams, and for the carrying out of community projects. In the case study discussed in her paper, Hanifan addresses a very small, low-density area defined by its school district.

2. Most of the familiar East Coast grocery chains such as Stop and Shop, A&P, Giant, and Krogers are wholly owned subsidiaries of multinationals, such as Ahold (Netherlands) and Sainsbury (UK).

References

Biggs, L. 1996. *The Rational Factory: Architecture, Technology, and Work in America's Age of Mass Production.* Baltimore: Johns Hopkins University Press.

Chandler, A. D. J. 1962. *Strategy and Structure: Chapters in the History of the Industrial Enterprise.* Cambridge: MIT Press.

Fishman, R. 1987. *Bourgeois Utopias: The Rise and Fall of Suburbia.* New York: Basic Books.

Hall, P. D. 1999. "Vital Signs: Organizational Population Trends and Civic Engagement in New Haven, Connecticut, 1850–1998." In *Civic Engagement in American Democracy.* Ed. by Theda Skocpol and Morris P. Fiorina. Washington, D.C.: Brookings.

Hanifan, L. J. 1916. "The Rural Community Center." *Annals of the American Academy of Political and Social Science* 67: 130–38.

Jacobs, J. 1961. *The Death and Life of Great American Cities.* New York: Random House.

Nye, D. E. 1998. *Consuming Power: A Social History of American Energies*. Cambridge: MIT Press.

Putnam, R. 2000. *Bowling Alone: The Collapse and Revival of American Community*. New York: Simon & Schuster.

Sennett, R. 1970. *The Uses of Disorder: Personal Identity and City Life*. New York: W. W. Norton.

Introduction

Scott L. McLean

David A. Schultz

Manfred B. Steger

The 1995 publication of Robert Putnam's article "Bowling Alone: America's Declining Social Capital" heralded the concept of "social capital" to new prominence in the debates on civil society and political participation. In this essay and a series of related publications that culminated in his magisterial study, *Bowling Alone: The Collapse and Revival of American Community* (2000), the Harvard political scientist argued that social capital has been declining since the end of the 1950s. For Putnam, social capital signifies the measurable number and density of a society's human connections and memberships that connect us in civil society. In his view, the diminishing stock of social capital in America is the leading cause of political disengagement and the public's widespread mistrust of politics. Putnam's haunting image of alienated Americans "bowling alone" in postmodern alleys dominated by omnipresent television screens captured the imagination of conservatives, liberals, and communitarians alike. His yearning for a society with higher levels of social trust has resonated strongly with American policy makers and researchers, sparking a conference on social capital at the White House and drawing increased scholarly attention to the subject. Even popular culture seems to be embracing the "bowling alone" theme. The popular television series *Ed* centers on a lonely New York lawyer who returns to his sleepy Ohio hometown and rescues a dilapidated bowling alley, only to discover that the only way to attract new bowlers is to offer them free advice on how to sue others in the community. The lesson, it seems, is that civic revival will have to contend with a larger political and cultural system that promotes the pursuit of self-interest and political indifference.

Indeed, dismal voting statistics in the United States seem to bear out Putnam's worst fears. Since the end of World War II, the percentage of the American population voting in presidential elections has dropped from around 65 percent to about 50 percent. At the state and local levels, it is not uncommon for less than 40 percent of the population to vote, with many school board elections generating turnouts of barely 5 percent. Today, the voter turnout in the United States is the lowest among major western European-style democracies. The Vietnam War and the Watergate scandal have contributed to a serious rise in the distrust, cynicism, and anger that Americans feel for government in general. The Iran-Contra affair and the impeachment of President Clinton have made matters even worse.

As the public's trust in governmental institutions has declined, many of the traditional modes of democratic participation—voting, campaigning, attending meetings, and even talking about politics—have also ebbed. It is perhaps a sign of the times that despite the stakes and competitiveness of the 2000 presidential elections, 49 percent of eligible voters did not bother to go to the polls. Voter interest in the election peaked only when the "boring" policy debates before election day gave way to the more entertaining struggle for power during the vote recount (Vanishing Voter Project 2000). Certainly the framers of the U.S. Constitution expected the clash of interests and distrust of government. Indeed, they believed self-interest, properly channeled by political institutions, with a dose of apathy, would actually serve to stabilize the regime (Madison, 1787; Dahl 2000; Huntington 1983). Thus the question: Is the rise in political distrust and indifference in our postmodern age of globalization a cause for alarm?

Scholars who argue that political disengagement is caused by the unraveling of "civil society" respond to this question affirmatively. In recent years, these scholars have begun to turn away from the political parties, interest groups, and individual rights to focus instead on what they see as the erosion of "civil society" (Barber 1998; Bellah et al. 1996; Carter 1999; Etzioni 1996; Fowler 1991; Rosenblum 1998). According to this view, citizen support for democratic government is weaker because society is less civil. Since the middle of the eighteenth century, European and American thinkers have used the term *civil society* to describe a type of political association which places its members under the influence of its laws and mores and thereby ensures peaceful order and good government (Keane 1988). Today's civil society enthusiasts argue that democratic political institutions depend on voluntary associations in civil society for their stability and vigor. In civil society we learn to cooperate with one another, trust one another, and create a shared civil respect for fellow citizens.

Robert Putnam's catchy metaphor for civic disengagement in America, "bowling alone," represents the most recent phase of the new fascination with civil society. His concept of "social capital" networks that bind us and lubricate our interactions offers a potential measure of the vitality of civil society. In his research, Putnam purported to show that the nation's stock of "social capital" has measurably declined since the 1950s. He notes that while more Americans than ever are bowling, they are no longer organized in networks of leagues, as was common during the 1950s. Instead, Putnam insists they are bowling alone, or at best, in small homogeneous groups of family and close friends.

In like manner, membership has declined in a vast array of voluntary associations. Associations like bowling leagues functioned as a bridge between individuals in different ethnic groups and classes. They strengthened individuals in their capacity to organize still more associations. But since the 1950s, regular, habitual, and active participation in formal associations with diverse others has given way to informal, sporadic, and individualized participation in small, more homogeneous groups. Gone are the Norman Rockwellian days when Americans joined clubs by the scores, regularly attended PTA meetings, and participated wholeheartedly in league sports such as bowling. Our image-driven, postmodern world is increasingly characterized by solitary television watching, alienation, declining membership in school and after-work functions, and flaccid forms of civic engagement.

Surely, Putnam is correct in emphasizing that democracies require citizen activism and involvement if they are to thrive (Dahl 2000). Yet, there remain open questions about social capital and civic engagement, including whether those social resources are really being depleted. In fact, some of Putnam's most vociferous critics are not convinced by his arguments at all, raising serious questions regarding the role voluntary associations play or ought to play in American society. Largely unquestioned in the academic debates on Putnam's empirical measurements, however, were the normative implications of his social capital theory. The Harvard scholar leaves little doubt that America experienced a decline in some face-to-face forms of participation in the last forty years, but what does that mean with respect to future values? Has it become impossible to rebuild a civic society? If citizens tried to revive the old patterns of American civic culture, would the country really be better off? If so, for whom and in what respects? These normative questions hold deep implications for political theory and political practice.

The original essays collected in this volume reflect the growing interest in the social sciences and humanities in social capital and the role it plays in facilitating collaborative and collective actions. In their critical encounter with the dominant "Putnam-school" approach, the contributors to this volume explore the concept of social capital from various historical, political, and philosophical perspectives. Overall, then, the main objective of this anthology is to respond to three basic questions about the relationship between social capital research, political theory, and democratic politics in America:

1. What are the normative, historical, and empirical foundations of social capital theory?
2. What role, if any, does social capital play in the maintenance of democratic political institutions?
3. To what extent does Robert Putnam's discussion of social capital provide a new theoretical conception of the relationship between the individual, civil society, and the democratic state?

Before turning to the contributors' responses to these questions, a brief history of the concept, as well as clarification of the conceptual tensions within social capital research, are needed.

Origins of Social Capital Theory

While Robert Putnam has done the most to bring social capital into vogue in the United States, he acknowledges that he did not invent the term. He offers several conceptualizations of social capital, noting that the term had been independently invented at least six times in the twentieth century (Putnam 2000, 19). He asserts that the core idea of social capital is that "social networks have value" and that increased "social contacts affect the productivity of individuals and groups" (19). Social capital refers to "connections among individuals—social networks and norms of reciprocity and trustworthiness that arise from them" (19). Putnam suggests this is a new twist on traditional ideals of "civic virtue" and "community"; he argues that social capital can be useful for bridging or bonding purposes; and he emphasizes its qualities as something which self-interested individuals invest in and which has important social externalities (22). In a word, social capital is good for individuals and for society.

The French sociologist Pierre Bourdieu appears to have first introduced the term "social capital" in the contemporary sense in a 1980 study (Bourdieu 1980; Portes 1998). Yet his use of *le capital social* received little attention in France and it was not until 1985 that his first English conceptualization of the term appeared. In seeking to understand the different forms of capital available to individuals, Bourdieu defined social capital as "the aggregate of the actual or potential resources which are linked to possession of a durable network of more or less institutionalized relationships of mutual acquaintance or recognition" (Bourdieu 1985, 248). This definition depicted social capital in functional terms—as something essential for building up economic capital and social status—and essential for maintaining the possibility for future social participation.

The sociologist Glenn Loury was the next major researcher to employ social capital in his work, using the concept to refer to intergenerational mobility and the assets and opportunities that families pass on to individuals (Loury 1981). Yet he offered no clear definition of the term. Instead, it was James Coleman (2000), a theorist of education, who became attached to the term to address crucial issues in the educational system. Seeking to explain the causes of social action, Coleman argues that social theorists have historically posited one of two claims. Sociologists tend to consider individuals embedded in a layer of social rules and norms, whereas economists often depict humans as independent agents who construct their own norms and values (Coleman 2000, 15). As an alternative to these dominant perspectives, Coleman employs the concept of social capital to describe human interaction as premised upon rational action:

> Social capital is defined by its function. It is not a single entity but a variety of different entities, with two elements in common: they all consist of some aspect of social structures, and they facilitate certain actions of actors . . . within the structure . . . Like other forms of capital, social capital is productive, making possible the achievement of certain ends that in its absence would not be possible. (Coleman 2000, 16)

For Coleman, social capital is, therefore, not a characteristic of individual agents but "inheres in the structure of relations between actors and among actors (Coleman 2000, 160). It is "the connective tissue" of society, which makes it easier for people to trust each other and build routinized relationships, especially in the area of commerce.

Put differently, Coleman sees social capital in functional terms as something that actors will pursue and attempt to accumulate. Its value lies in how it makes social, especially commercial, intercourse possible. According to Coleman, market exchanges, clandestine study circles, and letting children ride on mass transportation unescorted are three ideal-typical examples of actions that are facilitated by the existence of social capital. He differentiates among various types of social capital, which he discusses in the context of the family and the community, social norms and sanctions, and information channels. Finally, and most important, Coleman describes social capital as a public good that is created as a by-product of other activities. In his view, social capital is indispensable for the production of other forms of capital (Coleman 2000, 35).

Taken as a functional statement about society in general, Coleman's theory appears to be on the mark. Social capital constitutes a public good that people may utilize even when they are not well connected themselves. On the level of the individual, however, Coleman's argument is less persuasive. Like physical capital, social capital represents in capitalist societies a fundamentally private good, albeit one with significant social effects. Since cooperation is necessary for all persons as a means of achieving their self-interested ends, individuals will produce social capital as a fundamentally private good. Still, as in Adam Smith's "invisible hand," social capital (like physical capital) is inseparably linked to "externalities"—certain benefits (or harms) that other persons can receive without contributing anything or cooperating with anyone in its direct creation. In short, individuals may benefit—or be harmed—through social networks forged by others.

Bowling Alone

Robert Putnam has alternated between emphasizing social capital as a private good for individuals and a public good for groups. In his award-winning 1993 study *Making Democracy Work: Civic Traditions in Modern Italy*, he drew on Coleman and emphasized social capital as a public good. Social capital is defined there as "those features of social organization, such as trust, norms, and networks, that can improve the efficiency of society by facilitating coordinated actions" (167). Putnam attributes numerous benefits of social capital, including facilitation of voluntary and spontaneous cooperation, the ability to maintain credit associations, and other forms of social commerce. He seems to indicate that people will want to produce more social capital because it has instrumental value for the individual, but he also asserts that as a society we ought to try to produce social capital because it is good for making us a community. Moreover, he concludes that people's engagement in civil society not only improves a community's economic performance, but also has a significant impact on the quality of democratic governance (Putnam 1993, 117, 152). The economic success and governmental performance of the northern Italian communities, and the weakness of the same in the south, is explained by their differing amounts of "social capital" (Putnam 1993, 181–85).

Although *Making Democracy Work* emphasizes the positive impact of social capital on the market and the state, the book virtually ignores the possibility that social capital might have adverse effects on society. It was not until his influential essay "Bowling Alone: America's Declining Social Capital" (1995a) that Putnam provided a richer theoretical groundwork for his crucial distinction between benign, "bridging" forms of social capital and potentially destructive, "bonding" types of social capital. In a trilogy of essays in the *Journal of Democracy* (1995a), *PS: Political Science and Politics* (1995b), and *The American Prospect* (1996), Putnam extended his definition of social capital to refer to "those features of social life—networks, norms, and trust—that enable participants to act more effectively to pursue shared objectives" (Putnam 1996, 34). Rejecting most of the established hypotheses accounting for the decline in civic participation, increased mobility, suburbanization, pressures on time and money, generational change, and women entering the work force—he ultimately identifies television watching as the "main culprit" in the erosion of social capital.

He states that bowling leagues embody "bridging" forms of social capital and are more conducive to strengthening liberal democracy than associations like the Ku Klux Klan, which represent "bonding" types of social capital. Yet Putnam's theory does not explain how societies can generate bridging capital necessary for vibrant bowling leagues while at the same time also accumulating bonding capital that encourages the formation of such illiberal associations as the Klan or Militia groups. In other words, the generation of more social capital does not necessarily lead to a flowering of the "good aspects" of liberal democracy. As Peter Berkowitz (1999) and Michael Edwards (2000) have emphasized, social capital can be put to many uses, some of them undemocratic.

Putnam's methodology and data in his original article provoked a number of critical responses. For example, some skeptics questioned whether group memberships and civic activities are actually on the decline, or whether they are merely being replaced by new activities in smaller, less formal groups (Ladd 1999). As Nicholas Lehmann put it, we may be bowling alone, but we are also "kicking in groups" as soccer leagues have reached new heights of popularity in America (Lehmann 1996). Other critics accused Putnam of being caught in a "logical circularity" where social capital is theorized as both a cause and effect of civic action (Cobb et al. 1995; Edwards and Foley 1998; Portes 1998; Tarrow 1996). Still others maintain that Putnam neglects the crucial role played by public authorities in the creation of social capital (Maloney et al. 2000). The critics' focus on what they consider Putnam's faulty methodology was exacerbated by the discovery that the data utilized in the original "Bowling Alone" article were flawed.

In exemplary scholarly fashion, Putnam took some of these criticisms to heart and spent the next four years digging for stronger evidence of civic decline in America. The landmark publication of Putnam's *Bowling Alone: The Collapse and Revival of American Community* (2000) refines and develops many of his earlier claims. The study seemed to provide a resounding reposte to his detractors. Elaborating on his earlier argument and armed with a rich new data source—the DDB Needham Life Style surveys measuring decades of consumer preferences and behavior—Putnam hoped to put to rest any doubts about whether there had been a major change in civic activity in the United States since the 1960. His alarming conclusion is that the erosion of social capital has frayed the fabric of civil society.

Normative Dilemmas

While Putnam seems to have succeeded in detecting the disappearance of social capital in civil society, the wider political implications of these social changes remain unclear. For example, Putnam's evidence gives very little assistance in evaluating why an increase in social capital would necessarily lead to more democratic participation in the political realm (Barber 1998; Fukuyama 1995; McKnight 1995; Rosenblum 1998). Moreover, different cultures produce different visions of the relationship between democracy and civil society. In Asia, Eastern Europe, and Latin America, the concept is often attached to a utopian vision of a self-determined community resisting an authoritarian state. In such circumstances, the primary political goal is to establish the institutional foundations of civil society (Havel 1997). Conversely, in the United States and other Western liberal democracies, the idea of civil society is often connected to a nostalgic yearning for the rejuvenation of old customs and institutions (Barber 1998).

In short, Putnam's analysis misses the fact that civil society is historically amorphous and has an ambiguous relationship with order, revolution, and democratic politics. This shortcoming is especially obvious in the context of current discussions of international civil society and the phenomenon of globalization. Although the literature provides many definitions of globalization, James Mittelman (2000, 5–6) identifies two main categories. The first of these is to point to an increase in interconnections, or interdependence, a rise of transnational flows, and an intensification of processes such that the world is, in some respects, becoming a single global society. The second definition is more theoretical and emphasizes the compression of time and space. Globalization clearly alters the nature of any debate on civil society, because it implies the possibility of a global civil society emerging out of the conflict between capitalist and interstate spheres. As nationally based voluntary associations increasingly forge transnational links to other groups, the very character of civil society changes. Hence, Putnam's analysis of trends in American civil society remains incomplete without a comparative dimension that captures the significance of these burgeoning interconnections around the world. Indeed, the salience of globalization to any communitarian theory or study of civil society has to be exposed to critical examination (Jones 2000, 72).

Another issue concerns the implications of Putnam's view of social capital as an attribute of private individuals. Indeed, Putnam seems to be attracted to the rational-choice economists' definition of social capital as informal norms produced as a private good in order to facilitate cooperation. According to this perspective, social capital emerges spontaneously when there are habitual patterns of social interaction which are likened to repeated "prisoner's dilemma" games. In such a game, the purported rational strategy of humans is to defect, not to cooperate. Robert Axelrod (1984) argues that repeating this game over and over with the chance of meeting the same players again leads to a rational strategy of reciprocity, one in which cooperation is rewarded with cooperation, defection punished by defection: cooperation begets more cooperation from players in reiterated prisoner's dilemma. As individuals interact repeatedly over time, they develop a self-interested stake in having a reputation for honesty, reliability, and trustworthiness. Hence, we achieve an individualistic explanation for social mores.

Rational-choice theorists assert that such behavior is not a matter of altruism. People don't require more "civility" in order to have more social capital. As Immanuel Kant noted two centuries ago, even a society of "devils" will cooperate with each other along rational lines, so long as it serves their self-interest. If it becomes less likely that the players will encounter each other again in the future, however, or if players become anonymous to one another, the strategy of reciprocity will be displaced by a less cooperative strategy. Under such conditions, social capital will wither away. It leads to the question: Is it really possible to construct a public-spirited community on the privatistic motives of individuals? More likely, as Mancur Olson explained, civic engagement becomes rent-seeking by hyperactive interest organizations and corporations, competing to divert public resources to its own members at the expense of the common good.

We find, and the essays in this volume also reveal this, such rational-choice interpretations of social capital and civic engagement severely flawed because they are remarkably ahistorical and contextless. Ultimately, the rise and decline of social capital cannot be explained by rational-choice games alone. After all, many of society's norms and values are lodged in hierarchical structures of authority such as religion and traditional institutions. People tend to obey these norms and remain loyal to them, not out of enlightened self-interest, but for nonrational reasons such as identity, faith, and feelings of duty. Norms from these sources do not come about from bargaining patterns but are passed down from generation to generation through processes of socialization and habit. They change slowly, unpredictably, and often because of unforeseen developments such as war or dramatic economic change. Tradition—or "path-dependence" as Putnam prefers to call it sometimes—means that norms that are "suboptimal" for individuals can persist for a very long period of time in society. Hence, civic connections in institutions tend to precede individuals in time, rather than follow from their rational choices in a market (or politics).

To be sure, traditional norms are socially constructed, often by accident, but some of these values are more durable and more stubbornly held than others. It is precisely the erosion of those forms of civic participation that rely on a sense of faith and moral duty, rather than on economic self-interest or state coercion, which are said to be in decline (Wolfe 1998). A civic culture cannot simply be "re-invented," no matter how much social capital theorists such as Putnam would like to see that happen. Thus, to the extent that economistic assumptions are built into the social capital paradigm, it is difficult to see whether attempts to build up more social capital can successfully revive American community.

The Essays in This Volume

Our brief review of Putnam's work has mapped out the clusters of issues in social capital theory that are of shared concern to the contributors of this collection. All of them credit Putnam with effectively demonstrating that American civic life has dramatically changed since the 1950s. In addition, there is agreement among all the authors that civic engagement is important for democracy and that Putnam is correct that political partici-pation has declined. But do Putnam's interpretations of these trends and the concepts he develops adequately capture the politics of social engage-ment in the twentieth century? Do his prescriptions for rebuilding civic capacity in America offer the foundation for a practical democratic theory in the twenty-first century? The essays also complement each other in their areas of criticism—Putnam's account of American history, his assess-ment of economic forces, his relationship to the tradition of political phi-losophy, and his notions of cultural and political change.

Yet the contributors offer critical responses to Putnam's work from var-ious perspectives.

In chapter 1, Amy Fried offers a critical assessment of Putnam's debt to Alexis de Tocqueville's *Democracy in America*. She argues that Putnam's studies do not pay sufficient attention to the impact of political and social institutions on citizens' communal attitudes and actions—a key concern of Tocqueville's. Specifically, she points out that Putnam's social capital approach neglects how unequal distribution of economic resources di-rectly relates to concentration of political power and the decline of politi-cal participation.

John Ehrenberg in chapter 2 discusses the idea of civil society and the role it plays in *Bowling Alone*. Ehrenberg has reservations about the use of Putnam's view of civil society as a cure for our democratic ills. Civil soci-ety is asked to do too much—revive communities, train citizens, and build habits of trust and cooperation. But the corresponding role of national and state government in this hoped-for civic revival has not been developed.

David Schultz in chapter 3 continues this line of discussion by contrasting Putnam's understanding of "voluntary associations" with that of the postwar pluralist school as a way to clarify the role they play in his political ontology, that is, his conception of how groups and individuals are related to democratic participation in politics. Schultz argues that Putnam lacks a structuralist perspective on democracy, conceives of social capital as an individual attitude, and in so doing, he fails to appreciate forces in the polity and economy that cause civic indifference. We may be bowling alone, not by individual choice, but as a result of the vast growth of corporations and interest groups since the 1950s.

Michael Shapiro in chapter 4 focuses on Putnam's romanticization of "face-to-face" associations and how he discounts the civic possibilities for new technologies. Shapiro uses a postmodern perspective which challenges Putnam's nineteenth-century neo-Tocquevillian assumptions about civic space and association, arguing that new technologies alter the frame of social agency and transform traditional notions of territory, association, and citizenship and point toward a civic renaissance.

Steven Smith and Jessica Kulynych develop a critique of the language of social capital in chapter 5. They argue that the term *social capital* obscures distinctions crucial to several important traditions, including Greek ideals of virtue, classical liberalism, conservatism, and neo-liberalism. The result, according to them, is that social capital exiles political talk from civic discourse, and impedes our ability to conceive of politics other than in terms of market capitalism. Their chapter calls for political scientists to develop alternatives to the term *social capital,* and the authors suggest the term *social capacity. Social capacity* avoids implying, as *social capital* does, that economic capital is a substitute for the rich network of communal relations that makes civic engagement possible.

Chapter 6 by Scott McLean looks at Putnam's generational explanations for social capital decline. Putnam asserts that major national events have a formative impact on the future political behavior of age cohorts. Yet political scientists have found virtually no direct evidence that major events experienced during youth have any systematic impact on political views or patterns of political behavior later in life. Moreover, McLean argues, Putnam does not distinguish between personal memories—formative events that are immediate and personal—and events that are represented to citizens by media and shaped by national and international political leaders and movements. McLean argues therefore that any generational explanation for civic engagement must take into account the role of the state and the structure of the mass media in shaping collective memories, patriotic sentiments, and habits of civic action.

In chapter 7 R. Claire Snyder focuses on the rise of conservative reactions as an explanation for civic decline. She highlights how social capital has declined in large part because of reactionary attacks on the feminist movement, immigration, and the welfare state. She points out that the conservative ideas for increasing the nation's stock of social capital by restoring the traditional family, denouncing identity politics, and reducing the role of government are unlikely to resuscitate our civic life.

In a similar vein, Carl Boggs in chapter 8 focuses on Putnam's peculiar thesis that the placid 1950s were the height of civic America and that the politically turbulent 1960s are seen as the period of civic decline. Boggs argues that this counterintuitive conclusion stems from the limits of Putnam's methodology, namely, his focus on traditional, mainly unpolitical associations favored by older Americans. Boggs points out that Putnam might have had more success in understanding why political action is on the decline had he taken historical shifts of economic factors into consideration. Indeed, Putnam viewed capitalism as a constant and downplayed the momentous growth of the corporation in American life. Boggs concludes that the democratic potential of community associations and networks depends on the cultural and economic context in which they are rooted.

This volume concludes with four different efforts to focus more closely on the actual workings of civil society at the grassroots, and in the global system. These chapters not only represent interesting studies of community, but they also stand as critiques to Putnam's approach to civic engagement and his recommendations for building social capacity today. Yvette Alex-Assensoh addresses how poverty in inner cities affects people's access to associations and civic institutions, particularly among African Americans. Using data on Black and White residents in low-income neighborhoods in Columbus, Ohio, she shows that poverty is a crucial limiting factor in the creation of civic relationships and political activity.

Working along the same lines, Lane Crothers in chapter 10 focuses on "street level leadership." In his analysis of community-policing efforts, Crothers finds that leadership that is sensitive to the values, goals and ideals of local populations is far more successful than "top-down" efforts at community building.

In chapter 11 Michael Forman considers the implication of the social capital approach on the political activities of labor unions, environmental groups, and human rights organizations in the new era of globalization. Labor unions, unlike bowling leagues and reading circles, regularly confront powerful opposition to their activities from employers, police, and members of Congress. The recent resurgence of these groups, highlighted by the anti–World Trade Organization protests in Seattle, have occurred not because of any effort to build social capital, but because of their rediscovery of the notion of "social rights" within their own militant traditions. Forman's piece highlights once again the question of whether the social capital idea, which views the solidarity of groups in terms of investment resources, is an adequate guide for building community and solidarity in a postmodern global economic system.

Has Putnam investigated all of the prime suspects for the demise of social capital? Manfred Steger finds that Putnam inexplicably leaves globalization off of the list of potential culprits. Yet Steger points out that it is impossible to ignore the dramatic changes that global patterns of trade and investment have wrought on the very features of American community that Putnam says are declining—patterns of work, leisure, television, and politics. While Putnam sees political parallels between the community challenges of the 1890s and today, he does not extend the comparison to the economic transformations occurring in both periods. Great transformations in economic life have far-reaching effects on political and social life, and set the stage for movements that seek to revitalize the spirit of community. Steger recommends that future studies in the politics of social capital should take into consideration the increasing role of global trade, finance, investment, and communication on the quality of democracy in the world.

Overall, the essays in this volume question the viability of Putnam's understanding of forces affecting civic engagement and the role of the individual in the democratic state, suggesting that his discussion of social capital is theoretically deficient on many fronts. Yet despite the divergent criticisms, the consensus is that civic engagement in America has declined and that there is reason to be concerned. Moreover, as the essays in this volume demonstrate, the prescriptions for what ails American democracy do not necessarily follow one simple party line or solution. Instead, each of the contributors develops arguments suggesting a broad political spectrum of solutions.

References

Axelrod, Robert. 1984. *The Evolution of Cooperation.* New York: Basic Books.

Barber, Benjamin R. 1998. *A Place for Us: How to Make Society Civil and Democracy Strong.* New York: Hill and Wang.

Bellah, Robert, Richard Madsen, William M. Sullivan, and Steven M. Tipton. 1996. *Habits of the Heart.* Updated edition. Berkeley: University of California Press.

Berkowitz, Peter. 1999. *Virtue and the Making of Modern Liberalism.* Princeton: Princeton University Press.

Bourdieu, Pierre. 1980. "Le Capital Social: Notes Provisoires." *Actres de la Recherche en Sciences Sociales* 31: 2–3.

———. 1985. "The Forms of Capital." *Handbook of Theory and Research for the Sociology of Education.* Ed. by J. G. Richardson, 241–58. New York: Greenwood.

Carter, Stephen. 1999. *Civility.* New York: Harper Perennials.

Cobb, Clifford, Ted Halstead, and Jonathan Rowe. 1995. "If the GDP Is Up, Why Is America Down?" *Atlantic Monthly*: 59–78.

Cohen, Anthony P. 1985. *The Symbolic Construction of Community.* London: Tavistock Publications.

Coleman, James S. 2000. "Social Capital in the Creation of Human Capital." *Social Capital: Multifaceted Perspective.* Ed. by Partha Dasgupta and Ismail Serageldin, 13–39. Washington D.C.: World Bank.

Dahl, Robert. 2000. *On Democracy.* New Haven: Yale University Press.

Edwards, Michael. 2000. "Enthusiasts, Tacticians, and Skeptics: Civil Society and Social Capital." *Kettering Review* 18: 39–51.

Edwards, Bob, and Michael W. Foley. 1998. "Civil Society and Social Capital Beyond Putnam. *American Behavioral Scientist* 42: 124–40.

Etzioni, Amitai. 1996. *The New Golden Rule: Community and Morality in a Democratic Society.* New York: Basic Books.

Fowler, Robert Booth. 1991. *The Dance with Community: The Contemporary Debate in American Political Thought.* Lawrence: University Press of Kansas.

Fukuyama, Francis. 1999. "Social Capital and Civil Society." Paper delivered at IMF Conference on Second Generation Reforms, Oct. 1, 1999. International Monetary Fund.

———. 1995. *Trust: The Social Virtues and the Creation of Prosperity.* New York: The Free Press.

Green, Donald, and Ian Shapiro. 1994. *Pathologies of Rational Choice Theory: A Critique of Applications in Political Science.* New Haven: Yale University Press.

Havel, Vaclav. 1997. *The Art of the Impossible: Politics and Morality in Action.* New York: Knopf.

Hirschman, Albert O. 1970. *Exit, Voice, and Loyalty: Responses to Decline in Firms, Organizations, and States.* Cambridge: Harvard University Press.

Huntington, Samuel P. 1983. *American Politics: The Promise of Disharmony*. Cambridge: Harvard University Press.

Jones, Barry R. J. 2000. "Globalization versus Community: Stakeholding, Communitarianism and the Challenge of Globalization." In *Globalization and the Politics of Resistance*. Ed. by Barry K. Gills. New York: St. Martin's Press.

Keane, John. 1988. "Despotism and Democracy: The Origins and Development of the Distinction between Civil Society and the State 1750–1850." In *Civil Society and the State: New European Perspectives*. Ed. by John Keane. New York: Verso.

Ladd, Carll Everett. 1999. *The Ladd Report*. New York: The Free Press.

Lehmann, Nicholas. 1996. "Kicking in Groups." *Atlantic Monthly* (April): 22–26.

Loury, Glenn. 1981. "Intergenerational Transfers and the Distribution of Earnings." *Econometrica* 49: 843–67.

Maloney, William, Graham Smith, and Gerry Stoker. 2000. "Social Capital and Urban Governance: Adding a More Contextualized 'Top-Down' Perspective." *Political Studies* 48 (2000): 802–20.

McKnight, John. 1995. *The Careless Society: Community and Its Counterfeits*. New York: Basic Books.

Miller, D. W. 1999. "Perhaps We Bowl Alone, But Does It Really Matter?" *Chronicle of Higher Education* (July 16).

Mittelman, James H. 2000. *The Globalization Syndrome: Transformation and Resistance*. Princeton: Princeton University Press.

Olson, Mancur. 1965. *The Logic of Collective Action*. Cambridge: Harvard University Press.

Pollitt, Katha. 1996. "For Whom the Bell Rolls." *The Nation* 262 (April 15): 9.

Portes, Alejandro. 1998. "Social Capital: Its Origins and Applications." *Modern Sociology: Annual Review of Sociology* 24: 1–24.

Putnam, Robert D. 1993. *Making Democracy Work*. Princeton: Princeton University Press.

———. 1995a. "Bowling Alone: America's Declining Social Capital." *Journal of Democracy* 6: 65–78.

———. 1995b. "Tuning In, Tuning Out: The Strange Disappearance of Social Capital in America." *PS: Political Science and Politics* 28: 664–83.

———. 1996. "The Strange Disappearance of Civic America." *The American Prospect* (Winter): 34–49.

———. 2000. *Bowling Alone: The Collapse and Revival of American Community*. New York: Simon & Schuster.

Rosenblum, Nancy L. 1998. *Membership and Morals: The Personal Uses of Pluralism in America*. Princeton: Princeton University Press.

Sandel, Michael. 1996. *Democracy's Discontent: America in Search of a Public Philosophy*. Cambridge: Belknap Press of Harvard University Press.

Skocpol, Theda. 1999. "From Membership to Advocacy." In *Civic Engagement in*

American Democracy. Ed. by Theda Skocpol and Morris P. Fiorina. Washington, D.C.: Brookings.

Smith, Rogers M. 1997. *Civic Ideals: Conflicting Visions of Citizenship in U.S. History*. New Haven: Yale University Press.

Snyder, Claire R. 1999. "Shutting the Public Out of Politics." In *Kettering Foundation Occasional Paper*. Dayton: Kettering Foundation.

Tarrow, Sidney. 1996. "Making Social Science Work Across Space and Time: A Critical Reflection on Robert Putnam's *Making Democracy Work*." *American Political Science Review* 90: 389–98.

Vanishing Voter Project. "Interested but Discouraged: Americans' View of the Election Drama." Joan Shorenstein Center, Kennedy School of Government. http://www.vanishingvoter.org/releases/11-21-00.shtml.

Wolfe, Alan. 1998. *One Nation After All*. New York: Viking.

Part I

Tocquevillean Traditions and the Study of Civil Society

The Strange Disappearance of Alexis de Tocqueville in Putnam's Analysis of Social Capital

Amy Fried

How can we understand what Putnam (1995a) calls "the strange disappearance of social capital in America"? At the turn of the twenty-first century, Putnam invokes nineteenth-century writer Alexis de Tocqueville as someone who can provide insight into this issue, calling him the "patron saint of contemporary social capitalists" (Putnam 2000, 292) and the "patron saint of American communitarians" (21). In his work preceding the book *Bowling Alone*, Putnam repeatedly acknowledges his intellectual debt to Tocqueville. For instance, in *Making Democracy Work*, Putnam writes, "The norms and values of the civic community are embodied in, and reinforced by, distinctive social structures and practices. The most relevant social theorist here remains Alexis de Tocqueville" (Putnam 1993, 89). Tocqueville is summarized and quoted in the second and third paragraphs of one article (Putnam 1995b) and its fourth paragraph introduces modern social science work on civic engagement by calling such scholars "neo-Tocquevillean."

Bowling Alone (2000) includes eighteen separate mentions of Tocqueville, compared to six mentions of Dewey, two of Jefferson, two of Madison, and three of Coleman. While *Bowling Alone*'s references to Tocqueville largely concern the Frenchman's views about the prevalence of associations and about "self-interest properly understood" as growing out of associational activity, Putnam also cites Tocqueville on such disparate topics as religion and newspaper readership. The work of Alexis de Tocqueville on democracy in America clearly provides one of the most crucial theoretical bases for Putnam's analysis of social capital in America.

However, as this chapter demonstrates, Putnam gives insufficient attention to some of Tocqueville's important conceptual and methodological contributions as a social and political analyst. In addition, this chapter argues that a fuller appropriation of Tocqueville would benefit social capital scholarship and the political projects associated with this line of research.

The chapter considers three main gaps in Putnam's use of Tocqueville. First, Putnam slights Tocqueville's analysis of how equality influences Americans. Tocqueville argued that equality in the United States helps produce citizens who have drive, aspirations, and involvement in politics and their communities. In addition, Tocqueville saw America as a nation in which political institutions were open to citizens, and where there was relative equality in political input and power. To be sure, Putnam does not altogether ignore questions about equality and inequality. However, American equality is a decidedly subordinate concern in *Bowling Alone*. Thus, Putnam does not investigate how contemporary inequalities in Americans' political voices and economic positions affect community-oriented beliefs and actions, nor does Putnam recommend policies to mitigate inequalities.

Second, while Tocqueville—in both *Democracy in America* and *The Old Regime and the Revolution*—provides an analysis of historical shifts in political, social, and economic structures, Putnam's studies are inattentive to structural dynamics. As a result, Putnam is unable to assess how the organization, relations, and structures of current political and social institutions affect citizens' commitments to civic life. This is unfortunate, because there have been considerable changes in political institutions, campaigns, and elections; a new media regime, and a growing role of money as a form of political participation, each of which establishes a new context affecting citizen action and voice.

Third, Putnam's methodological approach of survey research could benefit from additional research methods, some of which were used by Tocqueville. For instance, Tocqueville interviewed a diverse array of citizens and leaders. Alternatives to surveys could better illuminate citizens' understandings of politics and the contexts in which Americans live. In addition, Tocqueville's germinal political sociology was centered on the intersections between individual choices and institutions. This approach provides a model worth emulating.

Two main objections to my discussion may be raised thus far. One, it may be pointed out that the Tocqueville found by Putnam is, perhaps unavoidably, one of "many Tocquevilles" (Nisbet 1976). One reason why these many Tocquevilles exist is because his key work, *Democracy in America,* is so large in conception and sweeping in its coverage, and filled with ambivalence and tension.[1] Some decades ago two historians noted:

> The *Democracy* is not a simple work and not an easy one for historians to utilize. It does not easily fit into historians' traditional categories of source materials. It is not, for most purposes, a primary source, but not, strictly speaking, a secondary source either. (Marshall and Drescher 1968, 512)

Nor is Tocqueville easily fit into the political science discipline. Although political theorists analyze Tocqueville's ideas and teach his works in classes on American political thought, Tocqueville's insights drew upon direct observations and studies. To this I argue that while many interpretations of Tocqueville are possible, Putnam's includes some gaps, which, if addressed, could improve our understanding of contemporary civic life. Putnam's work has been highly influential, entering the public sphere, stimulating elite discourse, and affecting scholarship.[2] Given its standing and impact, it is especially important to correct and reconstitute a disappearing, partial Tocqueville.

Second, in emphasizing the role of equality in Tocqueville's analysis and in arguing for more attention to inequality in social capital scholarship, the impression might be left that I see Tocqueville as an advocate for greater equality. However, as will be clear in the following section, I am well aware that Tocqueville saw great problems and dangers inherent in social equality, including forces that undermine the fragile sense of community, which could be developed by political and associational means. I do not recover a different Tocqueville in order to likewise proclaim him a paragon or patron saint. Indeed, we need not be bound by Tocqueville's fears about some of the results of equality to appreciate that a fuller appropriation of Tocqueville points us to the significance of equality in defining a previous century's political culture and suggests the place of equality and inequality in affecting our own.

Tocqueville on American Democracy and Equality

Tocqueville, Putnam's patron saint of contemporary social capitalists, was an observant and diligent "aristocratic liberal," who sought to explicate "what is to be hoped for and what is to be feared from the democratic revolution" (Mansfield and Winthrop 2000, xix, lii). In the course of his

American travels of May 9, 1831 to February 20, 1832, Alexis de Tocqueville acquired impressions of the United States that were to form the basis of *Democracy in America*. Tocqueville and his traveling companion Gustave de Beaumont arrived from France with a keen interest in the democratic experiment. Both Tocqueville and Beaumont were from aristocratic lineages; both were unsure of their place in the new French order and were apprehensive about the stability of the regime. They obtained the charge to investigate the American penitentiary system and to prepare a report, and this they did. However, their investigation of penitentiaries was largely an excuse for their excursion. As they readied themselves to examine American democracy, they prepared well, reading significant works and obtaining letters of introduction to well-known persons.[3] Once there, they spoke with and observed people of all social standings, from merchants in New York and President Andrew Jackson in Washington, D.C., to slaves, Native Americans, and persons living on the frontiers.

Tocqueville's examination was nearly all encompassing, yet a good deal of the book centered on a theme stated early on. In the very first sentence of the author's introduction to Volume I, Tocqueville emphasized equality: "No NOVELTY in the United States struck me more vividly during my stay there than the equality of conditions" (9; Volume I, Author's Introduction).[4] Equality, of course, should be seen in relative terms, and indeed Tocqueville repeatedly compares the equality in America to the inequality of aristocratic nations. According to Tocqueville's observations, the equality of America is both political and social,[5] and both are enormously consequential.[6]

Political equality, for Tocqueville, did not involve the occasional use of the suffrage or mere voting rights. Instead, citizens held fairly equal political ranks when it came to influencing their townships and local governments. In the early 1830s, the national government was fairly weak, but participatory institutional forms such as town meetings and juries were relatively common and active. Through involvement in local government, the average citizen "learns to rule society" (70; Volume I, Part I, Chapter 5). "Local institutions are to liberty what primary schools are to science; they put it within the people's reach; they teach people to appreciate its peaceful enjoyment and accustom them to make use of it" (63; Vol. I, Part I, Chapter 5).[7]

Americans, Tocqueville found, also experienced considerable social and economic equality.[8] Inheritance laws and a fair degree of intergenerational mobility decreased the stasis in class divisions. Yet Tocqueville was not altogether admiring about the degree of equality he found. Instead, Tocqueville was troubled because he believed equality was associated with majority tyranny and conformity. The majority's power has a political basis, as the elected legislature will be attentive to their will. However, in conditions of equality, there also develops "the moral authority of the majority" (247; Volume I, Part II, Chapter 7). While European kings can control people only physically, in America the majority "acts as much upon the will as upon behavior and at the same moment prevents both the act and the desire to do it" (254). In sections from Volume II of *Democracy in America* (surely familiar to public opinion and political behavior scholars, if only because of the fine work of Ginsberg [1986] and Noelle-Neumann [1984]), Tocqueville directly connected social equality with the power of public opinion.

> When standards are unequal and men unalike, there are some very enlightened and learned individuals whose intelligence gives them great power, while the multitude is very ignorant and blinkered. As a result men living under an aristocracy are naturally inclined to be guided in their views by a more thoughtful man or class, and they have little inclination to suppose the masses infallible. In times of equality the opposite happens. The nearer men are to a common level of uniformity, the less are they inclined to believe blindly in any man or any class. But they are readier to trust the mass, and public opinion becomes more and more mistress of the world (435; Volume II, Part I, Chapter 2).

Nor is the public's power minimal. Instead, Tocqueville says, individual thought may be bound by "tight fetters," as citizens' heads are held under a "yoke" (436; Volume II, Part II, Chapter 2).

Social equality has numerous other effects, many of which are no more salutary. In a veritable laundry list at the start of Volume II, Tocqueville gives numerous examples of the mediocrity and smallness of conception endemic among Americans. Because equality is a pervasive social condition and ideal, Americans pay little attention to philosophy, have no well-developed philosophical systems, concentrate on scientific applications rather than scientific theory, create acceptable crafts rather than excellent craftsmanship, have many writers who are bombastic, and do not create great plays or other works of art and literature. Furthermore, while American equality encourages Americans to pursue prosperity, they engage in this pursuit without satisfaction; no matter how much they gain, they are restless, dogged, and hurried. Equality also gives rise to something new in the world—individualism. Because people are not linked together in fixed stations, as they are in aristocratic societies, Americans have no definite ties to others. Thus, individualism arises; it is "a calm and considered feeling which disposes each citizen to isolate himself from the mass of his fellows and withdraw into the circle of family and friends . . ." (506; Volume II, Part II, Chapter 2).[9]

Putnam's interest in Tocqueville largely revolves around Tocqueville's solution to individualism. Tocqueville argues that associational life can overcome individualism by developing a trait Tocqueville calls "self-interest properly understood," the recognition that individuals are served by contributing to the collective good. Great sacrifices are not necessary, "but every day it prompts some small ones" (527; Volume II, Part II, Chapter 8). People may get involved in groups to serve their own interests, but those activities can teach other-regarding views. "[A]n enlightened self-love continually leads them to help one another and disposes them freely to give part of their time and wealth for the good of the state" (526). This solution is readily available to Americans because involvement in associations is widespread. Tocqueville claims that, "In democratic countries knowledge of how to combine is the mother of all other forms of knowledge . . ." (517; Volume II, Part II, Chapter 5).

Individualism arises from equality in America, but so does Americans' tendency to proliferate associations. This becomes clear as Tocqueville asks, "Is that just an accident, or is there really some necessary connection between associations and equality?" (514; Volume II, Part II, Chapter 5), and then answers, "Among democratic peoples associations must take the place of powerful private persons whom equality of condition has eliminated" (516).

In a section that is reminiscent of contemporary groups such as Alcoholics Anonymous or Promise Keepers, Tocqueville notes that associations in America have come to include groups that focus on personal moral choices. These, too, have grown because of American equality.

> The first time that I heard in America that one hundred thousand men had publicly promised never to drink alcoholic liquor, I thought it more of a joke than a serious matter and for the moment did not see why these very abstemious citizens could not content themselves with drinking water by their own firesides. In the end I came to understand that these hundred thousand Americans, frightened by the progress of drunkenness around them, wanted to support sobriety by their patronage. (516; Volume II, Part II, Chapter 5)

Thus, associations help Americans to buttress their will. In a land of equality, others provide moral sustenance in one's group.

While seeing equality as a crucial force in America, Tocqueville did not overlook two groups that suffered from egregious inequality: slaves and Indians (Native Americans). In fact, he foresaw difficulties facing the United States, as it would be forced to deal with inequality and its effects. Toward the end of Volume I (363; Part II, Chapter 10) Tocqueville predicted, "[S]lavery, amid the democratic liberty and enlightenment of our age, is not an institution that can last. Either the slave or the master will put an end to it. In either case great misfortunes are to be anticipated."

Another despotism Americans might choose and which Tocqueville fears is control by the state: a meta-association that will act more like a child's teacher than a tyrant. "They console themselves for being under schoolmasters by thinking that they have chosen them themselves. Each individual lets them put the collar on, for he sees it is not a person, or a class of persons, but society itself which holds the end of the chain" (693; Volume II, Part IV, Chapter 6). Equality, the fundamental political and social force Tocqueville saw, can develop participatory skills and a largeness of conception, or it can limit freedom and control the human spirit.

Despite the problems that can arise from an inordinately strong state, Tocqueville should not be seen as heralding private organizations in opposition to government. As Mansfield and Winthrop note, "Tocqueville is a critic of big government, not of all government" (2000, lxxii). In fact, Tocqueville argues that political institutions develop interests and skills needed to support other sorts of associations; these kinds of groups should not be seen in competition with each other.

Is it enough to see things separately, or should we discover the hidden link connecting them? It is through political associations that Americans of every station, outlook, and age day by day acquire a general taste for association and become familiar with the way to use the same. Through them large numbers see, speak, listen, and stimulate each other to carry out all sorts of undertakings in common. Then they carry these conceptions into the affairs of civil life and put them to a thousand uses (524; Volume II, Part II, Chapter 7).

In a democracy, suffused with the value of equality, ties between restless citizens are grounded in activities linked to a set of political institutions, which promote other useful and bonding associational activities.

Robert Putnam on Social Capital and
His Use of Alexis de Tocqueville

Putnam's project, most fully developed in *Bowling Alone*, is to understand what has happened to Americans' sense of being mutually bound together. Putnam argues (2000, 19) that social capital—"connections between individuals and the norms of reciprocity and trustworthiness"—has declined. Putnam finds numerous indicators of reductions in social capital, including decreased voting and other sorts of political participation, a drop-off in the number of picnics, family dining experiences, and dinner parties; decreases in voting and club attendance; and a fewer number of bowling leagues (but not other sorts of group bowling).[10] Using an index (which is heavily based in measures of community-level group involvement, interpersonal trust, and informal socializing) to assay state social capital, Putnam finds correlations between states' amount of social capital and states' levels of children's welfare, crime, health, tax evasion, and rudeness. Putnam explains the historical trends in social capital by four main factors: time and money pressures; suburbanization and sprawl; television watching; and generational change, and Putnam provides statistical estimates of the particular contribution each of these factors makes to its decline (see Putnam 2000, 283–84 for specific percentages).

As noted at the start of this chapter, Putnam repeatedly turns to Tocqueville to provide theoretical support for Putnam's contention that group activities are important for building a sense of community. However, Putnam removes Tocqueville's views about associations from their larger context and thus overstates the influence of group action on democratic culture. As Diggins points out:

> Today much attention is given to Tocqueville's purported abiding faith in America's capacity for starting up voluntary civil associations. Tocqueville's observations on that subject take up only about six pages in his massive, seven hundred-page *Democracy in America*, and the observations are tempered by his more telling perception that the American people have little will to sustain organizations—they seem to dissolve as quickly as they are formed. Those who cite Tocqueville as advocating communal civil society scarcely confront what undermines it every day. "Why Are Americans so Restless Amidst Their Prosperity?" is the title of one of his chapters . . . [H]appiness and equality was precisely what Tocqueville believed drove Americans to move ahead while leaving community behind. (2000, 108)

Groups cannot bear the burden Putnam attributes to them. Instead, their influence must be seen in the context of other social and political arrangements, including political institutions and patterns of equality or inequality, which can undermine or support a sense of connectedness.

Equality and Inequality in Putnam's Analysis

Despite the neo-Tocquevillean themes and the frequent citations of Tocqueville, Putnam presents a rather limited discussion of equality, whether political, social, or economic. Tocqueville argued that Americans experienced a high degree of political equality and were educated by their involvement with highly participatory local governments. In addition, Tocqueville warned that inordinate economic power could undermine democracy and the spirit of equality. In a chapter entitled "How an Aristocracy May be Created by Industry," Tocqueville cautioned that the emerging "manufacturing aristocracy" could threaten democracy: "[T]he friends of democracy should keep their eyes anxiously fixed in that direction. For if ever permanent inequality of conditions and aristocracy make their way into the world, it will have been by that door that they entered" (558; Volume II, Part II, Chapter 20).

However, Putnam does not recognize contemporary inequalities in political power which add up to "representational distortion" so that "the public's voice is often loud, sometimes clear, but rarely equal" (Verba, Schlozman, and Brady 1995, 509). To be sure, Putnam does not ignore variations in the citizenry. For example, in one article, Putnam notes that "highly educated people are much more likely to be joiners and trusters, partly because they are better off economically, but mostly because of the skills, resources, and inclinations that were imparted to them at home and in school" (Putnam 1995a, 667). However, issues regarding political inequality are certainly not a central element of Putnam's analysis in *Bowling Alone*. In an aside in a section introducing possible reasons for declining civic engagement, Putnam admits that "education is in part a proxy for privilege—for social class and economic advantage," but he never explores what consequences those unequal advantages might have in terms of decreased political efficacy or withdrawal from political life (2000, 186).

In contrast, Verba, Schlozman, and Brady note that

recent developments with respect to participation also have implications for citizen dissatisfaction . . . [M]aking contributions has assumed greater prominence in the mix of citizen activities. Among activities, contributing is far from the most rewarding . . . Thus, the activity that has gained in significance is one that is relatively unlikely to leave activists feeling satisfied. At the same time, the increasing importance of contributing as a form of participation is likely to feed public dissatisfaction with politics. (1995, 531)

Therefore, they recommend that debates about campaign finance reform should be framed "in terms of the extent to which a money-based politics contributes to skepticism about politics among citizens or undermines the ability of the less well heeled to take part on an equal footing with those who are better off and thus jeopardizes equal protection of interest" (532).

Putnam also overlooks growing economic inequality in the United States, despite the centrality of American equality in Tocqueville's argument. True, Putnam notes declines in real wages and increasing wage insecurity (2000, 189). However, he does not acknowledge that these changes have taken place as income as been redistributed—upward. From 1977 to 1990, the bottom 60 percent of the population had a decline in their family income, while the top 10 percent went up by almost 20 percent. The top 1 percent had an increase of 45 percent (Phillips 1993, 21). A 1995 study for the Organization for Economic Cooperation and Development found that the gap between rich and poor is higher in the United States than in fifteen other wealthy industrialized nations (Atkinson, Rainwater, and Smeeding 1995). Since 1960, the average CEO has gone from making forty-one times as much as an average factory worker to one hundred and fifty-seven times as much in 1992 (Palley 1998, 58). Furthermore, even as the economy grew and the stock market rose in the 1990s, the poverty rate among full-time workers in America increased (Conference Board 2000).

Bowling Alone does more to address such issues than Putnam's earlier work. However, the book continues to skirt the issue, sometimes briefly mentioning inequalities, while other times starting with the assumption that equality has negative consequences for political and social involvement. For instance, Putnam examines comparative data that could have been used to explore equality along the lines of *Democracy in America*. Instead, Putnam frames equality issues in terms of whether there is an incompatibility between social capital on the one hand and social welfare spending or equality on the other. For instance, Putnam says that "big government" does not appear to be a cause of decreasing social capital because, "Among the advanced Western democracies, social trust and group membership are, if anything, *positively* correlated with the size of government; social capital appears to be highest of all in the big-spending welfare states of Scandinavia" (2000, 281; italics in original). Putnam's analysis of U.S. states demonstrates strong positive relationships between social capital and both economic and civic equality (2000, 358–61). While one might expect the theorist termed the patron saint of social capitalists to be referenced here, Putnam overlooks Tocqueville's arguments on the effects of American equality.

This oversight is unfortunate because growing economic inequality could have a number of effects and not just on the less-than-wealthy. As Schrag notes:

> The people at the upper end of those income scales . . . each of them modemed, cell-phoned, electronically banked—are themselves, of course, much more closely connected to their peers in New York or Tokyo, or Hong Kong or London, than they are to the people on the street below. They are members of a "community," real or virtual, that has no fixed geographic base and fewer real communitarian loyalties with each passing day, people whose dreams seem, perhaps for the first time in our history, to be connected to no geographical region or place—certainly few that celebrate social diversity. (1998, 116)

In this context of economic sequestration, individuals who are beneficiaries of the economic system have less in common with many of their fellow citizens and thus develop less of a collective identity, leading them to separate themselves and to focus on their own loved ones. (Such a condition sounds a good deal like what Tocqueville identified as individualism.) To be sure, Putnam (2000) discusses suburbanization and its effects on separating various groups from others. However, this analysis focuses more on the tendency for individuals to shuttle themselves around in isolation and the time drain of commuting than on groups' settlement patterns and resulting different and unequal life styles.

Nor does Putnam consider whether poor individuals, many of whom have been left behind in deindustrialized cities, could come to believe that their efforts mean little and, discouraged, would be less inclined to participate. Putnam's discussion of economic prosperity overlooks factors such as the loss of well-paid working class jobs and the poor condition of schools in low-income neighborhoods. Furthermore, Putnam does not

acknowledge or assess the impact of ill-conceived highway and urban
planning projects which cut, disrupted, and damaged city neighborhoods
across the United States. Instead, he argues that citizens in poor areas do
not have enough strong connections with the right sort of people. For example, Putnam quotes a study which found "that not only do residents of
extreme-poverty areas have fewer social ties but also that they tend to have
ties of less social worth, as measured by the social position of their partners, parents, siblings, and best friends, for instance" (2000, 321). In short,
they possess lower volumes of social capital. Putnam also finds that "networks tend to be more lucrative for whites than for members of minority
groups," but he does not consider whether this could be attributed, even in
part, to a legacy of racial inequality and discrimination (2000, 322). Building stronger connections within poor communities is Putnam's preferred
strategic starting point for economic development.

It is when Putnam turns to historical precedents that he comes closest
to directly addressing the role of political, social, and economic equality.
However, Putnam does not place this issue in a position of analytical importance and therefore paints equality as but one element in his portrait
of American development. Chapter 23 of *Bowling Alone*, "Lessons of History: The Gilded Age and the Progressive Era," argues that "In a number of
deep respects the challenges facing American society at the end of the
nineteenth century foreshadowed those that we face in our own time," and
that, "some unexpectedly relevant—and in many respects optimistic—
lessons can be found" (Putnam 2000, 367). Here, more than in any other
chapter of *Bowling Alone*, Putnam's view is broad and integrative, addressing a range of historical circumstances and events, such as patterns of
technological change, urbanization, immigration, concentrations of
wealth, racism, declines in community ties, the initiation of new associations, reforms in the political process, and new policies to protect workers,
children, consumers, and the environment.

Conditions of inequality run through Putnam's historical analysis as a
diffuse but almost surreptitious subtext. At one point Putnam notes,
"Then, as now, new conditions of wealth and corporate power raised
questions about the real meaning of democracy" (2000, 381). Given Putnam's glimpse into the importance of economic inequality for structuring
political power, it is even more striking that his analysis of the contemporary civic condition has so little to say about rising inequality today. There
is no sustained analysis of changing patterns of wealth today, although the
assiduous reader can find a footnote noting that economic inequality "cer-

tainly declined from roughly 1940 to 1970, and it certainly rose from roughly 1970 on" (Putnam 2000, 498).

Putnam alludes to inequality in another historical period as part of his explanation of age cohorts' variations in associational activity. Putnam argues that this generational effect is so strong that it, along with different cohorts' exposure to television during youth, accounts for about half of the overall decline in civic engagement and social capital (2000, 283–84). The most involved generation "is the cohort born in 1925–1930, who attended grade school during the Great Depression, spent World War II in high school (or on the battle field), first voted in 1948 or 1952, set up housekeeping in the 1950s, and watched their first television when they were in the late twenties" (Putnam 1995b, 675). He contends that the war years promoted a sense of shared adversity and civic and economic equality (2000, 268–71). Furthermore, he acknowledges that World War II "was probably the most leveling event in American economic history. The fraction of all personal wealth held by the top 1 percent of adults fell from 31 percent in 1939 to 23 percent in 1945 . . ." (2000, 271). Yet, while Putnam gives equality during World War II as an important reason why the civic generation was civic, Putnam neglects growing inequality in discussing today's civic condition.

Furthermore, Putnam's solutions do not include policies to create greater equality or to mitigate inequalities in areas (such as access to extracurricular activities and flexibility in the workplace) that he does discuss (2000, 268–71).[11] Instead, Putnam's solutions are rather more generic, starting with the call that "[W]e desperately need an era of civic inventiveness to create a renewed set of institutions and channels for a reinvigorated civic life that will fit the way we have come to live" (2000, 401). The self-identified neo-Tocquevillean Putnam does not promote equality in America, despite its importance in his examination of American history and generational change, and in Tocqueville's analysis of American democracy.

Putnam and Tocqueville as Political and Social Analysts

Since the publication of *Democracy in America*, Tocqueville's work has been acclaimed both because of his substantive conclusions and his approach as a political and social analyst. While Putnam's examination of social capital trends is, to be sure, quite extensive, social capital scholarship could benefit from Tocqueville's explanatory model, particularly Tocqueville's attention to the intersections between structural conditions and individual action, politics and society, and subjectivity and context.

Throughout Tocqueville's work, and most particularly in *Democracy in America* and *The Old Regime and the French Revolution*, Tocqueville's theoretical approach "involves the determination of certain structural traits of modern societies and then the comparison of the various modalities of these societies" (Aron 1965, 183). In defining and explaining these societies, Tocqueville's analysis is multilayered and focused on the interactions between historical conditions, institutional forms, social relations, and values. While Tocqueville identifies important elements influencing the shape and direction of social and political developments, it is clear (perhaps most in *The Old Regime*) that individuals retain agency and act within but also to change institutions and structures. Mitchell notes "Tocqueville's commitment to a concept of linkage between human choice and an underlying, if hidden structure in human events" (Mitchell 1996, 145).

Tocqueville's influence on Putnam comes through *Democracy in America*, a work that explains American society in terms of a variety of historical precedents and political and social conditions. One sociologist extracts three main explanations from *Democracy in America* (276; Volume I, Part I, Chapter 9); these are: "1) the accidental and particular situation in which American society happened to be, 2) the laws, and 3) the customs and manners" (Aron 1965, 192). "Laws" do not mean legislation but rather encompass the American constitutional scheme, national and local institutions, the jury system, and a free press. Pre-existing conditions—ranging from geographical to cultural and administrative—set the context in which particular changes are more or less likely to occur.[12] Although *Democracy in America* places a strong emphasis on social relations, Tocqueville makes it clear that the social and cultural are intermingled with political dynamics (see Mansfield and Winthrop 2000, xliii). Furthermore, while Tocqueville's analysis of American democracy is often comparative—in that it draws out the ways that democracy diverges from aristocracy—Tocqueville defines American democracy on its own terms and in terms of Americans' subjective views.

Thus, Tocqueville offers an analysis of the role of social and political institutions as influences on (and influenced by) individuals' acts and beliefs.[13] In *Souvenirs*, Tocqueville noted that existing patterns of thoughts, traditions, and institutions influenced how new events emerged and were perceived. Tocqueville wrote, "Antecedent facts, the nature of institutions, turns of mind, the state of manners and morals—these are the materials with which chance constructs those impromptu events which surprise and alarm us."[14] As Stone and Mennell note, "Tocqueville not only saw but pursued the connections between aspects of social life which latter-day intellectual Taylorism has placed in hermetically sealed subdivisions of a discipline which, even taken as a whole, would to Tocqueville have seemed unduly limited" (Stone and Mennell 1980, 24).

In contrast, Putnam's emphasis on social capital as an attribute of individuals leads him to assess how the choices of those individuals—to do such things as live in suburbs and commute, to vote, to watch television, to join a bowling league, or to socialize by playing cards on a regular basis, among other things—are related to decreasing social capital. When looked at as a matter of individual choices, which in the aggregate tend to go in the same direction, participatory declines indeed seem strange, even if it is not really disappearing. However, when looking at contemporary American life, Putnam does not examine the structures and institutions that frame the choices individuals make.

Take one example, "suburbanization, commuting, and sprawl," which Putnam says contributes about 10 percent to the overall decline of social capital (Putnam 2000, 283). However, Putnam does not acknowledge that suburbs are themselves products of dynamics such as post–World War II economic growth, government policies that promoted home ownership and built highways, declining urban tax bases, and disinvestment. Furthermore, suburbs today bring with them particular demographic, metropolitan, economic, and transportation systems that set frameworks in which people make choices. Certainly, citizens today, like citizens before, can choose to commute long distances, little, or not at all. However, people's choices about where they live are not made in the same context as they were decades ago, and so should not be viewed as simply a matter of individual preference.

The same case can be made about women working outside of the home. Putnam is sensitive to arguments that he is blaming women for civic disengagement, even as he argues that the growing number of two-career families has a "visible" role in eroding social capital and civic disengagement (Putnam 2000, 201, 202). While I appreciate Putnam's attempt to refrain from censuring women who work full time, the analysis suffers because it is again decontextualized. Putnam's discussion of the impact of working women suffers from inattention to changing economic patterns, which have led to stagnation and decline in middle-class incomes, in part due to deindustrialization, as well as new educational requisites for income-earners, the professionalization of the caring professions, the diminishing numbers of neighbors available for assistance and socializing to women who stay at home rather than working outside of the home, and the social values which have led families to now cook (and bowl) together.[15] Again, the context in which any particular woman decides to work is not the same as it once was, and therefore the context must be understood as part and parcel of the choice and the larger trend.

When Putnam turns to past periods—the Gilded Age, the Progressive Era, and World War II—his analysis incorporates a broad range of contextual elements affecting individual choice. But this approach is not applied to contemporary society. In fact, one of Putnam's most important explanations for trends in social capital—generational change, as seen in differences between members of different age cohorts—could be easily understood as an *indicator* of the impact of differing contexts, but is instead viewed as an independent variable in and of itself. In contrast, Tocqueville used a contextually aware approach, which, if adopted, could encourage Putnam to attend to how new social and political circumstances have transformed the American polity and society.

Surely one of the structural conditions worth more investigation is the class structure. Putnam (2000) acknowledges that differences in trust related to class and race are based in differential experiences (138) and notes (339) that churches are one of few institutions where the poor can learn civic skills. However, Putnam does not recognize that not all associations and sets of skills are as important within the overall set of political and civic organizations. In contrast, Schlozman, Verba, and Brady note in a comparison between churches and unions:

> [T]hese institutions are not interchangeable when it comes to reducing participatory inequality. Churches and unions are not simply politically neutral sites that encourage political participation as a by-product of other purposes; they are institutions with political concerns of their own. It has long been a union mission to represent the less advantaged in the halls of government . . . Though the issue of priorities of American religious institutions are likely to continue to evolve, there is no reason to expect them to act as a substitute for unions or other organizations representing the less well off in bringing to the attention of elected officials the economic needs and preferences of the disadvantaged. (456–57)

In addition, paying attention to different participatory patterns by class would itself help us better understand declining voting participation, which has affected the class profile of the electorate as a whole.[16] As Rosenstone and Hansen note, "Class equality in participation was greatest in the high-turnout elections of the 1960s and least in the low-turnout elections of the 1990s. As turnout declined between 1960 and 1988, class inequalities multiplied" (Rosenstone and Hansen 1993, 241).

Putnam also neglects other important developments in American politics that constitute the context for contemporary civic choices. The very nature of politics has changed since the end of World War II, with the decline of direct campaigning by political parties, the rise of big-money politics (which buys advertisements that are frequently negative and alienating), and the formation of a political regime that encourages a demobilizing politics of scandal.[17] Interest groups rely on perils to their mission to raise funds; they are increasingly professionalized organizations in which members are prompted to write checks to counter policy threats. Polarization within institutions has increased, as elites engage in a permanent campaign in which they strategically promote partisanship, political divisiveness, and highly charged negative characterizations of political opponents and government.[18]

As media ownership has become increasingly concentrated, efforts to cut costs have led to a decline in the number of working journalists who pursue substantial news stories and a turn to easily produced and distributed soft news.[19] Citizens' views—often more nuanced, complex, and ambivalent than the opinions presented by pundits and politicians through the media—are frequently excluded or slighted in public discourse.[20] At the same time, the news media contribute to political polarization by emphasizing conflict, drama, sensationalism, and personal characteristics.[21] What place do citizens have in this system? Political leaders may claim that they are responsive to public opinion, but the public will is frequently ignored or misunderstood, and some research suggests that responsiveness is threatened by manipulative and inadvertent acts of elected officials, other political leaders, and the media.[22] While some citizens remain enthusiastic participants, these conditions alienate many others. Of these myriad changes (which interact and add up to a very different sort of political culture), Putnam considers only those involving the organization and activities of political parties and interest groups.

In fact, in looking over Putnam's entire work on social capital, Putnam's interest in politics clearly wanes in *Bowling Alone*. If Tocqueville was correct that political action and open, democratic institutions were requisites for other sorts of civic action, Putnam's increasing emphasis on private actions such as family dinners leads him away from understanding the dynamics involved in shifts in social capital.[23] Putnam's apolitical tendency is consistent with his avoidance of concrete policy positions, which, if included, would have required Putnam to enter in conflicts over the distribution of resources and thus would make it more difficult for people with diverse ideologies to agree with his conclusions. Furthermore, a more political take on social capital might require some analysis and assessment of the actions of media and political elites that have contributed to public cynicism and withdrawal. Tocqueville, it should be recalled, was willing to criticize and warn Americans of the 1830s regarding their treatment of those with the least power: Native Americans and slaves. Putnam almost never criticizes political and economic leaders, but instead concludes his book by leaving the reader with his hope that citizens will "become reconnected with our friends and neighbors," and with Beecher's advice to "multiply picnics" (Putnam 2000, 414).

Lessons from Tocqueville's Research Methods

Tocqueville's analytical approach brings with it a set of methods that could be used today for understanding the condition of American democracy. While it would be ahistorical to equate Tocqueville's methodologies with contemporary techniques, there are at least family resemblances to certain methods. This section discusses two such approaches, neither of which is employed in Putnam's *Bowling Alone*.

One method is tied to Tocqueville's contextual and historical approach. A range of social and political conditions constitutes the context for political and social life today. In addition to the predominantly political conditions discussed in the last section, new time binds affect our work and lives (Hochschild 2001) and there are new ways that money can be used to separate citizens from each other (McKenzie 1994). Because political and social contexts have changed, citizen participation today does not have the same meaning or impact as participation in Tocqueville's time.

While Putnam does not adopt a contextual approach, scholarship by "new institutionalists," philosophers of social science proposing greater attention to the agent-structure divide, and contextually oriented re-searchers[24] demonstrate that the hermetically sealed subdivisions which Tocqueville avoided in the 1830s can be escaped today. While Putnam's approach "stress[es] the socialization of individuals into shared norms and cooperative societal action . . . historical-institutionalists probe chang-ing organizational patterns, shifts in resources for collective social and po-litical activity, and transformations in the relations between elites and or-dinary citizens," and represent an approach closer to that used by Toc-queville (Skocpol and Fiorina 1999, 13).

While this first method emphasizes historical context, the second stresses individual subjectivities, which are themselves affected by contex-tual conditions. Tocqueville repeatedly wrote about Americans' values and the ways they saw themselves, each other, the community, and the political world. Tocqueville's approach thus bears a likeness to interpretive social sci-ence, which is attuned to the understandings of everyday people (Winch 1958; Bernstein 1976). With this approach comes a set of methods quite un-like Putnam's. Tocqueville's work today might be characterized as involving participant-observation, intensive interviews, textual study, and grounded theory (Glaser and Strauss 1967). Those approaches allow analysts to un-derstand what various acts mean to those they study. While Putnam muses about why younger cohorts lack a sense of community, intensive interviews with individuals in different cohorts could have revealed more about the sources of a sense of connectedness (or its absence).[25]

My argument is not that Tocqueville would have eschewed quantitative methods in favor of other approaches for understanding civic values and behavior. For one thing, we cannot know if this is so simply because Toc-queville could not choose to use the sophisticated statistical techniques available to Putnam because these had not yet been developed. In addition, statistics would have been useful to Tocqueville in helping him describe more precisely certain elements of American political, economic, and civic life, and Tocqueville's approach of combining different sorts of research ap-proaches suggests that he likely would have chosen a variety of tools, in-cluding quantitative methods, if statistical information and techniques had been at hand. What can be maintained is that, given Tocqueville's interests in understanding Americans' particular "motives, tastes, concerns [and] thoughts" (Poggi 1972, 34) and the institutions and structures that framed and encouraged those, research that claims to take Tocqueville as a prime inspiration should take on a Tocquevillean commitment to exploring Americans' subjective states and behaviors and the ways they are constituted.

This more subjective approach keeps in mind this reality: citizenship and civic values do not just change in terms of how much they relate to a particular standard, but also qualitatively—in terms of their substantive meanings. As Cruikshank argues, the modern democratic self, like other versions of citizenship, are created and "the political itself is continually transformed and reconstituted at the micro-levels of everyday life where citizens are constituted" (Cruikshank 1999, 5). Researchers have sought to understand both subjectivity and context in analyzing different understandings of citizenship; the ways that class is socially constructed and related to particular conditions and experiences; as well as diverse meanings and uses of other values, including patriotism, the American Dream, and distributive justice.[26] But a good deal more work is needed to comprehend how today's citizens see themselves as civic, political, and private actors. An interpretive approach, in concert with attention to context, would recognize that "political actors act on the basis of identities that are themselves shaped by political institutions and governance."[27]

Concluding Comments

Despite Tocqueville's status as (according to Putnam) a patron saint of social capitalists, Tocqueville's ideas and approach have a more partial than robust presence in *Bowling Alone*. This essay contends that a more fully recovered Tocqueville casts attention to the issue of equality as a main element influencing American democracy, encourages scholarship that is contextual, institutional, and historical in nature, and invites methodological approaches oriented toward structural analysis and interpretive exegesis.

Some readers may believe that this is precisely the wrong path for research on civic engagement and that a better alternative is to look to someone other than Tocqueville. For example, they may agree with Ehrenberg's two main criticisms regarding Tocqueville and the social capital research agenda. One problem for Ehrenberg is that "neo-Tocquevillean orthodoxy" is too conservative and antipolitical. Ehrenberg contends:

> Contemporary thought is characterized by a pervasive skepticism of the state and of the possibilities afforded by broad political action. Now it is civil society that is supposed to revive communities, train effective citizens, build habits of respect and cooperation, provide a moral alternative to self-interest, limit intrusive bureaucracies, and reinvigorate the public sphere—all this in an environment of small government and local politics. Indeed, a

narrowed sense of public purpose and political responsibility is central to contemporary public life and thought . . . Good feelings, volunteerism, nostalgia, and community constitute civil society in an antipolitical period. (1999, 233)

Yet this purportedly Tocquevillean turn to the private is not, as my previous discussion supports, the only credible or best interpretation of Tocqueville.[28] Indeed, Tocqueville makes it clear that democratic political institutions are crucial to building civic skills and encouraging citizens to act in other associations. Tocqueville does not argue that family life, picnics, sports groups, and private associations are adequate bases for developing democratic bonds and casts of mind.

But what of social capitalists' attention to local involvement? Ehrenberg points to a second problem in using Tocqueville, arguing, "Tocqueville is not particularly helpful in these conditions. Categories derived from the face-to-face democracy of early nineteenth-century New England towns cannot furnish a credible model for public life in a highly commodified mass society marked by unprecedented levels of economic inequality" (Ehrenberg 1999, 234). However, while the New England experience of the past cannot be brought back to our time, Tocqueville's focus on the ways that those institutional settings affect activities and understandings of citizenship is helpful. Tocqueville's contextual and institutional analysis brings with it essential tools for assessing our time and determining useful directions.

To be sure, Tocqueville was not a full-throated advocate for greater equality and he saw many problems associated with its presence. However, Tocqueville's insistence that equality in the democratic America he saw was particularly important in shaping that world can be helpful now in reminding us about the impact of contemporary inequality. Even if Tocqueville cannot provide a complete model for those concerned with understanding and improving America's civic condition, a more fully recovered Tocqueville is a beneficial place to start. Putnam and scholars affected by Putnam's work should take heed of what their patron saint, properly understood, may provide.

Notes

The author thanks the University of Maine for financial support, Nicole Poliquin and Daniel Schlaefer for research assistance, and the editors for comments.

1. Thus Tocqueville is used by scholars and political actors across the political spectrum (Mansfield and Winthrop 2000, xviii). President Clinton and House Speaker Gingrich both drew from Tocqueville in major speeches in 1995, and "Tocqueville's words also are routinely incorporated into Supreme Court decisions, presidential election campaigns, and across the political spectrum from Pat Buchanan to Progressives attempting to renew the American left" (Drescher 1998, vii).

2. See, for instance, Bennett 1998; Brehm and Rahn 1997; Foley and Edwards 1997; Green and Brock 1998; Heying 1997; La Due Lake and Huckfeldt 1998; National Commission on Civic Renewal 1998; Rahn et al. 1999; Rahn and Transue 1998; Shah 1998; Smith 1999; Symposium 1999; and Uslaner 1998.

3. Pierson (1938, 34–37); see 718–38 on reading and analysis undertaken when composing *Democracy in America;* also see Jardin (1988, chapters 14).

4. All quotations from *Democracy in America* use the George Lawrence translation (Tocqueville 1966 [1835/1840]).

5. There is scholarly disagreement about the relative importance of these different sorts of equality. For example, Aron (1965) argues that Tocqueville stressed social equality, while Mansfield and Winthrop argue that Tocqueville viewed equality in political institutions and activities as key elements in creating a democratic culture, but that Tocqueville also avoids "the contest over causality between politics and society" (Mansfield and Winthrop 2000, xliv).

6. At the same time, Tocqueville does not consider equality to be the only important factor affecting the American development. In the author's preface to Volume II (417), Tocqueville states: "Noting how many different effects I hold due to equality, [the reader] might suppose that I consider equality the sole cause of everything that is happening now. That would be a very narrow view to attribute to me."

7. Tocqueville's view about the educative effect of participation is much like Mill's. In *Considerations on Representative Government,* Mill argues, "Giving [the ordinary man] something to do for the public . . . if the circumstances allow the public duty assigned him to be considerable, it makes him an educated man."

8. Tocqueville's contentions about equality in this period are consistent with the analysis offered by historian Gordon Wood (1993). For some criticisms of Wood, see the forum in the October 1994 *William and Mary Quarterly.*

9. Tocquevillean individualism is distinct from economic individualism. Fried (1993) argues that empirical researchers have more fully investigated economic individualism.

10. Ladd (1996, 1999) contends that associational activity has not declined.

11. On p. 405 of *Bowling Alone,* Putnam calls for increasing support for extracurricular activities and notes that funds for this purpose have been cut in recent decades. However, Putnam does not note that these opportunities are differentially available to various groups of students. Yet a study conducted for the U.S.

Department of Education (U.S. Department of Education 1996, 92) has found that students' involvement in many of these activities has become more skewed by class over time. In 1972, 17.6 percent of high school seniors with low socioeconomic status and 22.8 percent of those with high socioeconomic status were involved in the school's newspaper or yearbook; 5.2 percentage points separated the groups. However, in 1992, 14.2 percent of the low socioeconomic group worked on the newspaper or yearbook and 25.5 percent of the high socioeconomic group did, yielding an 11.3 percentage point gap between the classes—more than twice the earlier one. The class gap opened even more when it came to participation in academic clubs. In 1972, with participation by 24.4 percent of the low socioeconomic status group and 27.7 percent of the high socioeconomic economic group, the class gap was only 3.3 percentage points. However, in 1992, 19.4 percent of the low socioeconomic group was involved in academic clubs, compared to 31.7 percent of the high socioeconomic students, creating a nearly fourfold gap than that in 1972. In addition, Putnam does not address a key public policy issue relevant to educational offerings in public schools: their reliance on property tax as the main basis of funding, a factor which best explains the money available for programs and purchases.

12. On Tocqueville's historical analysis in *The Old Regime*, see Aron (1965) and Herr (1962).

13. See Giddens 1989; Kincaid 1994; and Little 1991 for contemporary philosophy of social science discussions of the relationship between structures and individual choice.

14. Quoted in Stone and Mennell 1980, 30.

15. I acknowledge Joel Blank for suggesting to me that, with changes in gender roles, families are increasingly cooking together.

16. Another structural shift is that local economic and political control is less meaningful in our increasingly nationalized and globalized political economy. Putnam (2000, 282–83) notes this only in passing, and in discussing the impact of this changing economy on elite involvement.

17. See Martin Wattenberg, *The Decline of American Political Parties, 1952–1994* (Cambridge: Harvard University Press, 1996); Elizabeth Drew, *The Corruption of American Politics* (Seacaucus, N.J.: Birch Lane Press, 1999); and David S. Broder and Dan Balz, "Scandal's Damage Wide, If Not Deep," *Washington Post* (February 11, 1999): A1.

19. On increasing polarization within institutions and the development of the permanent campaign, see Eric M. Uslaner, *The Decline of Comity in Congress* (Ann Arbor: University of Michigan, 1993); Barbara Sinclair, *Legislators, Leaders, and Lawmaking: The U.S. House of Representatives in the Postreform Era* (Baltimore: Johns Hopkins University Press, 1995); and Amy Fried and Douglas B. Harris, "On Red Capes and Charging Bulls: How and Why Conservative Politicians and Interest Groups Promoted Public Anger." In *What Is It About Government That Americans*

Dislike? Ed. by John Hibbing and Elizabeth Theiss-Morse (New York: Cambridge University Press, 2001).

19. See Robert W. McChesney, *Rich Media, Poor Democracy* (New York: New Press, 1999); and Thomas E. Patterson, *Doing Well and Doing Good—How Soft News and Critical Journalism Are Shrinking the News Audience and Weakening Democracy—And What News Outlets Can Do About It* (Harvard Univeristy: Joan Shorenstein Center on the Press, Politics, and Public Policy, 2000).

20. On citizens' relationship to the public sphere and public discourse, see James W. Carey, "The Press, Public Opinion and Public Discourse." In *Public Opinion and the Communication of Consent,* ed. by Theodore Glasser and Charles Salmon (New York: Guilford Press, 1995); Jurgen Habermas, *The Structural Trans-formation of the Public Sphere* (Cambridge: MIT Press, 1989); and Susan Herbst, *Numbered Voices* (Chicago: University of Chicago Press, 1993).

21. On the media and its impact, see Thomas E. Patterson *Out of Order* (New York: Knopf, 1994); Joseph Cappella and Kathleen Hall Jamieson, *Spiral of Cyni-cism* (Oxford: Oxford University Press, 1997); Stephen Ansolabehere and Shanto Iyengar, *Going Negative* (New York: Free Press, 1995); and Bill Kovach and Tom Rosenstiel, *Warp Speed: America in the Age of Mixed Media* (New York: The Cen-tury Foundation Press, 1999).

22. On legislators' responsiveness to public opinion, see Lawrence R. Jacobs and Robert Y. Shapiro, *Politicians Don't Pander: Political Manipulation and the Loss of Democratic Responsiveness* (Chicago: University of Chicago Press, 2000); Amy Fried, *Muffled Echoes: Oliver North and the Politics of Public Opinion* (New York: Columbia University Press, 1997); and Amy Fried and Timothy M. Cole "Talking about Public Opinion and Public Opinion Yet To Come: Media and Legislator Constructions of Public Opinion in the Clinton-Lewinsky Scandal," *Communica-tion Review* 4(2000): 219–51.

23. I have argued that Putnam is not a Tocquevillean in his analytical ap-proach because he has overlooked the importance of contextual factors such as structures and institutions. My emphasis on context and institutions rather than social ties and individual values is, however, consistent with a historical-institu-tional approach, in which "the trouble with American democracy today does not lie in sheer social disconnection or simply in the generalized growth of social and political distrust. Institutionalists examine changing patterns of organization and resource balances. They ask who relates to whom, and who is organized for what purposes. They are especially interested in forms of participation and power that include—or exclude—average and less-privileged citizens" (Skocpol and Fiorina 1999), 16.

24. See Smith (1992), Giddens (1989), and Steinmo, Thelen, and Longstreth (1992).

25. See Eliasoph (1998) and Lichterman (1996) for intensive studies of community groups. Another subjectively oriented approach is Q-methodology.

(See Steven R. Brown, *Political Subjectivity* (New Haven: Yale University Press, 1980).

26. See Robert Bellah, R. Madsen, W. Sullivan, A. Swidler, and S. Tipton, *Habits of the Heart* (New York: Harper and Row, 1985); John Dryzek, *Discursive Democracy* (Cambridge: Cambridge University Press, 1990); J. Schwartz, "Participation and Multisubjective Understanding," *Journal of Politics* 46(1984): 1115–41; and Elizabeth Theiss-Morse, "Conceptualizations of Good Citizenship and Political Participation," *Political Behavior* 15(1993): 355–80. On construction of class, see, for example, Paul Willis, *Learning to Labor* (New York: Columbia University Press, 1977); David Croteau, *Politics and the Class Divide* (Philadelphia: Temple University Press, 1995); and E. P. Thompson, *Making History: Writings on History and Culture* (New York: New Press, 1994). On values, see John Bodnar, ed., *Bonds of Affection: Americans Define Their Patriotism* (Princeton: Princeton University Press, 1996); Morris Janowitz, *The Reconstruction of Patriotism* (Chicago: University of Chicago Press, 1983); Jennifer Hochschild, *What's Fair? American Beliefs about Distributive Justice* (Cambridge: Harvard University Press, 1981); Jennifer Hochschild, *Facing Up to the American Dream* (Princeton: Princeton University Press, 1995); and John L. Sullivan, Amy Fried, and Mary G. Dietz "Patriotism, Politics, and the Presidential Election of 1988," *American Journal of Political Science* 36(1992): 200–34.

27. James G. March and Johan P. Olsen, *Democratic Governance* (New York: Free Press, 1995, 45).

28. At the same time, Ehrenberg is correct that Tocqueville has been employed by conservatives to support their vision of civil society based on local, volunteer-staffed community institutions. Putnam's involvement with Bush's inaugural speech is but one example of the connections between conservative policy endeavors and Putnam's analysis of the impact of community endeavors (which Putnam claims is closely linked to Tocqueville's ideas). See Dana Milbank, "Needed: Catchword for Bush Ideology," *Washington Post* (February 1, 2001, A1), regarding Putnam's role with respect to the Bush speech and on whether Bush is a communitarian.

References

Aron, Raymond. 1965. *Main Currents in Sociological Thought I*. Trans. by Richard Howard and Helen Weaver. New York: Basic Books.

Atkinson, Anthony B., Lee Rainwater, and Timothy Smeeding. 1995. *Income Distribution in OECD Countries*. Paris: OECD.

Bennett, W. Lance. 1998. "The UnCivic Culture: Communication, Identity, and the Rise of Lifestyle Politics." *PS* 31: 741–61.

Bernstein, Richard J. 1976. *The Restructuring of Social and Political Theory*. Philadelphia: University of Pennsylvania Press.

Brehm, John, and Wendy Rahn. 1997. "Individual-level Evidence for the Causes and Consequences of Social Capital." *American Journal of Political Science* 41 (3): 999–1023.

Coleman, James. 1990. *Foundations of Social Theory*. Cambridge: Harvard University Press.

———. 1988. "Social Capital in the Creation of Human Capital." *American Journal of Sociology* 94: S95–120.

Conference Board. 2000 (June). *Does a Rising Tide Lift All Boats?* New York: Conference Board.

Cruikshank, Barbara. 1999. *The Will to Empower*. Ithaca: Cornell University Press.

Diggins, John Patrick. 2000. *On Hallowed Ground*. New Haven: Yale University Press.

Drescher, Seymour. 1998. Foreword. In *Tocqueville and the French*, ed. by Francoise Melonio and trans. by Beth G. Raps. Charlottesville: University Press of Virginia.

Ehrenberg, John. 1999. *Civil Society: The Critical History of an Idea*. New York: NYU Press.

Eliasoph, Nina. 1998. *Avoiding Politics: How Americans Produce Apathy in Everyday Life*. Cambridge: Cambridge University Press.

Foley, Michael W., and Bob Edwards. 1997. "Escape from Politics? Social Theory and the Social Capital Debate." *American Behavioral Scientist* 40: 550–61.

Fried, Amy. 1993. "Is Political Action Heroic? Heroism and American Political Culture." *American Politics Quarterly* 21: 490–517.

Giddens, Anthony. 1989. *Central Problems in Social Theory: Action, Structure, and Contradiction in Social Analysis*. Berkeley: University of California Press.

Ginsberg, Benjamin. 1986. *The Captive Public: How Mass Opinion Promotes State Power*. New York: Basic Books.

Glaser, Barney G., and Anselm L. Strauss. 1967. *The Discovery of Grounded Theory*. New York: Aldine.

Green, Melanie C., and Timothy C. Brock. 1998. "Trust, Mood, and Outcomes of Friendship Determine Preferences for Real Versus Ersatz Social Capital." *Political Psychology* 19: 527–44.

Herr, Richard. 1962. *Tocqueville and the Old Regime*. Princeton: Princeton University Press.

Heying, Charles H. 1997. "Civic Elites and Corporate Delocalization: An Alternative Explanation for Declining Civic Engagement." *American Behavioral Scientist* 40: 657–68.

Hochschild, Arlie. 2001. *The Time Bind: When Work Becomes Home and Home Becomes Work*. New York: OWI Books.

Jardin, Andre. 1988. *Tocqueville*, trans. by Lydia Davis and Robert Hemenway. New York: Farrar Straus & Giroux.

Kincaid, Harold. 1994. "Reduction, Explanation, and Individualism." In *Readings in the Philosophy of Social Science*, ed. by Michael Martin and Lee C. McIntyre. Cambridge: MIT Press.

Ladd, Carll Everett. 1999. *The Ladd Report*. New York: Free Press.

———. 1996. "The Data Just Don't Show Erosion of America's Social Capital." *The Public Perspective* 7: 7–16.

La Due Lake, Ronald, and Robert Huckfeldt. 1998. "Social Capital, Social Networks, and Political Participation." *Political Psychology* 19: 567–84.

Lichterman, Paul. 1996. *The Search for Political Community*. Cambridge: Cambridge University Press.

Little, Daniel. 1991. *Varieties of Social Explanation*. Boulder: Westview Press.

Mansfield, Harvey C., and Delba Winthrop. 2000. "Editors' Introduction," *Democracy in America*. Alexis de Tocqueville trans. and ed. by Mansfield and Winthrop. Chicago: University of Chicago Press.

Marshall, Lynn, and Seymour Drescher. 1968. "American Historians and Tocqueville's *Democracy*." *Journal of American History* 55: 512–32.

McKenzie, Evan. 1994. *Privatopia: Homeowner Associations and the Rise of Residential Private Government*. New Haven: Yale University Press.

Melonio, Francoise. 1998. *Tocqueville and the French*, trans. by Beth G. Raps. Charlottesville: University Press of Virginia.

Mitchell, Harvey. 1996. *Individual Choice and the Structures of History: Alexis de Tocqueville as Historian Reappraised*. Cambridge: Cambridge University Press.

National Commission on Civic Renewal. 1998. *A Nation of Spectators: How Civic Disengagement Weakens America and What We Can Do About It*. Available at the Website of the National Commission on Civic Renewal (www.puaf.umd.edu/civicrenewal).

Nisbet, Robert. 1976. "Many Tocquevilles." *American Scholar* 46: 59–75.

Noelle-Neumann, Elisabeth. 1984. *The Spiral of Silence*. Chicago: University of Chicago Press.

Palley, Thomas I. 1998. *Plenty of Nothing: The Downsizing of the American Dream and the Case for Structural Keynesianism*. Princeton: Princeton University Press.

Phillips, Kevin P. 1993. *Boiling Point: Republicans, Democrats and the Decline of Middle-Class Prosperity*. New York: Random House.

Pierson, George Wilson. 1938. *Tocqueville and Beaumont in America*. New York: Oxford University Press.

Poggi, Gianfranco. 1972. *Images of Society: Essays on the Sociological Theories of Tocqueville, Marx, and Durkheim*. Stanford: Stanford University Press.

Putnam, Robert. 1993. *Making Democracy Work*. Princeton: Princeton University Press.

———. 1995a. "Tuning In, Tuning Out: The Strange Disappearance of Social Capital in America." *PS: Political Science and Politics* 28: 664–83.

———. 1995b. "Bowling Alone: America's Declining Social Capital." *Journal of Democracy* 6:65–78.

————. 2000. *Bowling Alone: The Collapse and Revival of American Community.* New York: Simon & Schuster.

Rahn, Wendy M., John Brehm, and Neil Carlson. 1999. "National Elections as Institutions for Generating Social Capital." In *Civic Engagement in American Democracy,* ed. by Theda Skocpol and Morris P. Fiorina. Washington, D.C.: Brookings.

Rahn, Wendy M., and John E. Transue. 1998. "Social Trust and Value Change: The Decline of Social Capital in American Youth, 1976–1995." *Political Psychology* 19: 545–65.

Rosenstone, Steven J., and John Mark Hansen. 1993. *Mobilization, Participation, and Democracy in America.* New York: Macmillan.

Schlozman, Kay Lehman, Sidney Verba, and Henry E. Brady. 1999. "Civic Participation and the Equality Problem." In *Civic Engagement in American Democracy,* ed. by Theda Skocpol and Morris P. Fiorina. Washington, D.C.: Brookings.

Schrag, Peter. 1998. *Paradise Lost: California's Experience, America's Future.* New York: New Press.

Schudson, Michael. 1998. *The Good Citizen: A History of American Civic Life.* Cambridge: Harvard University Press.

Shah, Dhavan V. 1998. "Civic Engagement, Interpersonal Trust, and Television Use: An Individual-Level Assessment of Social Capital." *Political Psychology* 19: 469–96.

Skocpol, Theda. 1999. "How Americans Became Civic." In *Civic Engagement in American Democracy,* ed. by Theda Skocpol and Morris P. Fiorina. Washington, D.C.: Brookings.

Skocpol, Theda, and Morris P. Fiorina. 1999. "Making Sense of the Civic Engagement Debate." In *Civic Engagement in American Democracy,* ed. by Theda Skocpol and Morris P. Fiorina. Washington, D.C.: Brookings.

Smith, Elizabeth S. 1999. "The Effects of Investments in the Social Capital of Youth on Political and Civic Behavior in Young Adulthood: A Longitudinal Analysis." *Political Psychology* 20: 553–80.

Smith, Rogers M. 1992. "If Politics Matters: Implications for a 'New Institutionalism.'" *Studies in American Political Development* 6: 1–36.

Steinmo, Sven, Kathleen Thelen, and Frank Longstreth, eds. 1992. *Structuring Politics: Historical Institutionalism in Comparative Analysis.* Cambridge: Cambridge University Press.

Stone, John, and Stephen Mennell. 1980. Introduction. *Alexis de Tocqueville on Democracy, Revolution, and Society,* ed. by John Stone and Stephen Mennell. Chicago: University of Chicago Press.

Symposium (Joel Lieske, John Splain, Stephen Frantzich, Daniel J. Elazar, and John Kincaid). 1999. "Tocqueville and Democracy in America." *PS: Political Science and Politics* 32: 194–226.

Tocqueville, Alexis de. 1985. *Letters on Politics and Society,* ed. by Roger Boesche, trans. by James Toupin and Roger Boesche. Berkeley: University of California Press.

———. 1966 [1835/1840]. *Democracy in America,* trans. by George Lawrence. New York: Harper and Row.

U.S. Department of Education, National Center for Education Statistics. 1996. *Youth Indicators, 1996: Trends in the Well-Being of American Youth.* NCES 96-027, by Thomas Snyder and Linda Shafer. Washington, D.C.: Government Printing Office.

Uslaner, Eric M. 1998. "Social Capital, Television, and the 'Mean World': Trust, Optimism, and Civic Participation." *Political Psychology* 19: 441–67.

Verba, Sidney, Kay Lehman Schlozman, and Henry Brady. 1995. *Voice and Equality.* Cambridge: Harvard University Press.

Winch, Peter. 1958. *The Idea of a Social Science.* London: Routledge and Kegan Paul.

Wood, Gordon S. 1993. *The Radicalism of the American Revolution.* New York: Knopf.

Chapter Two

Equality, Democracy, and Community from Tocqueville to Putnam

John Ehrenberg

A conservative young aristocrat from a family suspected of Bourbon sympathies, Alexis de Tocqueville came to the United States in 1831 to escape the turmoil of French politics and study American penal reform.[1] But a wider project gradually took shape as he began to wonder whether the New World had anything to offer Europe about their common future. Uneasy about the rise of the modern state, troubled by democracy's instability and mediocrity, and unsure if equality and liberty could be reconciled in an age of mass politics, Tocqueville became convinced that American traditions of localism and voluntary activity could help Europeans learn how to attenuate modernity's contradictory impulse to atomize and centralize. An astute observer, he knew it was important to start at the beginning and wasted no time getting to the heart of the problem. "Among the novel objects that attracted my attention during my stay in the United States," he wrote at the very beginning of *Democracy in America*, "nothing struck me more forcibly than the general equality of condition among the people."

> I readily discovered that the prodigious influence of this fact extends far beyond the laws of the country, and that it has no less effect on civil society than on the government; it creates opinions, gives birth to new sentiments, and modifies whatever it does not produce. The more I advanced in the study of American society, the more I perceived that this equality of condition is the fundamental fact from which all others seem to be derived and the central point at which all my observations constantly terminated. (Tocqueville 1990, I: 3)

As we will see, Tocqueville's conviction that the American future would be relatively free of Europe's history of class warfare *was* decisive to the way he understood civil society—even though historians disagree about whether he was right.[2] But his central insight is of little interest to most of his contemporary disciples. For all their elaborate genuflection in his direction, communitarian theory does not take seriously the Frenchman's most basic finding. It shares his suspicion of politics, his hostility to the state, his preference for the local and the small, and his inability to adequately understand the logic of capitalism. But many of the politicians, professors, and pundits who regularly refer to *Democracy in America* refuse to consider the economic and political determinants of civil society—even though Tocqueville based his entire analysis on equality of condition and free political institutions. Their indifference to the historically unprecedented levels of inequality in America makes their appropriation of Tocqueville theoretically tendentious, empirically misleading, and politically suspect.

Almost any theory can be invoked to support any political project, and the neo-Tocquevillean heart of contemporary American thinking about civil society is no exception. Fresh from his 1994 victory, Speaker Newt Gingrich declared from the well of the House of Representatives that the triumphant Republicans had based their program on *Democracy in America*'s celebration of voluntary activity and Friedrich von Hayek's hostility to the regulatory state. Even as Gingrich regularly quoted Tocqueville in support of the Contract With America's frontal assault on the New Deal, Bill Clinton would find occasion to use the Frenchman's admiration for American voluntary organizations to quietly transfer much of the responsibility for social justice and economic equality from the state to a "civil society" of local volunteerism. Indeed, the President spent eight years promoting community service and urging Americans to dedicate themselves to family, faith, and community. We are likely to hear more of the same from George W. Bush.

Like many other thinkers, Robert Putnam nods in Tocqueville's direction—or seems to. *Bowling Alone* is sprinkled with suggestions that economic inequality compromises the democratic potential of civil society, and its hope that a new Progressive Era might stimulate civic and political revitalization seems attentive to the ways in which broad economic and political trends can encourage—or constrain—civil society's intermediate organizations. "Community and equality are mutually reinforcing, not mutually incompatible," Putnam says, and he follows this observation with a recommendation that "efforts to strengthen social capital should go hand in hand with efforts to increase equality" (Putnam 2000, 358, 360).

But Putnam's agreement with Tocqueville's central insight, the one from which "all others seem to be derived and the central point at which all my observations constantly terminated," is more apparent than real. Tocqueville's presumption of equality took social justice off the table, but he consistently paid attention to the constitutive role of economics and politics. He may have gotten America wrong, but contemporary theorists who propose to examine the democratic potential of civil society have no business ignoring the fact that the United States is now the most unequal advanced society on Earth. Study after study document unprecedented transfers of wealth and power to smaller and smaller sections of the population; the most recent example is a report from the World Health Organization that places the United States dead last among industrialized countries in accessibility to medical care—and this after a decade of uninterrupted economic expansion and enormous budget surpluses. Unprecedented economic, social, and political inequality is the central and determinative fact of contemporary American life, and Putnam is too good a social scientist to ignore its effects. But the substance of *Bowling Alone* presents a normalizing, integrating, and moralistic communitarianism instead of a serious examination of how markets and states condition political activity and shape civic attachments. Putnam impressively documents his thesis that "for the first two-thirds of the twentieth century a powerful tide bore Americans into ever deeper engagement in the life of their communities, but a few decades ago—silently, without warning—that tide reversed and we were overtaken by a treacherous rip current. Without at first noticing, we have been pulled apart from one another and from our communities over the last third of the century" (Putnam 2000, 27). If political, social, and civic engagement have unraveled as dramatically as Putnam suggests, his surprising indifference to what Tocqueville considered essential might help us understand why he talks so much about "us," "we," and "our."

From Tocqueville . . .

We have to begin by taking Tocqueville at his word about the importance of "equality of condition." *Democracy in America* set out to investigate how equality and freedom shaped political and civil affairs. Tocqueville's hope that they could strengthen one another depended on whether equality of condition and popular sovereignty could be blended with the "habits, ideas and customs" generated by and supportive of a vigorous tradition of local activity. He knew that the feudal ideal of the disinterested search for the common good no longer made sense in an individualistic environment dominated by commercialism, materialism, and the competitive search for individual advantage. He frequently observed how commercially minded Americans were, recognized the "cupidity" which rested at the heart of their "philosophical method," and hoped that their persistent elevation of private judgment over received wisdom would help them hold the public at arm's length. But Tocqueville was aware of an important contradiction, and it haunts contemporary theories of civil society as powerfully as it shaped his own attempt to link the reality of an individualistic social order to the desirable necessity of civic-minded cooperation. If liberal civil society is the sphere of individual autonomy, personal freedom, private gratification, and the pursuit of self-interest, how can it anchor the ethically based community that Putnam and so many others want to see? To paraphrase a rich tradition of English liberalism, how can public virtue be built on a foundation of private vice? "Individualism," Tocqueville accurately observed, "is a mature and calm feeling, which disposes each member of the community to sever himself from the mass of his fellows and to draw apart with his family and friends, so that after he has thus formed a little circle of his own, he willingly leaves society at large to itself" (Tocqueville 1990, II: 98)?

Putnam is as aware of this problem as Tocqueville was, and he makes good use of *Democracy in America*'s hope that self-interest "rightly understood" will encourage individualistic citizens to associate with one another in an age when equality and democracy constantly erode the basis of that cooperation. "When social conditions are equal," Tocqueville had observed, "every man is apt to live apart, centered in himself and forgetful of the public" (1990, I: 256). He was confident that American localism could offset equality's atomizing impulses. Whether it was the township system of government or local voluntary activity in civil society, the small scale and restricted horizons of Americans' political and civic activities enabled self-serving individuals to cooperate with one another in conditions of freedom protected from the leveling inclination of the nation-state. Equality of condition and political democracy might define America's politics and condition her civil society, but Tocqueville expected New England localism to temper the tendency to equalize too much. The town meeting was his favorite political example, for municipal institutions constitute the strength of free nations. Town meetings are to liberty what primary schools are to science; they bring it within the people's reach, they teach men how to use and how to enjoy it. A nation may establish a free government, but without municipal institutions it cannot have the spirit of liberty. Transient passions, the interests of an hour, or the chance of circumstances may create the external forms of independence, but the despotic tendency which has been driven into the interior of the social system will sooner or later reappear on the surface. (1990, I: 61)

American decentralization, municipal sovereignty, and the virtual absence of central political institutions made town meetings the domesticated versions of the Greek polis where "the passions that commonly embroil society change their character when they find a vent so near the domestic hearth and the family circle" (Tocqueville 1990, I: 67). Localism protected liberty.

The native of New England is attached to his township because it is independent and free; his co-operation in its affairs ensures his attachment to its interests; the well-being it affords him secures his affection; and its welfare is the aim of his ambition and of his future exertions. He takes a part in every occurrence in the place; he practices the art of government in the small sphere within his reach; he accustoms himself to those forms without which liberty can only advance by revolutions; he imbibes their spirit; he acquires a taste for order, comprehends the balance of powers, and collects clear practical notions on the nature of his duties and the extent of his rights. (Tocqueville 1990, I: 68)

Tocqueville's appreciation of localism drove his analysis of the American tendency to voluntarily organize. Indeed, his signature contribution to contemporary theories of civil society is conditioned by his respect for the way American small-scale, parochial activities fused the private strivings of self-interested individuals with the necessities of cooperation and community. Americans had learned how to reconcile equality of condition and political democracy with freedom because their powerful traditions of local autonomy kept the modern state at bay. Observation taught him that in democratic countries "it is not a portion only of the people who endeavor to improve the state of society, but the whole community is engaged in the task; and it is not the exigencies and convenience of a single class for which provision is to be made, but the exigencies and convenience of all classes at once" (1990, I: 249).

It is not impossible to conceive the surprising liberty that the Americans enjoy; some idea may likewise be formed of their extreme equality; but the political activity that pervades the United States must be seen in order to be understood. No sooner do you set foot upon American ground than you are stunned by a kind of tumult; a confused clamor is heard on every side, and a thousand simultaneous voices demand the satisfaction of their social wants. Everything is in motion around you; here the people of one quarter of a town are met to decide upon the building of a church; there the election of a representative is going on; a little farther, the delegates of a district are hastening to the town in order to consult upon some local improvements; in another place, the laborers of a village quit their plows to deliberate upon the project of a road or a public school. Meetings are called for the sole purpose of declaring their disapprobation of the conduct of the government, while in other assemblies citizens salute the authorities of the day as the fathers of their country. Societies are formed which regard drunkenness as the principal cause of the evils of the state, and solemnly bind themselves to give an example of temperance. (1990, 249–50)

Tocqueville had no doubt that America's formidable level of political activity and civic vitality resulted from her marriage of equality, democracy, and localism—even if the communitarians who so regularly quote him often seem to suffer from selective judgment and diminished memory. "In no country in the world," he said admiringly, "has the principle of association been more successfully used or applied to a greater multitude of objects than in America. Besides the permanent associations which are established by law under the names of townships, cities, and counties, a vast number of others are formed and maintained by the agency of private individuals" (1990, 191). Whether it was in politics or in civil society, Americans had learned to organize. Shaped in the final instance by economic equality and political democracy, local activity transforms self-interested individuals into community-minded citizens:

The general affairs of a country engage the attention only of leading politicians, who assemble from time to time in the same places; and as they often lose sight of each other afterwards, no lasting ties are established between them. But if the object be to have the local affairs of a district conducted by the men who reside there, the same persons are always in contact, and they are, in a manner, forced to be acquainted and to adapt themselves to one another.

It is difficult to draw a man out of his own circle to interest him in the destiny of the state, because he does not clearly understand what influence the destiny of the state can have upon his own lot. But if it is proposed to make a road cross the end of his estate, he will see at a glance that there is a connection between this small public affair and his greatest private affairs;

and he will discover, without its being shown to him, the close tie that unites private to general interest. Thus far more may be done by entrusting to the citizens the administration of minor affairs than by surrendering to them in the control of important ones, towards interesting them in the public welfare and convincing them that they constantly stand in need of one another in order to provide for it. (Tocqueville 1990, II: 103–4)

Impressed by the way localism deflected attention from the general and national to the local and particular, Tocqueville admired how Americans had learned how to "combat the effects of individualism by free institutions." He knew how important—and difficult—it was to get people to cooperate in a democratic and individualistic society marked by equality of condition. The relatively narrow organizations of civil life might be organized around the pursuit of private advantage and the broader associations of the political sphere might be constituted by the search for the general welfare, but they are mutually reinforcing and dependent (Tocqueville 1990, II: 105). Independent civil associations need political liberty, and free political groupings function best in conditions of equality. Tocqueville was mightily impressed by the proliferation of political activity, but contemporary theories of civil society tend to be more suspicious of politics than he was and have focused instead on his description of "those associations that are formed in civil life without reference to political objects":

The political associations that exist in the United States are only a single feature in the midst of the immense assemblage of associations in that country. Americans of all ages, all conditions, and all dispositions constantly form associations. They have not only commercial and manufacturing companies, in which all take part, but associations of a thousand other kinds, religious, moral, serious, futile, general or restricted, enormous or diminutive. The Americans make associations to give entertainments, to found seminaries, to build inns, to construct churches, to diffuse books, to send missionaries to the antipodes; in this manner they found hospitals, prisons, and schools. If it is proposed to inculcate some truth or foster some feeling by the encouragement of a great example, they form a society. Wherever at the head of some new undertaking you see the government in France, or a man of rank in England, in the United States you will be sure to find an association. (1990, II: 106)

Associations were distinctly American alternatives to French statism and English aristocrats. Nurtured in conditions of economic equality and political democracy, they compensated for the individual weakness of modernity's isolated citizen. America was showing Europe the way toward a future that would temper individualism with the ties of affiliation. Association does not come naturally to the modern citizen, but Tocqueville was as alert to his beneficial effects as is Putnam. But his approach to the moral benefits of a vibrant civil society was not driven by a moralizing viewpoint. "Feelings and opinions are recruited, the heart is enlarged, and the human mind is developed only by the reciprocal influence of men upon one another. I have shown that these influences are almost null in democratic countries; they must therefore be artificially created, and this can only be accomplished by associations" (Tocqueville 1990, II: 109).

But there is more to Tocqueville's admiration of associations than meets the eye. In the end, his respect for the way they shaped American democracy was driven by an aristocratic suspicion of the leveling state. He looked to local centers of power and influence to blunt the universalizing thrust of democratic politics and of the modern state—a tendency that is shared by a good deal of contemporary communitarian thinking. Local power and voluntary association can moderate the fact that "every central government worships uniformity; uniformity relieves it from inquiry into an infinity of details, which must be attended to if rules have to be adapted to different men, instead of indiscriminately subjecting all men to the same rule" (Tocqueville 1990, II: 295). In an era when the state's influence was spreading everywhere, the key problem of modern politics was how to adapt Montesquieu to democracy. The Old World's future problem found an answer in the New World's present.

> The notion of secondary powers placed between the sovereign and his subjects occurred naturally to the imagination of aristocratic nations, because those communities contained individuals or families raised above the common level and apparently destined to command by their birth, their education, and their wealth. This same notion is naturally wanting in the minds of men in democratic ages, for converse reasons; it can only be introduced artificially, it can only be kept there with difficulty, whereas they conceive, as it were without thinking about the subject, the notion of a single and central power which governs the whole community by its direct influence. (1990, II: 289)

Tocqueville's admiration of "artificial" intermediate associations was directly anti-statist in tone, and this is one reason why he has been of such interest to contemporary theories of civil society. Putnam is not as overtly hostile to broad political action as many of his peers, but his effective failure to consider the implications of inequality is of a piece with the claim that local voluntary activity is the indispensable heart of democracy and the suggestion that "reviving community" is a credible project absent meaningful state action to mitigate inequality. Tocqueville was aware that the state's increasing influence was a consequence of democracy, equality, industrialization, urbanization, and the other accompaniments of modernity. Distinct duties and different rights had conditioned medieval legislation, but the eclipse of feudalism only intensified the threat that central power posed to the local differences and particularities that constitute civil society and provide the grounding for liberty. "However enlightened and skillful a central power may be, it cannot of itself embrace all the details of the life of a great nation," Tocqueville warned. "Such vigilance exceeds the powers of man" (1990, I: 90).

American localism and habits of voluntary organization would safeguard liberty by restraining the universal application of the law. Associations would temper "the dangers to which the principle of equality exposes the independence of man," and this would be the American lesson that could help Europe after the French Revolution's success in sweeping away the remnants of feudalism. "A government can no more be competent to keep alive and to renew the circulation of opinions and feelings among a great people than to manage all the speculations of productive industry. No sooner does a government attempt to go beyond its political sphere and to enter upon this new track than it exercises, even unintentionally, an insupportable tyranny; for a government can only dictate strict rules, the opinions which it favors are rigidly enforced, and it is never easy to discriminate between its advice and its commands" (1990, II: 109).

Equality, then, was both problem and cure. Tocqueville knew how hard it would be to contain it; if people do not differ by very much, there doesn't seem to be much reason for anything but the uniform application of the law. "The Americans hold that in every state the supreme power ought to emanate from the people; but when once that power is constituted, they can conceive, as it were, no limits to it, and they are ready to admit that it has the right to do whatever it pleases. They have not the slightest notion of peculiar privileges granted to cities, families, or persons; their minds appear never to have foreseen that it might be possible not to apply with strict uniformity the same laws to every part of the state and to all its inhabitants" (1990, II: 290). Equality and democracy were irresistibly conditioning modern life, and Tocqueville's desire to restrain their effects was driven by his understanding of how quickly the American present was be-

coming Europe's future. At a time when equality and democracy were beginning to transform European politics, Tocqueville appealed to the so-
phistication of her leaders:

> The government of a democracy brings the notion of political rights to the
> level of the humblest citizens, just as the dissemination of wealth brings the
> notion of property within the reach of all men; to my mind, this is one of its
> greatest advantages. I do not say that it is easy to teach men how to exercise
> political rights, but I maintain that, when it is possible, the effects which re-
> sult from it are highly important; and I add that, if there ever was a time at
> which such an attempt ought to be made, that time is now. Do you not see
> that religious belief is shaken and the divine notion of right is declining;
> that morality is debased and the notion of moral right is therefore fading
> away? Argument is substituted for faith, and calculation for the impulses of
> sentiment. If, in the midst of this general disruption, you do not succeed in
> connecting the notion of right with that of private interest, which is the
> only immutable point in the human heart, what means will you have of
> governing the world except by fear? When I am told that the laws are weak
> and the people are turbulent, that the passions are excited and the authority
> of virtue is paralyzed, and therefore no measures must be taken to increase
> the rights of the democracy, I reply that for these very reasons some mea-
> sures of the kind ought to be taken; and I believe that governments are still
> more interested in taking them than society at large, for governments may
> perish, but society cannot die. (1990, I: 245–46)

The paradox that an America that had never experienced feudalism could
offer local institutions and intermediate associations to a Europe whose
democratic revolutions threatened to sweep the ground clear was not lost
on Tocqueville. He was worried that, since the Continent did not have extensive experience with either equality or democracy, the modern drift toward centralization would be more intense there than in the United States
(1990, II: 297). Americans had been free before they had become equal,
and their English roots generated political institutions and civic associations, which were defending liberty against state power before equality
began to shape the New World's economic relations. Never having under-
gone a deeply democratic revolution, the Americans had built a political
order based on "the notion of private rights and the taste for local freedom; and they have been able to retain both because they have had no
aristocracy to combat" (299).

Tocqueville knew that the drive toward centralization and despotism
was becoming powerful in Europe precisely because the Old World's

democratic revolutions had eliminated many of the intermediate bodies that had once protected aristocratic privilege. From one end of Europe to the other the privileges of the nobility, the liberties of cities, and the powers of provincial bodies were disappearing. The problem was clear to him: "all these various rights which have been successively wrested, in our time, from classes, guilds, and individuals have not served to raise new secondary powers on a more democratic basis, but have uniformly been concentrated in the hands of the sovereign. Everywhere the state acquires more and more direct control over the humblest members of the community and a more exclusive power of governing each of them in his smallest concerns" (1990, II: 304). The nobility can no longer defend Liberty, but Europeans can learn the vital American lesson:

> I firmly believe that an aristocracy cannot again be founded in the world, but I think that private citizens, by combining together, may constitute bodies of great wealth, influence, and strength, corresponding to the persons of an aristocracy. By this means many of the greatest political advantages of aristocracy would be obtained without its injustice or its dangers. An association for political, commercial, or manufacturing purposes, or even for those of science and literature, is a powerful and enlightened member of the community, which cannot be disposed of at pleasure or oppressed without remonstrance, and which, by saving its own rights against the encroachments of the government, saves the common liberties of the country. (1990, II: 324)

Tocqueville's celebrated analysis of civil society was organized around the promise and the threat of equality and democracy. His neo-feudal appreciation for secondary organizations sought to defend the locally based freedom of those with "great wealth, influence, and strength" from the centralizing and universalizing thrust of the modern state. His suspicion of mass democracy in an age of equality has carried over to contemporary communitarian theory—but a good deal of his work has been distorted and lost in the process. Taking shape as it has in a period of increasing inequality, diminished political expectations, lower levels of activity, heightened degrees of cynicism and disengagement, and endless reassertions of orthodox moral categories, communitarian theory routinely tries to adapt Tocqueville to conditions that are radically different from what he thought he had encountered in America. In so doing, it often ignores what is most useful and retains what is most problematic.

. . . To Putnam

Economic equality and political democracy are the twin anchors of Tocqueville's analysis of American political and civic associations. He may have assumed too much, but it's important that *Democracy in America* went from economics and politics to civil society. Tocqueville welcomed self-interested voluntary activity in an egalitarian, democratic civilization precisely because he hoped its parochialism would blunt the intrusive thrust of the universal state. It was his concern with matters of economic equality and political democracy that drove his famous appraisal of intermediate organizations. He knew community, social capital, and civil society require economic equality and political democracy.

Apart from some scattered references here and there, *Bowling Alone* demonstrates little such understanding. It is surprisingly silent on economics and politics, presenting instead a normalizing and integrating moralism in a period marked by historic degrees of economic and political inequality. Putnam demonstrates that high levels of political and civic activity come with safe neighborhoods, good schools, happy citizens, and healthy lives. There is no reason to doubt his findings or question his methodology, but his repeated invocations of "we," "our," and "us" reveal a great deal about the book's ultimate project and demonstrate how much communitarians leave behind when they move away from Tocqueville's understanding that economics and politics constitute civil society. The best way to uncover this is to start with *Bowling Alone*'s presentation of the Progressive Era as a model of present and future reform.

To be fair, Putnam does attribute the erosion of social capital to a variety of economic, technological, and social developments—but he explicitly denies that historic levels of economic inequality play an important role in the current crisis. "Television, two-career families, suburban sprawl, generational changes in values—these and other changes in American society have meant that fewer and fewer of us find that the League of Women Voters, or the United Way, or the Shriners, or the monthly bridge club, or even a Sunday picnic with friends fits the way we have come to live. Our growing social-capital deficit threatens educational performance, safe neighborhoods, equitable tax collection, democratic responsiveness, everyday honesty, and even our health and happiness" (Putnam 2000, 367). Aware of the possibility that communitarianism can arouse reactionary, anti-democratic, and nostalgic yearnings for a vanished Golden

Age of Association, Putnam calls for a new era of civic inventiveness founded on the proposition that contemporary American civilization bears striking similarities to the end of the Gilded Age:

> It was, in short, a time very like our own, brimming with promise of technological advance and unparalleled prosperity, but nostalgic for a more integrated sense of connectedness. Then, as now, new modes of communication seemed to promise new forms of community, but thoughtful men and women wondered whether those new forms would be fool's gold. Then, as now, optimism nurtured by recent economic advances battled pessimism grounded in the hard realities of seemingly intractable social ills.
>
> Then, as now, new concentrations of wealth and corporate power raised questions about the real meaning of democracy. Then, as now, massive urban concentrations of impoverished ethnic minorities posed basic questions of social justice and social stability. Then, as now, the comfortable middle class was torn between the seductive attractions of escape and the deeper demands of redemptive social solidarity.
>
> Then, as now, new forms of commerce, a restructured workplace, and a new spatial organization of human settlement threatened older forms of solidarity. Then, as now, waves of immigration changed the complexion of America and seemed to imperil the *unum* in our *pluribus*. Then, as now, materialism, political cynicism, and a penchant for spectatorship rather than action seemed to thwart idealistic reformism.
>
> Above all, then, as now, older strands of social connection were being abraded—even destroyed—by technological and economic and social change. Serious observers understood that the path from the past could not be retraced, but few saw clearly the path to a better future.
>
> By the turn of the century, complacency bred of technological prowess was succeeded by dissatisfaction, civic inventiveness, and organized reform efforts fueled by a blend of discontent and hopefulness. Over the succeeding decade this flourishing, multifaceted movement—sprouting from seeds sown in the Gilded Age and dependent on new tendrils of social connectedness—would produce the most powerful era of reform in American history. (Putnam 2000, 381–82)

On Putnam's reading, Progressive leaders forged an egalitarian communitarianism, which translated the face-to-face values of small-town life to a rapidly industrializing country faced with unprecedented levels of immigration, economic transformation, urbanization, social conflict, and political corruption. A sustained, conscious program of political reform and social renewal replenished American social capital and set the conditions for a long period of political and civic health. *Bowling Alone*'s central thesis is that similarly dramatic measures are called for now. "Just as did our predecessors in the Progressive Era," Putnam writes, "we need to create new structures and policies (public and private) to facilitate renewed civic engagement." And, since the book documents an impressive falling-off of engagement over the past twenty-five years, nothing less than a full-court press will do: "leaders and activists in every sphere of American life must seek innovative ways to respond to the eroding effectiveness of the civic institutions and practices that we inherited" (Putnam 2000, 403).

Bowling Alone offers a "new Progressive agenda" in six spheres that deserve special attention from aspiring "social capitalists": youth and schools; the workplace; urban and metropolitan design; religion; arts and culture; and politics and government" (2000, 404). Despite the book's alarmed tone, though, it is remarkably short of credible solutions. Indeed, the reader is left with a surprisingly modest set of proposals which range from ensuring that workplaces will be more "family-friendly and community-congenial" to encouraging "new forms of electronic entertainment and communication engagement." After having seen Putnam at his best in the first three-fourths of the book, several commentators have noted the insipid and thin quality of his specific proposals. They *do* look superficial at first blush, but the book's precipitous decline is the result of its fundamental ideological orientation. Having left Tocqueville behind for a foray into the vaporous world of "we," "us," and "our," *Bowling Alone* proposes an analysis of the Progressive Era shorn of most of its important economic and political content. It is unable to account for the ways in which the Progressive leadership was compelled to confront concentrated economic and political power by powerful movements from below, and—reflecting its author's political orientation—it is unable to furnish an accurate account of the important ways native-born workers, immigrants, and African Americans organized themselves and created a rich civil society whose social capital took shape as they directly confronted and indirectly resisted the existing order.[3] When *Bowling Alone*'s desire to provide a measure of social integration and ideological normalization is added, we are left with a decidedly unsatisfying vessel from which to draw meaningful suggestions about how to address the contemporary crisis in social capital and civil society.

The Progressive Era was a specific political response to the economic consequences of the Gilded Age's laissez-faire social Darwinism—chief among which were economic inequality and political weakness. Even though its leadership was decidedly middle class, it was marked by a remarkable level of broad political action driven by acute class conflict, economic transformation, and programs to redistribute wealth and de-mocratize politics. The social capital it created resulted from a long strug-gle for economic justice and political democracy—a struggle that was largely created from below. But Putnam's treatment effectively severs Pro-gressivism's politics from its economic foundation and treats it as if it were animated by the selfless, benign community-building activity of the re-formist middle class. *Bowling Alone*'s elitist and top-down version of Pro-gressivism is a good example of how easy it is to forget the lessons of his-tory in a conservative era driven by a suspicion of broad political action and hostility toward the welfare state.

The period was organized around the eminently republican notion that concentrated economic wealth threatened political democracy. As had been the case throughout much of the nineteenth century, this theme had been articulated most clearly by small farmers and the labor movement during the Gilded Age; what was special about the Progressive Era is that alarm about the social and political consequences of inequality spread to the middle class as well. Progressivism simply cannot be understood apart from a very broad, popular movement against economic polarization, in-dustrial concentration, the appearance of the trusts, the rise of finance capital, and the activities of corrupt urban political machines. Many orga-nizations and associations appeared during the period, only some of which pursued the integrating and normalizing agenda that is so dear to Putnam. A lot of them were organs of combat and did not speak about "we," "us," and "our." Middle-class Progressives could not cope with much of their activity then, and Putnam largely ignores them now.

Whether they were Finnish community centers, choruses, hiking groups, and sports clubs or Jewish socialist associations, apprenticeship programs, literary societies, and the Yiddish theater, the Progressive period was propelled by a massive and largely spontaneous self-organization of the working class. Driven by stifling inequality, political powerlessness, pervasive exclusion, and numbing exploitation, German workers estab-lished vibrant community beer gardens and supported a wide variety of newspapers; Italian workers set up political debates and opera groups; Irish workers congregated in neighborhood bars and organized their col-lective lives around an enormous variety of Catholic women's groups, bur-ial societies, parochial schools, and fraternal organizations. For its part, the nascent trade union movement began to put in place a remarkable set of class-based civil and political organizations that reflected labor's determi-nation to acquire literacy, civilization, and knowledge—a development that was deeply connected to the way workers were organizing their own education, leisure, and culture. When Eugene V. Debs warned the working class that capitalism was trying to turn it into "a hand," he expressed a deeply rooted and class-based desire for culture which gradually coalesced as immigrant and native-born workers across the country organized themselves and created institutions which allowed them to fight and survive. None of this would have happened without the conviction that workers should be self-reliant and independently acquire the knowledge and culture that the new age required.

Nowhere was this expressed more strongly than in the 1912 strike by immigrant women textile workers in Lawrence, Massachusetts. When they expressed their desire for culture and knowledge, they were very clear in articulating a desire for "bread and roses." Astonished by their clarity and threatened by their activity, mainline Progressives stayed away from them. Assisted by the Industrial Workers of the World, the strikers' songs, poetry, leaflets, literary societies, discussion groups, and theaters carried their desire for decent wages, humane treatment, and modern knowledge from their homes and communities to the rest of the country.

Urban working-class neighborhoods generated hundreds of newspapers, political clubs, literary societies, dance halls, religious circles, fraternal associations, debating organizations, civic leagues, and business fellowships. The Progressives had virtually nothing to do with them; their New York leadership wouldn't go near Irish neighborhoods, for example, because it distrusted the "papist" influence of the Catholic Church, hated Tammany Hall, and had serious misgivings about labor associations—the three institutions creating so much of the social capital that Putnam celebrates. There is an important historical lesson about the Progressive Era here, and it should not be lost on those who look to middle-class leaders for inspiration: not all organization and enlightenment came from above. Putnam rightly points out that the Progressives were often suspicious of initiatives from below and were prone to a top-down managerialism, but his own account of the period is equally elitist because of its basic project. For all of *Bowling Alone*'s communitarian talk, a powerful integrating drive makes it difficult to address the partisan and combative class content of much of the social capital that was created during the Progressive Era.

The same could be said of southern and northern blacks. Confined by a legally expressed and state-enforced system of racial exclusion and segregation, southern blacks developed intricate networks of mutual aid, churches, schools, vocational training, newspapers, and community leadership and preserved these institutions in the face of relentless white hostility and violence. The farmers' alliances, sharecroppers' unions, voluntary schools, self-defense leagues, ministers' associations, and women's clubs tested the limits of American apartheid and cannot be understood apart from the South's history of racialized oppression and resistance (McMillen 1989). The same was true of the North. Even before the Great Migration changed the face of industrial cities during World War I, urban blacks organized neighborhood juke joints, social clubs, churches, newspapers, baseball leagues, consumer cooperatives, a thriving underground economy, and a lively tradition of public discourse on the street whose character was directly influenced by formal and informal efforts to keep them spatially confined and economically marginalized. Caribbean immigrants built churches, benevolent associations, newspapers, dance troupes, and mutual aid societies, which provided the social capital for interracial solidarity and national identity alike. The most important black urban mass movement of the World War I era, Garveyism added to a solid foundation of social capital that had been built during the Progressive Era but which Putnam's emphasis on the middle-class NAACP and Progressives largely ignores (James 1998; Watkins-Owens 1996).

The social capital created during the Progressive Era simply cannot be understood apart from the independent activity of workers and the poor. Many of the period's most important initiatives came as the result of independent and confrontational pressure from below, a fact that is largely missing from Putnam's communitarian account. To characterize the Progressive Era as the great creator of middle-class communitarian social capital is a good measure of how far contemporary political discourse has fallen—and how uncomfortable Putnam is with conflict and politics. When they were at their best—that is to say, when they were most responsive to the economic and political demands of their labor and farmer constituencies—Progressive leaders talked of "industrial democracy," a term which signified their understanding that extending equality and freedom was a class project pitting the interests of the many against those of the few. Whether they sought to protect beleaguered small proprietors or looked to the positive state to protect workers and consumers in an era dominated by predatory corporations and banks, the most advanced Progressives knew that equality and democracy required partisan and class-based political combat.

The period's social movements, immigrant associations, reform groups, labor unions, funeral societies, tenant circles, and suffragette organizations agreed that important measures of economic and political redistribution were required if American democracy was to survive industrialization, urbanization, and immigration. This is not to say that the Progressive Era was a single undivided whole; as Putnam points out, its disposition to use political power to deepen economic equality and extend democracy paid no serious attention to the consolidation of a brutal racial dictatorship in the South and urban apartheid in the North.[4] Even as civic organizations like the League of Women Voters and the NAACP appeared, middle-class Progressives were often disposed to create nonpartisan organizations in an effort to reduce the influence of mass class-based political parties. The success of that endeavor was measured by declines in political participation, particularly in voting.

It is important to be nuanced about a complicated phenomenon like the Progressive movement, but at the same time it is important to recognize what rested at the heart of the era's politics. As Eric Foner observes, "Progressivism occupied a broad political spectrum that ranged from socialists who advocated state control of the economy to forward-looking businessmen who realized that workers must be accorded a voice in economic decision-making. But at its core stood a coalition of middle-class reformers, male and female, often linked to trade unions, who sought to humanize capitalism by making it more egalitarian and to reinvigorate democracy by restoring political power to the citizenry and civic harmony to a fractured society" (1998, 141). What made many of its political and civic organizations special was their recognition that inequality threatened democracy, that broad political struggle was necessary to defend and deepen it, that the interests and activity of workers would determine its future, and that civic harmony depended on engaging the vital economic and political issues of the day. For all of its ritual invocations of civicness and togetherness, this is more than can be said of *Bowling Alone*.

Measures to establish "industrial freedom" recognized the intimate connection between economic redistribution and political democracy. Driven by working-class organizations from below, some Progressive leaders talked of the right to work, encouraged the formation of labor unions, promoted a "living wage," rearranged workplace relations in favor of workers, and established social controls over plant relocations, layoffs, and the distribution of profits. They were powerfully influenced by mass labor and socialist movements that were outgrowing their European roots and assuming a distinctively American political identity—a development that introduced a radically new political orientation to the country's politics. A broad coalition of organized women, labor leaders, socialists, and reformist intellectuals recognized how important it was to establish an activist national state. They did so for very different reasons, but much of their activity was powered by a simple conviction that does not appear in *Bowling Alone*: that the Gilded Age's laissez-faire social Darwinism was socially destructive and profoundly anti-democratic. Moving away from the constricted categories of earlier periods, this conviction generated a reform movement of unprecedented breadth and depth.

Civilizing the marketplace and democratizing the state now meant "busting" the trusts, protecting consumers, organizing the immigrant poor, and empowering workers and farmers. The period's combative social capital helped create the most striking and durable feature of the Progressive movement: the appearance of the "positive" state. National administrative agencies and regulatory commissions worked to set uniform rules of behavior which imposed limits on capital and interfered with the rights of property in the name of a measure of democratic supervision over the market. Local control and states' rights were widely derided as excuses for inaction and masks for class privilege as economic justice and political democracy became national projects whose parameters were defined and defended at the level of the nation-state. Herbert Croly expressed the new understanding by observing that the "Hamiltonian" means of a government-directed national economy had become necessary to realize the "Jeffersonian" ends of democratic self-government, individual freedom, and local autonomy. Economic redistribution and political democracy meant that the face-to-face interactions of community would have to be supplemented by state regulatory activity (Croly 1909).

It is important to reiterate that Progressivism was a deeply contradictory movement—but that is because the interests of its participating classes often clashed. If the labor and socialist movements generated important activity from below, a powerful elitist, managerial, and top-down regulatory thrust expressed a bureaucratized and administrative approach whose drive for order and efficiency often clashed with democracy. Thus, millions of Southern and Northern blacks, native-born workers, and recent immigrants were eliminated from the voting rolls even as millions of middle-class white women were added. Leading reformers promoted referendum, initiative, recall, residency, and literacy requirements, and other "good government" measures *because* they would remove politics from particular group interests, impose order in the workplace, combat the factionalism against which Madison warned, reorient the movement toward the pursuit of the common good, reform urban machines, and—most importantly—paralyze the dangerous tendency of the lower orders to use mass political power in ways which threatened property and order. "Enlightened" businessmen recognized that their capital-intensive firms would benefit from federal regulation rather than being left to the vicissitudes of local and state politics.

But this does not change the fact that it was labor that drove the creation of social capital during the Progressive Era. The problem is that *Bowling Alone*'s preference for moralistic integration over political analysis makes it impossible to acknowledge how class conflict shaped the period's politics. It wasn't as hard for those who were actively engaged in the fight—and a fight it was. Many of the most effective activists who fought for women's suffrage linked political power to a broad demand for state intervention on behalf of female immigrant laborers. This class alliance anchored the activity of a broad coalition of middle-class club women, socialists, settlement house workers, and trade unionists whose class consciousness and militancy does not appear in Putnam's account. As the movement shed its early nativism it became steadily more democratic, and this led it to combine the struggle for political democracy with the fight for economic equality. The movement grew progressively more comprehensive in its understanding and broad in its organization. Middle-class women sought to uplift the urban poor in concrete ways, but they brought their own skills to a vibrant civil society that had already been created— and this is why they went considerably further than moralizing paeans about the virtues of cooperation and community. The organizations which demanded state provision of social services, the right to work, economic regulation, protection from disease, decent housing, and universal education certainly created social capital—but it was not the sort with which contemporary communitarians are comfortable.

The real lesson of the Progressive Era is lost in Putnam's account, and it is *Bowling Alone*'s elitism which explains why it can't even consider the possibility that creating social capital might require a political movement aiming at consistent, partisan state action to democratize the market and establish a measure of conscious social direction over the blind destructiveness of unregulated economic processes. The Progressives might have been naive in assuming that the modern administrative state could be the impartial guardian of the public good, but they certainly shared Tocqueville's understanding that the fusion of concentrated economic and political power would effectively end the American experiment which

Democracy in America had so presciently outlined. Such an understanding is absent in the accounts of scholars who would reinvigorate community by changing the bad habits of the poor.

Because he doesn't go deep enough, Putnam doesn't enable us to get to the roots of how Progressivism reinvigorated democracy and strengthened community. This is why his desire to, say, "ensure that by 2010 America's workplace will be substantially more family-friendly and community-congenial" stands in such a pale imitation of the struggle for women's suffrage, federal supervision of industrial activity, universal national labor and health legislation, an eight-hour day, a living wage for all workers, a national system of health and social insurance, and the unimpeded right to form trade unions. It is likely that American social capital would be substantially richer if the remains of the century-old Progressive agenda were implemented than if Putnam's recommendations were to take shape.

The relative weakness of the book's conclusion is based on a deeper conceptual failure. More is needed to reinvigorate community than reducing suburban sprawl, encouraging more part-time work, and the other measures Putnam suggests. In trying to explain the precipitous decline of the trade union movement, for example, he pays lip service to structural matters like the transition to a post-industrial economy but really ends up saying that unions have been declining because fewer people want to join, and they don't want to join because of the generational shifts charted in *Bowling Alone*. But a highly conscious, state-supported offensive against American labor is now well into its third decade. It features the usual suspects: bitter employer resistance, illegal firings, hostile courts, Taft-Hartley, unfriendly labor law, congressional contempt, presidential indifference. In light of the remarkable report on "Unfair Advantage" from Human Rights Watch, which documents the contours of a class war so brutal that it violates the most elementary international human rights standards, Putnam's account of the decline in trade union membership is more than a little superficial (Human Rights Watch 2000). It is insulting, inaccurate, and misleading to blame the television habits of the working class for the weakness of organized labor.

Conclusion

"The touchstone of social capital," Putnam says, "is the principle of generalized reciprocity—I'll do this for you now, without expecting anything immediately in return and perhaps without even knowing you, confident that down the road you or someone else will return the favor" (2000, 134). This is certainly an attractive ideal, and Putnam's claim that "generalized reciprocity" is good for health, prosperity, community, and morale is eminently plausible. The problem is how to get from here to there, and *Bowling Alone* would be considerably stronger if it took Tocqueville more seriously.

The fact that it doesn't shouldn't be surprising. Unfortunately, a moralized, depoliticized, and self-righteous communitarianism is a perfect ideological reflection of contemporary disengagement, materialism, individualism, cynicism, and inequality. Rebuilding communities cannot happen with an approach that refuses to take sides, engage the political issues of the day, and address contentious questions of social justice. For all their limitations, many Progressive leaders and activists were fueled by a desire to fight political corruption, economic injustice, and social exclusion. That militancy, not some deracinated desire to build "community," is what explains their success.

Strengthening social capital is a worthwhile project, but it won't come easily. Tocqueville was perfectly correct when he observed that a healthy civil society requires equality of conditions and democratic political institutions. There's more to his observations than the ritual communitarian references to *Democracy in America* are willing to consider. Other developed societies, after all, are somehow able to provide quality healthcare, decent public education, manageable workweeks, affordable housing, and living wages—not to mention reasonably honest national elections. Large swaths of the United States are littered with industrial cities whose hearts were cut out by capital flight and deindustrialization. It might be useful to consider how a German law that prevents corporations from closing manufacturing plants without recompensing their home communities helps preserve social capital. Local funding of education guarantees that the quality of the training that American children receive is in direct proportion to the market value of their parents' houses. It might be useful to consider how nationalized French funding of universal education helps enrich social capital. It would be disgracefully easy to list similar examples. The dismal American record in matters of equality, justice, and democracy is a political problem at bottom, and it cannot be addressed without broad and comprehensive activity, which communitarians abhor. The real lesson of the Progressive Era is that no conceivable combination of charitable donations, student volunteerism, employer-donated spaces for community meetings, or neighborhood arts groups can revitalize community without a broad commitment to social justice. *Bowling Alone*'s failure to engage these potentially disruptive issues has serious consequences, for encouraging citizens to think in terms of what "we" share in conditions of scandalous inequality can subvert the most basic requirements of a decent society. It's simply not enough to urge people to get along because "we" will benefit. Building community will require more universal categories, more partisan struggle, more politics, more courage—and, most importantly, more thinking which pits "us" against "them."

NOTES

1. The following analysis is like that of my 1999 *Civil Society: The Critical History of an Idea*. New York: NYU Press.

2. See, for example, Pessen (1971) and (1978).

3. See Kelley (1996) for a fruitful adaptation of James Scott's notion of "the hidden transcript" developed in Scott (1985). I am grateful to Mark Naison for his valuable help with regard to working-class social capital.

4. As McMillen (1989) points out, the worst and most violent years of "Negrophobia" in Mississippi ran from 1890 to the outbreak of World War I—exactly during the Progressive Era.

REFERENCES

Croly, Herbert. 1909. *The Promise of American Life*. New York: MacMillan.

Ehrenberg, John. 1999. *Civil Society: The Critical History of an Idea*. New York: NYU Press.

Foner, Eric. 1998. *The Story of American Freedom*. New York: Norton.

Human Rights Watch. 2000. *Unfair Advantage: Workers' Freedom of Association in the United States under International Human Rights Standards*. http://www.hrw.org/reports/2000/uslabor/.

James, Winston. 1998. *Holding Aloft the Banner of Ethiopia: Caribbean Radicalism in Early Twentieth-Century America*. London: Verso.

Kelley, Robin D. G. 1996. *Race Rebels: Culture, Politics, and the Black Working Class*. New York: Free Press.

McMillen, Neil R. 1989. *Dark Journey: Black Mississippians in the Age of Jim Crow*. Urbana: University of Illinois Press.

Pessen, Edward. 1971. "The Egalitarian Myth and the American Social Reality: Wealth, Mobility, and Equality in the `Era of the Common Man.'" *American Historical Review* (October) 70:4.

————. 1978. *Jacksonian America: Society, Personality, and Politics*. Homewood, Ill.: Dorsey Press.

Putnam, Robert. 2000. *Bowling Alone: The Collapse and Revival of American Community*. New York: Simon & Schuster.

Scott, James. 1985. *Weapons of the Weak: Everyday Forms of Peasant Resistance*. New Haven: Yale University Press.

Tocqueville, Alexis de. 1990. *Democracy in America*. 2 Vols. New York: Random House.

Watkins-Owens, Irma. 1996. *Blood Relations: Caribbean Immigrants and the Harlem Community, 1900–1930*. Bloomington: Indiana University Press.

Chapter Three

The Phenomenology of Democracy
Putnam, Pluralism, and Voluntary Associations

David A. Schultz

Democratic theories have ontologies. Each defines its object of inquiry, the critical components of what makes a political system work, and what forces, structures, and assumptions are core to its conception of governance. This ontology will not only include a discussion of human nature but also an examination of concepts such as representation, consent, political parties, liberty, equality, and a host of other ideas and institutions that define what a democracy is and how it is supposed to operate (Pennock 1979; Sartori 1987).

Civic engagement, voluntary associations, and social capital occupy essential ontological positions in Robert Putnam's conception of democracy. From his *Making Democracy Work* (Putnam 1993) through his trilogy of essays on American democracy in 1995 and 1996 and especially in *Bowling Alone* (Putnam 2000), civic engagement and voluntary associations are described as important generators of social capital, resulting in the enhanced performance of democratic institutions and instilling in its members "habits of cooperation and public-spiritedness" (2000, 338–41). While Putnam no longer describes voluntary associations as the panacea for the ills of American democracy (341), they nonetheless remain important in his vision of political theory and practice.

Robert Putnam acknowledges Tocqueville's discovery of voluntary associations in *Democracy in America* as critical to the maintenance and production of social capital in a democratic society (48). Yet this appeal to voluntary associations is not unique. After World War II, advocates of pluralism and pluralist theory also appropriated Tocqueville's notion of voluntary associations, reaching different conclusions about democracy and participation in an effort to support their claims regarding the importance of groups as intermediate associations critical to stabilizing democracy (Baumgartner and Leech 1998, 87). As a result, voluntary associations occupied an important role in their vision of democracy. They spatially configured democracy and defined public space in specific ways that defined relationships among and between individuals and groups (Warren 2001). Yet if concepts derive their meaning from use and their relationship to other concepts (Wittgenstein 1968, paragraphs 82, 340, 432, 693), then the voluntary associations of Tocqueville and the pluralists are very different from the ones Putnam describes.

This chapter examines Robert Putnam's appropriation of Tocqueville's voluntary associations and contrasts it to that of the pluralists. The primary claim here will be that unlike Putnam who seems to emphasize group membership as a means of enhancing individual social capital, psychological attributes, and participation, the focus of the pluralists and Tocqueville was more on the structural role that groups played in making democracies stable. For the pluralists, emphasis on group involvement was not centrally premised upon a concern to encourage individual participation or efficacy. For them, the ontology and epistemology of political analysis and involvement shifted away from the individual and to the group, and voluntary associations were seen as one of several critical structural forces essential to maintaining a stable democratic system. In contrast, Putnam's view of democracy is incomplete, seeing it as one that is the sum of the individual attributes and attitudes of its members, while lacking a structural component. In short, Putnam lacks a theory of the state and the role it plays in fostering the conditions that make it possible for voluntary associations to form, exist, and interact.

A second claim here is that the value of groups for the pluralists resided not so much in how they protect individual freedom but in how they struck a balance between consensus and conflict, producing the conditions for a stable democracy. Third, unlike the pluralists who seemed conscious or aware of the structural role of wealth or class upon the operations of a democracy, at least in some circumstances, Robert Putnam appears blind to how structural forces, such as economic capital, can impact democratic performance.[1] Overall, the claim to be made is that Putnam's view of what social capital is and how it makes a democracy work changes dramatically from *Making Democracy Work* to *Bowling Alone* such that structural and relational issues important in the earlier work fade in importance as social capital increasingly becomes viewed more as an individual attitude and attribute. The significance of that movement is important because it represents an important ontological shift in Putnam's thinking regarding how democracies operate and what is required to fix them. As this chapter will show, by the time Putnam reaches *Bowling Alone,* the causes of democratic dysfunction, including a lack of trust and civic engagement, rest with the individual, thereby causing Putnam to ignore important structural forces that may be at the root of the decline of political participation and alienation in the United States. Finally, Putnam's effort to produce social capital as a way of encouraging sociality is misguided. Putnam's wrongheaded tactic of trying to build social consciousness from the individual up reveals an incomplete vision of democracy and human nature, as well as an incomplete understanding of human intersubjectivity. Overall, Putnam's conception of social capital reveals his failure to see structural causes for democratic disengagement.

Tocqueville, Equality, and Voluntary Associations

Tocqueville's *Democracy in America* approaches an explanation of American democracy from a structural perspective more characteristic of theories of Karl Marx and Emile Durkheim than of a methodological and epistemological individualist such as Thomas Hobbes (Pope 1986). The latter sought to build and explain society up from the individual, whereas Marx and Durkheim placed central importance in understanding more structural forces to describe society, such as the worker-capitalist relationship for Marx or the division of labor for Durkheim. What this means is that for Tocqueville, society is more than merely the sum of individuals. Ontologically, social structures exist, and their existence is important to describing the social context in which individuals act.

Tocqueville's observations begin with his noting that one of the most striking characteristics of the United States was of a general equality of conditions that pervaded American society and institutions. It was this underlying equality of conditions, a structural prerequisite to democracy, along with the social mores of the nation, which influenced much of his discussion of the United States in *Democracy in America* (Pope 1986, 51). This equality—politically, socially, and economically—was critical to the maintenance of a democratic society and it was at the center of why America, Americans, and groups had the character they did.

Tocqueville saw excesses of wealth as a threat to popular government because the wealthy bourgeoisie would tend to pursue private interests and abuse their economic and political power (Boesche 1987, 78, 83). In a bourgeois society, excesses of wealth destroy public life by atomizing it and isolating people (88). Should wealth control or rule in America, popular participation, which Tocqueville described as important to the maintenance of a public life, would be threatened (121–22). Additionally, Tocqueville states "private citizens, by combining together, may constitute great bodies of wealth, influence, and strength, corresponding to the persons of an aristocracy" (Tocqueville 1960, vol. II, 387). In *Democracy in America*, the Frenchman even describes the new manufactures in negative terms, saying that its aim was to "use" citizens and that it tends to create a private-spirited "aristocracy" (1960, vol. II, 193). To check these early nineteenth-century manufactures, which are clearly different from the large corporations of the late twentieth century, de Tocqueville advocated the use of public or government institutions to help contain their threat (1960, vol. II, 130–31).

Tocqueville's observations on wealth carry over into his views of voluntary associations. These associations are part of the fabric of democracy's social structure, significantly defining how individuals act and behave. Not only does participation in voluntary associations have an impact on the private attitudes of citizens, but also these associations play an important role in the maintenance of a democracy. What Tocqueville meant by associations are not private groups serving private interests. Instead, these associations pursue their ideas for the public good and serve public ends (Boesche 1987, 128; Pessen 1977, 59–62). For instance, in describing the public nature of these groups, he describes groups as including towns and cities as examples of political associations (Tocqueville 1960, vol. I, 216). Their activities included founding hospitals, prisons, and schools, and serving other activities that in the nineteenth century were considered as furthering the public good (Tocqueville 1960, vol. I, 216–17). Thus, contrary to the pluralists, Tocqueville's discussion of interest groups is not an unequivocal defense of pluralist interest group politics, but a critique of it. While these associations could help promote participation and the protection of interests, these were mostly public—regarding groups composed of citizens banding together for public purposes. However, even these groups need to be regulated. Tocqueville saw occasions where these associations were a threat to popular government and required checks upon them via popular suffrage (Tocqueville 1960, vol. I, 224).

The voluntary (political) associations that Tocqueville praised generally are not private groups or civil associations like large corporations seeking to further their private interests through groups such as local chambers of commerce. Tocqueville distinguishes the *public* nature of *political* associations from the *private* nature of *civil* associations (Tocqueville 1960, vol. II, 128). Few scholars seem to note this important distinction that Tocqueville made. The latter type of groups are much more akin to Madison's factions which (in James Madison's mind) did pose a threat to the public good by pursuing private interests at the expense of the commonweal. Instead, in describing the composition of political associations, Tocqueville depicts them as composed of "private individuals" and "citizens" and not corporations seeking to pursue more public ends (Tocqueville 1960, vol. I, 217–18). As Mark Warren (2001) points out, not all voluntary associations perform the same functions or occupy the same role in society; some groups pursue political ends and produce certain outputs, while other groups secure private goals and outputs. Thus, Tocqueville's notion of voluntary association does not apply to just any group.

The point is that when Tocqueville spoke of voluntary associations, he did not seem to be referring either to bowling leagues, chambers of commerce, or economic corporations. His voluntary associations were public-regarding entities that fostered civic-mindedness within the context of an overall economic and political equality of conditions. Similarly and perhaps more significantly, voluntary associations were important not simply in terms of the individual attitudes they fostered in citizens, but because they functioned to improve, nurture and help organize institutions such as juries, administrative decentralization, manners, mores, and the laws (Pope 1986, 51–52).

Thus, as will be noted below, Tocqueville's views on voluntary associations differ from that of the pluralists in that he would not have considered all interest groups to be of equal value in the maintenance of a democratic spirit. Contrary to Nancy Rosenblum's (1998) recent claim that all voluntary associations—even those banding together neo-Nazis—are valuable in that they impart social capital and mediate extremism by inculcating moral restraint, both Tocqueville and even the pluralists would have recognized that there are good and bad groups and not all of them foster democratic values. Tocqueville would have agreed with the claim that membership does help foster important democratic values, yet he would not have agreed that all forms of group membership do so or that group membership alone secures that goal (Warren 2001).

Robert Putnam, Voluntary Associations

The role of voluntary associations has changed dramatically in the course of Robert Putnam's writings, and so has the meaning of social capital. In addition, the role assigned by Putnam to these associations is different from the usage assigned to them by Tocqueville.

In *Making Democracy Work* (Putnam 1993), the focus was on explaining institutional performance by way of an examination of the northern and southern Italian regions. In noting that the wealthier, more modern regions of the North have a head start over their poorer counterparts in material and human resources, Putnam ties economic performance to the performance of public and civic institutions (85). Speculating on the causes of the strength of these civic institutions, he identifies active citizen engagement and participation in public affairs as important (87), along with political equality (88), and solidarity, trust, and tolerance (89). However, these norms, according to Putnam, are "embodied in, and reinforced by, distinctive social structure and practices," and the most important of these institutions are civil associations (89). Borrowing from Tocqueville, Putnam argues that these associations instill internally in their members a sense of cooperation, trust, public-spiritedness, a tempering of self-interest, and other important values critical to democratic practice (89–90). Externally, these groups have a wider impact upon the polity, producing moderation of group conduct and cross-pressures (90).[2]

The performance of representative government is facilitated by the social infrastructure of civic communities and by the democratic values of both officials and citizens. Most fundamental to the civic community is the social ability to collaborate for shared interests. Where norms and networks of civic engagement are lacking, the outlook for collective action appears bleak. Generalized reciprocity thus generates high social capital and underpins collaboration. This type of harmony in society illustrates how voluntary collaboration can create value that no individual, regardless of income and intelligence, could produce alone (183). In the civic community, associations proliferate, memberships overlap, and participation spills into multiple arenas of community life. Overall, the performance of democratic institutions is enhanced by a developed civil society (182).

Critical to Putnam's equation is how involvement in voluntary associations generates social capital. Quoting from James Coleman's conception of the term, Putnam here defines social capital as those "features of social organization, such as trust, norms, and networks, that can improve the efficiency of society by facilitating coordinated actions" (Putnam 1993, 167). In drawing upon this definition of social capital and the way it is employed in *Making Democracy Work*, social capital has more of a, well, social aspect to it. Social capital is not the sole property of any individual. Instead, it is the connective tissue, shared norms, and community values that undergird social cooperation and intercourse. Social capital is not divisible; instead, it is a structural byproduct of engagement, in and through voluntary associations (Tarrow 1996). Moreover, voluntary associations are part of an embedded social structure, one part of several institutions necessary to making democracies work.

Putnam significantly abandons this structural approach to democracy, voluntary associations, and social capital in his later writings. In *The American Prospect* (1996), and *PS: Political Science and Politics* (1995), Putnam draws upon social capital, which he defines as "features of social life—networks, norms, and trust—that enable participants to act more effectively to pursue shared objectives" (Putnam 1996, 34), while in *Bowling Alone* social capital refers to "connections among individuals—social networks and norms of reciprocity and trustworthiness that arise from them" (19). The changes in definition are subtle, yet profound. First, and most importantly, social capital is now viewed as more of a psychological or attitudinal factor than a structural force.[3] By that, civic engagement seems to produce individual attributes in specific individuals that are lacking in persons who do not get involved. Therefore, those who opt to watch television have less social capital than those who do not (303). Similarly, those engaged in religious or other forms of participation have a greater sense of trust, honesty, voluntarism, and philanthropy than those not engaged. Social capital thus is conceived something that individuals can acquire via personal investment (323, 388).

Second, and related to the first point, social capital in *Bowling Alone* no longer appears to be a social attribute, if by social one means "a shared or collective good." Though Putnam contends that social capital has a collective aspect (2000, 20), his definition of a collective aspect is discussed in terms of how it individually benefits someone, or in how it enhances the productivity of the individual (20, 323). Moreover, in distinguishing two forms of social capital—bonding and bridging (22)—both are really individuated forms of social capital. Bonding capital provides "social and psychological support" to individuals and it helps with providing real capital, such as financing, in the marketplace (22). Bridging capital is similarly individual, such as access to information that one can use to find jobs (22).

Third, voluntary associations and their production of social capital have a different role in *Bowling Alone* than they did in *Making Democracy Work*. In the former, there is a much more confused relationship between social capital, voluntary associations, and the democratic polity. In *Bowling Alone* Putnam provides impressive data to document the decline in membership in civic organizations, charting the demise of dozens of organizations over time (48–65, Appendix III). Bracketing whether there is really a decline in civic engagement or simply a shift from these sorts of organizations towards others, ostensibly the message is that a decline in membership in these groups has resulted in a decline in social capital and such capital is necessary for trust, etc. However, equally plausible is that a decline in social capital is making it harder for people to join these groups. Both of these causal claims are asserted in *Bowling Alone* (294).

Diminished social capital is seen both as the cause and result of the failure to join civic associations (Edwards and Foley 1998; Portes 1998). In either case, civic associations have developed an important instrumental role in democracy; they are important to the furthering or manufacturing of social capital and the creation of a democratic society but they do not, per se, appear to be part of the structural organization of democracy the way they were in *Making Democracy Work*.

This suggests that in Putnam's early works, the emphasis was upon groups as prerequisites to democracy and social capital is viewed structurally and as a connective tissue like Coleman's conception, but it has changed into attitudinal attributes by Putnam's later definitions. Ontologically, this is a profound shift in Putnam's views on democracy. If the early Putnam was closer to the pluralists or even Tocqueville in seeing democracy from the top down, and in seeing an important role of the state or government in organizing society, the later Putnam sees democracy from the bottom up. By that, the creation of democracy resides in the installation of the proper democratic attitudes or beliefs in people, not in developing specific institutions and structures. The poor performance of a democracy is our fault—we do not participate, we do not engage, we do not do our duty in producing social capital—and not the fault of other overarching forces such as structural inequalities in the economy.[4] Thus, it is ironic that when Putnam discusses the Progressive Era in *Bowling Alone* and he notes the polarization of income as contributing to the loss of social capital in that era (370), he does not draw similar parallels between the polarization of income today and the decline of social capital. Similarly, in offering remedies to the decline of social capital today, with the notable exception of a weak plea for campaign finance reform (412), his solutions are more individual—travel less (408), be friendlier (406), become more religious (409), watch less television and movies (410), and join others in singing Kumbaya (410).

Putnam's views on voluntary associations also contrast to that of Tocqueville. Tocqueville never placed all of his democratic hope in voluntary associations. His description of democracy in America ontologically commenced with the equality of conditions and social mores, and it was these conditions and values that helped define and make group membership possible and, in turn, group membership reinforced democratic individualism and values. The same is not true with Putnam. Groups seem almost architectonic and magical in their ability to impart social capital, yet ignored is the epistemological and ontological issue of where the values and energy come from for individuals initially to join groups. Groups must presuppose some initial social or moral capital to encourage individuals to join them before social capital can be imparted (Berkowitz 1999, 187–89). Much like the dilemma John Locke faced in explaining why individuals would leave an almost Eden-like state of nature to join civil society, Putnam and other social capitalists face a dilemma of explaining how groups can impart social capital unless individuals have this capital already to join groups. Putnam is undecided: Are we social or solitary by nature?

Ontologically, Putnam's democracy is premised upon the aggregation of individual attitudes and beliefs who, when they acquire the requisite social capital, are more willing to join organizations, trust others, and cooperate than if these attitudes are lacking. A well-functioning democracy occurs when there is a sufficient reserve of social capital such that a large number of individuals are poised for civic engagement. In effect, Putnam seems to employ "social capital" in a similar way to "political culture" (21, 346) and, more importantly, the term also seems to be a surrogate for what others call "intersubjectivity." Intersubjectivity refers to the capacity to understand or empathize with others (Husserl 1977), or to be engaged in a conscious sense of sociality with others (Dewey 1957; Heidegger 1962; Schutz and Luckmann 1973), or to see the essential internal connections or bonds that connect individuals together (Ollman 1984).

If Putnam is in fact using social capital in this way, his discussion of the decline of social capital is really an effort to explain why individuals in contemporary America are alienated from one another. Putnam's solution to alienation is individual and, conversely, his solution to alienation is similarly individual, asking subjects to reconstruct the public sphere, or the intersubjective, by undertaking specific acts. Unfortunately, Putnam's solution is bound to fail much in the same way Edmund Husserl's efforts to prove the existence of other minds failed or any other effort to aggregate individual preferences into a collective choice will be unsuccessful (Arrow 1963). One cannot reconstruct intersubjective experiences or create some collective social unit simply by aggregating individual social capital (Jung 1973, 138–39; Merleau-Ponty 1973; Schutz 1966, 77).[5]

A large part of Putnam's problem is rooted in his ontology of individualism. He begins with a theory of human nature as essentially one of isolated *homo economicus* and from that starting point hopes to construct a theory of the social. Such an aggregating task is impossible (Jung 1973, 138–39; Schutz 1966, 77). It is illogical to begin with an individual rational maximizer and ask that person to join groups, participate, or develop a sense of sociality. As Mancur Olson pointed out, it makes no sense for individuals to engage in this type of collective action (Olson 1971). Individuals who are expected to produce economic capital for themselves cannot also be expected to engage in the type of altruistic or social action Putnam calls for.

Putnam's individualist approach to democracy's woes suggests that more structural approaches to addressing the problem are foreclosed. There is almost no role that the state or other institutions can play in creating social or political institutions that can bring people together or otherwise provide a context for shared experiences or a sense of the social.[6] Putnam is left with a vision of democracy that is incomplete, premised mostly upon individual attitudes, while missing the social constructs and institutions that make those attitudes possible.

The Context of Pluralist Thought

In contrast to Putnam, pluralist writers adopted a more structural view on democracy and how democracies work. Tocqueville's views on voluntary associations and the prerequisites for democratic stability influenced political scientists after World War II. At this time a predominant concern of political scientists was democratic stability and two questions dominated the discipline: First, why or how did Fascism and Nazism develop out of ostensibly democratic states and, second, what could be done to stabilize democracies so that they would not degenerate into either authoritarian or communist states? In short, the political science literature of the 1950s and 1960s was dominated by the question of how to maintain liberal democracies (Ceaser 1993, 41, 46).

Numerous studies sought to locate those institutions and values necessary to maintain stable democracies (Lijphart 1968; Neubauer, 1967). Factors that were deemed important included economic wealth and modernization (Dahl 1971, 60–62; Huntington 1984, 193, 199; Lipset 1959; Lipset 1963, 28, 87, 116; Needler 1968; Rostow 1971; and Rustow 1968); political participation (Lipset 1959, 116); civilian control of the government (Diamond et al. 1989, 344; Huntington 1956); and widely supported and regularized political mechanisms to resolve conflict (Almond and Verba 1965, 363; Dahl 1976, 364). They stressed the importance of a democratic political culture that inculcated tolerance and a reasonable balance of both social consensus and cleavage, including a respect for differences and a commitment to resolve these differences through the political process (Almond and Verba 1965, 363; Christoph 1965; Dahl 1971, 105; Lipset 1963, 1, 4, 78, 250). Equally important though, democracy required a social pluralism with crosscutting loyalties, expressed through multiple, competing groups (Lipset 1963, 78). The significance of overlapping loyalties among social cleavages was to prevent the emergence of social alignments polarizing a nation along race, ethnicity, religion, or other traditional lines of conflict and division.

Hence, the postwar political science paradigm argued that the trick to maintaining democratic stability rested in part on the encouragement of secular national values which all groups supported (Lipset 1959, 68), the maintenance of overlapping loyalties, and the replacement or amelioration of the divisive forces of race, ethnicity, and religion with less divisive interest politics that could be politically compromised through the electoral and political processes (Budge 1970; Easton 1965; Huntington 1968; Kornhauser 1959; Lijphart 1977, 19; Pennock 1979, 206–59; Rabushka and Shepsle 1972). These empirical studies stated that democracies depend on support for broad social and political toleration of diverse groups and dissident views as well as a set of regularized and peaceful mechanisms to reconcile disputes without censorship or force. Finally, these studies also emphasized that attainment of a certain level of economic conditions or affluence was required, or that a strong middle class was needed, or that the gaps between the rich and the poor could not be too great such that there was unchecked class conflict or antagonisms. It was within the context of democratic stability that Tocqueville and the role of interest groups in fostering stability made their pluralist entrance. All of these factors were structural prerequisites for democracy.

Pluralism was a political science effort to rethink what made liberal democracies stable. Drawing upon Arthur Bentley (1949, originally published in 1908), political scientists after World War II gave increasing attention to the role of interest groups in the political process. Works such as William Kornhauser's *The Politics of Mass Society* (1959), Seymour Martin Lipset's *Political Man: The Social Bases of Politics* (1963, originally published in 1960), and David Truman's *Governmental Process* (1971, originally published in 1951) were among a host of many other studies that turned to Tocqueville's *Democracy in America*. Bentley's impetus to turn to interest groups to explain how governments work, Tocqueville's emphasis on voluntary associations as important to American democracy, and the concern to stabilize democracies and explain the rise of fascism, all contributed to the pluralists forging a theory that depicted the encouragement of interest groups as important intermediary associations critical to democratic stability.

Kornhauser

Kornhauser's *The Politics of Mass Society* (1959) sought to distinguish between pluralist and mass tendencies in modern society, and to show how social pluralism supports liberal democracy (13). The book's stated aim was to examine the major social factors weakening democratic order and to argue that intermediating associations serve democracies (17).

Kornhauser defined a mass society as "a social system in which elites are readily accessible to influence by non-elites and non-elites are readily available for mobilization by elites" (39). Such a society would be highly vulnerable to totalitarianism (36) because mass behavior is unstable (46), diverts us from our personal experiences of daily life to more remote experiences (43–44), and produces social alienation and atomization (33). Mass societies level the distinctions between individuals, leaving no barriers or forces to limit the ability of some group or individual to dominate others. Overall, mass societies, such as Germany in the 1920s and 1930s (113), are particularly fluid and prone to democratic breakdown because there is no barrier between the people and the state and because there is no group in which individuals may associate.

Intermediate associations, which are missing in mass society, are critical to producing social insulation in a liberal society (75). For Kornhauser, individual freedom requires social insulation and differentiation (26). Conditions in which all are equal are dangerous. Quoting from Tocqueville's *Democracy in America* (26):

> I believe that it is easier to establish an absolute and despotic government among a people in which the conditions of society are equal than among any other; and I think that if such a government were once established among such a people, it not only would oppress men, but would eventually strip each of them of several of the highest qualities of humanity.

Interest groups are necessary to the creation of a liberal society because they render governmental elites less accessible to influence by nonelites. According to Kornhauser: "More than one hundred years ago, Tocqueville also argued that French political upheavals were related to the lack of independent group life" (87–88). Again, drawing upon the French nobleman:

> In aristocratic nations the bodies of nobles and the wealthy are in themselves natural associations that check the abuses of power. In countries where such associations do not exist, if private individuals cannot create an artificial and temporary substitute for them I can see no permanent protection against the most galling tyranny. (127)

According to Kornhauser, intermediate associations are a bulwark against tyranny in that they replace the breakup or social distinction in society lost when the aristocracies faded. They provide for political stability (78), by acting as a buffer between the individual and the state and by also being a forum for individual political expression. Overall, interest groups fulfilled important structural needs and balanced critical tendencies or forces in society. If a society encouraged a multiplicity of groups, mass society could be averted, pluralism fostered, and the result would be a democracy.

Finally, in discussing the conditions making mass society possible, Kornhauser quotes Tocqueville in the context of a discussion of how democratic orders accommodate conflict between the upper and lower classes by gradually assimilating more of the latter into the governing and voting class (133). Kornhauser recognized how socioeconomic status influenced political attitudes and participation (68), and he argued that societies that failed to address class issues were more likely to become antidemocratic and mass than those that did.

Lipset

Lipset's *Political Man* states very clearly that its goal is to locate the "social conditions making for democracy" (1). The social basis of a successful democracy resides in a tension between class conflict and social consensus and the ability of democracies to mediate this conflict and consensus. According to Lipset:

> Surprisingly, as it may sound, a stable democracy requires the manifestation of conflict or cleavage so that there will be struggle over ruling positions, challenges to parties in power, and shifts of parties in office; but without consensus—a political system allowing the peaceful "play" of power, the adherence by the "outs" to decisions made by the "ins," and the recognition by the "ins" of the rights of the "outs"—there can be no democracy. The study of the conditions encouraging democracy must therefore focus on the sources of both cleavage and consensus. (1)

Thus, *Political Man* is a perfect example of the pluralist concern with the stability of democratic structures that preoccupied many political scientists after World War II and in the face of the spread of communism.

Part I of the book is titled "The Conditions of the Democratic Order," and numerous passages relate to democratic stability. For example, Lipset states that the "stability of any given democracy depends not only on economic development but also on the effectiveness and legitimacy of its political system" (64). A table of social prerequisites to foster stable democracies includes an open class system, economic wealth, literacy, and a capitalist economy (61). Sufficient economic development produces "increased income, greater economic security, and widespread higher education" that permits "the lower strata to develop longer time perspectives and more complex and gradualist views of politics" (45). In fact, Lipset cites Tocqueville (51) as recognizing before Marx that increased wealth and education of the lower classes make them less susceptible to extremist ideology and antidemocratic sentiments.

Lipset tells the reader it "is obvious that the conditions related to stable democracy . . . are most readily found in the countries of northwest Europe and their English-speaking offspring" (57), and offers a list of stable and unstable democracies and contrasts them to stable and unstable dictatorships (32). Overall, there is no question that democratic stability is the theme and goal of *Political Man* and the various social and economic prerequisites to democracy are important in helping states manage social conflict and consensus. Yet critical to achieving a balance between consensus and conflict are social groups, and here is where Lipset notes his debt to Tocqueville.

Lipset credits Tocqueville as "the first major exponent of the idea that democracy involves a balance between the forces of conflict and consensus" (4). Contrasting Marx to Tocqueville, Lipset states that while the former saw classes as the social unit striking the balance, it was Tocqueville who first described local communities and voluntary associations as securing this balance. According to Lipset: "Private associations which are sources of restrictions on the government also serve as major channels for involving people in politics. In short, they are the mechanisms for creating and maintaining the consensus for a democratic society" (7). Tocqueville, then, is the first pluralist, at least according to Lipset, and much of the focus of *Political Man* and the arguments in the book on using voluntary groups both as buffers between the individual and the state and as a mechanism to preserve democracy are clearly indebted to him. In fact, *Political Man* makes scores of references to Tocqueville.

Elsewhere in *Political Man*, Lipset demonstrates how a mass society is an authoritarian society made possible by the absence of intermediary associations. Such associations act as "countervailing power to a centralized state (52), contributing to democratic attitudes including political tolerance and participation (52–53). Voluntary associations are also credited with increased voting activity (189), the production of crosscutting social cleavages (77–78), the breakup of social conformism (448), and the mediation of class conflict (310).

In sum, the value of interest groups resides less in how they enhance the efficacy and participatory activity of individuals, although that does occur. Instead, democracy is less about the individual than it is about the group and how its efficacy and political activity should be encouraged. The voluntary association—not the individual—is the savior of democracy, and it was Tocqueville's genius to first discover this.

Truman

David Truman's *The Governmental Process* is one of the single most important statements on pluralism, developing a theory of interest groups in a competitive political environment that serves to distribute political power. Truman defines an interest group "as a shared-attitude group that makes certain claims upon other groups in the society" (37). This definition is reminiscent of the first half of Madison's *Federalist* number 10 depiction of a faction as a number of citizens united and actuated by some common impulse, passion, or interest, yet it ignores the second half of the definition, which casts factions in a negative light.

With this definition of interest group in mind, Truman begins his work by referencing *The Federalist Papers* and the importance that Madison places on factions and the need to control them (Truman 1971, 4). Truman's claim is that *The Federalist* is "one of the most skillful and important examples of pressure group activity in American history" (5). Yet Truman's sanitized reading of Madison led to the conclusion that factions carried none of the overtones of corruption and selfishness associated with modern groups (6). From Madison, Truman then moves on to Tocqueville, invoking him as further evidence of the importance of groups in the American political process. Here, he cites approvingly from *Democracy in America*: "In no country of the world . . . has the principle of association been more successfully used or applied to a greater multitude of objects than in America" (7). By invoking Tocqueville and Madison, Truman thus demonstrates the important contributions interest groups make to the political process and how democracy would not be possible without group mobilization.

Having recast interest groups in a favorable light, Truman's *Governmental Process* articulates an argument about interest groups and government power. Governmental institutions are described as centers of interest-based power where groups will seek to influence the political process by gaining access to various points of the government (Truman 1971, 506). Government decisions are the result of the contest of organized interests using many access points to advocate their members' interests in the policy process (507). In many ways, the government is almost like a blank slate, with the policies written onto it by different groups. What keeps any one group from possessing too much power is the competition from other groups similarly seeking access. Yet Truman notes that stability and equilibrium within a group are disturbed by the loss or entry of a leader (26–27), and similarly, in the political arena, the entry of new groups will affect the stability and equilibrium of the interest group competitive political process. Second, overlapping group membership also serves as a stabilizing force by overcoming class stratification and the single-minded preoccupation an individual may have with pursuing only one interest (520).

Truman's debt to Tocqueville resides not in the social capital that interest groups afford the individual. The clear focus of *The Governmental Process* is not on the individual but on the group and how groups are important to making democracies work.

Summary

The leading pluralists after World War II premised their studies of democracy on the promotion of regime stability. They argued that competition between a diverse array of interest groups makes for a stable democracy. In supporting their views, pluralists cited Tocqueville as first discovering the importance of voluntary associations in promoting a stable democratic regime. These associations were seen as important less because they would enhance individual participation and more because groups in themselves were important and primary units of political participation. Groups were seen as protectors of interests, buffers between the government and citizen, channels of political communication, and forces to mediate class and other forms of social and political conflict. Groups, along with other variables, were described as important structural determinants of democracy. Voluntary organizations played a major role in pluralist epistemology as well as being for them the ontological basis for a free society. Thus, while groups were comprised of individual citizens, pluralists sought to understand and build a democratic society upon the former. In that sense, they were closer to Tocqueville's understanding of groups in the political process.

Finally, even though many have criticized pluralism as inattentive to the impact of wealth and class upon group mobilization (Lowi 1969; McConnell 1966; Schattschneider 1960), pluralists often recognized the problem of economics and class divisions in the maintenance of a stable democracy. Many pluralists held that political participation and democratic attitudes were influenced by socioeconomic status. In making these claims, the pluralists seemed closer to Tocqueville than did the social capital school.

Conclusion

The number of bowling leagues in America continues to decline as the percentage of Americans who do decide to bowl do it alone (Johnson 1999).[7] Robert Putnam no doubt views such trends as worrisome, prompting him to yearn for the golden days of yesterday when we bowled together, mom stayed home with the 2.1 children while dad went off to work, and we all had more time to socialize. Bowling leagues are thus a metaphor for the change in American habits, emphasizing the importance of voluntary associations to democracy. In advocating the importance of group membership, Robert Putnam harkens back to Alexis de Tocqueville's views. Yet he is not the first to do this, and his efforts are a significant departure from what Tocqueville sought.

Earlier in the twentieth century, pluralists envisioned voluntary associations as the savior of democracy. They saw them not as a font of individual social capital but as the new focus of political activity that could stabilize democracy in the face of erratic political participation. Voluntary associations thus became the ontological center of democratic theory, and the epistemology of democracy recognized groups as real entities. In contrast, Robert Putnam's vision of democracy lacks a structural context. While social capital in *Making Democracy Work* was something individuals were embedded in and shared, he sees social capital in *Bowling Alone* as a mere attribute of distinct individuals. Social capital is not social but rather proprietary, divisible, and individual.

For Putnam, civic engagement and voluntary associations produce individual attributes and psychological attitudes in citizens so that they participate, and such attitudes are at the basis of the democratic political culture that makes democracies work. Phrased otherwise, contemporary democracy is failing because it is our fault—we watch television instead of joining groups, and we have the wrong attitude to make democracy flourish. Putnam's approach situates the individual as the ontological center of democracy, and in turn, his epistemology is also individualistic, although groups are acknowledged as important to the maintenance of important social traits. Unlike the pluralists and even Tocqueville's view of groups, he overlooks their structural role in defining the conditions in which individuals act. Putnam also overlooks the role of wealth and how different types of voluntary associations impact democratic government differently. Tocqueville saw this. Even more, perhaps as Karl Marx noted over 150 years ago, Putnam ignores the alienating aspects of capitalism that strip individuals of their essential human attributes and bonds that connect them to one another (Ollman 1984).

We may be bowling alone not by individual choice but as a result of structural forces in the polity or economy that are breaking the essential human sociality that Putnam wishes to construct out of isolated egos and *homo economicus*. There may be several structural reasons why people have disengagement from democracy—economic inequalities, bureaucratization of society, and the alienation of work—that are not sourced in the individual behavior and attitudes of people. Watching television or disengaging from many types of activity may be a rational response or exit strategy to a problem in democratic legitimacy (Hirschman 1970). At a time when about half of the American public chose not to vote in the 2000 elections, many reasons, such as the role of big money in politics, mediocre candidates, poor or limited political choices, and the belief that the election would not make a difference, all provide good reasons for why people disengage. In addition, if Abraham Maslow is correct, people cannot participate in this type of activity unless sufficient basic physiological, safety, and love needs are first met (Maslow 1943). When millions of people lack health insurance, live at or below poverty level, face racism in their lives, it is no wonder there is disengagement.

Additionally, nowhere in the dissection of voluntary associations by Putnam is there a differentiation among types of groups and the values they impart. Not all groups or voluntary associations perform the same functions or roles (Warren 2001), and the ontological space that individuals versus groups occupy in Tocqueville, many of the pluralists, and Putnam's *Bowling Alone* are very different. Just as Bentham stated that poetry is as good as pushpin, so too for Putnam a bowling league is as good as a political rally.[8] Phrased otherwise, in their rush to praise groups, Putnam ignores the other view of voluntary associations as factions that have the capacity to corrupt the political process, or become corrupted themselves, thus driving away members (Ladd 1999, 33). It is perhaps this vision of groups as special interests, factions, and political action committees as despoiling democracy that most Americans think of when they think about groups and therefore discourage participation.[9]

Putnam's *Bowling Alone* thus provides a view of democracy that shifts back to individuals. Yet it is a confused view. As with the pluralists, social capitalists see individuals as simultaneously at the ontological and epistemological center of democracy. But at the same time they are no more than *tabula rasa* to be molded by bowling leagues. There is something eerie in this construction, reminiscent of the distinction David Riesman et al. (1953) made between the inner- and other-directed individual. For Riesman, the inner-directed individual was like a gyroscope, where the source of direction for individuals was achieved from internal values implanted by elders in youth. The other-directed individual was like a radar system, finding the source of direction from other contemporaries rather than ancestors.

Riesman's sociology criticized the change in American character. According to him, at the time Tocqueville wrote, Americans were inner-directed and their primary source of values came not from the group but the family and in other activities antecedent to group involvement (Riesman et al. 1953, 35). The American of the 1950s was now other-directed, taking behavioral and attitudinal cues from peers. The result? Individuals were less free and more prone to manipulation by social forces than in the past. Ironically, where Riesman saw America in the 1950s as a lonely crowd, Putnam sees the 1950s as a civic golden age. Putnam may be correct that group membership is important to democracy, but the harkening back to values last characteristic of the 1950s—a decade of McCarthyism, rising consumerism, and segregation—may not be appropriate. In the process of saving democracy, Robert Putnam has exorcised autonomy from politics.

Notes

1. Putnam (1996) in passing dismisses economics—both affluence and poverty—as the decline in civic life in America even though the best evidence suggests that political participation and engagement seem correlated with class and socioeconomic status. See Miller and Shanks (1996).

2. Here Putnam cites *The Civic Culture* on this point.

3. On page 288 of *Bowling Alone,* Putnam describes in individual terms how joiners "develop or maintain character traits" such as being more tolerant, less cynical, and more empathetic, and they also have better social network. On page 291, the measures of social capital, including numbers of meetings person attend, committees served on, or attitudes toward specific social issues. On pages 318–23, those with social capital are described as those who can better accumulate economic capital. On pages 331–33, those who are joiners and have social capital are described as healthier and happier, and on pages 343–44 civic engagement and social capital are linked to "psychic engagement." Overall, all of these measures are individual and measures of attitudinal or attitudinal changes that accompany possession of social capital.

4. On pages 283–84 of *Bowling Alone* Putnam provides a guesstimate of several factors and how they contribute to the decline in social capital. Work and sprawl each are 10 percent; television and the media alone are 25 percent; and television and generational effects are 50 percent. (Even the generational effects on pages 254, 255, and 272 are described in individual terms.) All of these factors, as described by Putnam, are ultimately if not exclusively described in terms

of individual choices and actions on individuals that have contributed to a loss of social capital. This suggests that 80 percent or more of the fault lies with the individual.

5. Evidence that Putnam simply aggregates individual social capital can be found in several places, but in his discussion on pages 322–23 he notes how "social capital can benefit individuals" and that "social capital among economic actors can produce economic growth." Presumably, social capital is aggregated much like economic capital is to produce some quanta of social capital. However, if Putnam claims that social capital is not divisible even though it is individual, then any effort to aggregate it into a collective good runs aground of either the ecological or individualistic fallacy (Frankfort-Nachmais and Nachmias 2000, 48).

6. For example, Powell (2000) indicates how the choice to create majoritarian or proportional representation systems can have a significant impact on how and what interests are represented and, presumably, how citizens relate to one another.

7. The number of league bowlers has declined by almost 50 percent since 1988, and the number of bowling alleys has dropped by over 9 percent since then. As a result, bowling alleys have turned to casual bowlers—families with children and young singles—for business. Additionally, smoking laws challenge bowling as some alleys report 50 percent of their customers to be smokers. Alas, not all the news is bad. Increased customer service and video games have turned business around, and some alleys report that the busiest night of the week is Mondays because "people love to get together with friends and watch the game when it isn't their turn to bowl" (Johnson 1999). Ironically, this suggests that television and video games may be the solution to solitary bowling and smoking laws may actually be a hindrance to social behavior, trust, and capital.

8. While Putnam (2000, 350–54) does acknowledge a dark side to social capital, he does not really see a downside to the role of groups in the political or social process.

9. Additionally, if Robert Michels (1962) is correct that organizations eventually come to be run by an elite, then it is unclear how well they impart democratic values or encourage individuals to remain with a group and engage in the type of meaningful participation that would foster social capital. The decline in membership of some groups and the increase in membership of others that Ladd (1999) notes is simply individuals opting for exit over voice or loyalty (Hirschman 1970).

References

Almond, A. Gabriel, and Sidney Verba. 1965. *Civic Culture: Political Attitudes and Democracy in Five Nations.* Boston: Little, Brown.

Arrow, Kenneth J. 1963. *Social Choice and Individual Values.* New Haven: Yale University Press.

Baumgartner, Frank R., and Beth L. Leech. 1998. *Basic Interests: The Importance of Groups in Politics and in Political Science.* Princeton: Princeton University Press.

Bentley, Arthur F. 1949. *The Process of Government: A Study of Social Pressures.* Bloomington, Ind.: Principia Press.

Berkowitz, Peter. 1999. *Virtue and the Making of Modern Liberalism.* Chicago: University of Chicago Press.

Boesche, Roger. 1987. *The Strange Career of Alexis de Tocqueville.* Ithaca: Cornell University Press.

Budge, Ian. 1970. *Agreement and the Stability of Democracy.* Chicago: Markham.

Ceaser, James W. 1993. *Reconstructing Political Science.* In *A New Constitutionalism: Designing Political Institutions for a Good Society,* ed. by Stephen L. Elkin and Karol Edward Soltan. Chicago: University of Chicago Press.

Christoph, James B. 1965. "Consensus and Cleavage in British Political Ideology." *American Political Science Review* 59: 629.

Coleman, James S. 2000. "Social Capital in the Creation of Human Capital." In *Social Capital: A Multifaceted Perspective,* ed. by Partha Dasgupta and Ismail Serageldin, 19–39. Washington, D.C.: The World Bank.

Dahl, Robert A. 1971. *Polyarchy: Participation and Opposition.* New Haven: Yale University Press.

———. 1976. *Democracy in the United States: Promise and Performance.* New Haven: Yale University Press.

———. 1979. *Who Governs? Democracy and Power in an American City.* New Haven: Yale University Press.

———. 1989. *Democracy and Its Critics.* New Haven: Yale University Press.

Dasgupta, Partha, and Ismail Serageldin. 2000. *Social Capital: A Multifaceted Perspective.* Washington, D.C.: The World Bank.

Dewey, John. 1957. *Reconstruction in Philosophy.* Boston: Beacon Press.

Diamond, Larry, et al., eds. 1989. *Democracy in Developing Countries: Latin America.* Boulder, Colo.: Lynn Reinner.

Durkheim, Emile. 1964. *The Division of Labor in Society.* New York: Free Press.

Easton, David. 1965. *A Framework for Political Analysis.* Englewood Cliffs, N.J.: Prentice-Hall.

Edwards, Bob, and Michael W. Foley. 1998. "Civil Society and Social Capital beyond Putnam." *American Behavioral Scientist* 42: 124–39.

Frankfort-Nachmais, Chava, and Nachmias David. 2000. *Research Methods in the Social Sciences.* New York: Worth.

Heidegger, Martin. 1962. *Being and Time.* New York: HarperCollins.

Hirschman, Albert O. 1970. *Exit, Voice, and Loyalty: Responses to Declines in Firms, Organizations, and States.* Cambridge: Harvard University Press.

Huntington, Samuel P. 1956. "Civilian Control and the Constitution." *American Political Science Review* 50: 676–99.

————. 1968. *Political Order in Changing Societies*. New Haven: Yale University Press.

————. 1984. "Will More Countries Become Democratic?" *Political Science Review* 99: 193–99.

Husserl, Edmund. 1970. *The Crisis of European Sciences and Transcendental Phenomenology*. Evanston: Northwestern University Press.

————. 1977. *Cartesian Meditations: An Introduction to Phenomenology*. The Hague, Netherlands: Martinus Nijhoff.

Johnson, Robert. 1999. "Proprietors Put a New Spin on Their Bowling Alleys." *Wall Street Journal*, September 14, p. B2.

Jung, Hwa Yol. 1973. "A Critique of the Behavioral Persuasion in Politics: A Phenomenological View." In *Phenomenology and the Social Sciences*, vol. 2, ed. by Maurice Natanson, 133–74. Evanston: Northwestern University Press.

Key, V. O. 1967. *Politics, Parties, and Pressure Groups*. New York: Thomas Y. Crowell.

Kornhauser, William. 1959. *The Politics of Mass Society*. Glencoe, Ill.: Free Press.

Ladd, Carll Everett. 1999. *The Ladd Report*. New York: Free Press.

Lijphart, Arend. 1968. "Typologies of Democratic Systems." *Comparative Political Studies* 1: 3–35.

————. 1977. *Democracy in Plural Societies*. New Haven: Yale University Press.

Lipset, Seymour M. 1959. "Some Social Requisites of Democracy: Economic Development and Political Legitimacy." *American Political Science Review* 53: 69–105.

————. 1963. *Political Man: The Social Bases of Politics*. New York: Anchor Books.

Lowi, Theodore J. 1969. *The End of Liberalism*. New York: Norton.

Maslow, Abraham H. 1943. "A Theory of Human Motivation." *Psychological Review* 50: 370–96.

McConnell, Grant. 1966. *Private Power and American Democracy*. New York: Knopf.

Merleau-Ponty, Maurice. 1973. "Phenomenology and the Sciences of Man." In *Phenomenology and the Social Sciences*, vol. 1, ed. by Maurice Natanson, 47–108. Evanston: Northwestern University Press.

Michels, Robert. 1962. *Political Parties: A Sociological Study of the Oligarchical Tendencies of Modern Democracy*. New York: Free Press.

Miller, Warren E., and J. Merrill Shanks. 1996. *The New American Voter*. Cambridge: Harvard University Press.

Natanson, Maurice, ed. 1973. *Phenomenology and the Social Sciences*, 2 vols. Evanston: Northwestern University Press.

Needler, Martin C. 1968. "Political Development and Socioeconomic Development: The Case of Latin America." *American Political Science Review* 62: 889–97.

Neubauer, Deane E. 1967. "Some Conditions of Democracy." *American Political Science Review* 61: 1002–9.

Ollman, Bertell. 1984. *Alienation.* New York: Cambridge University Press.

Olson, Mancur. 1971. *The Logic of Collective Action.* Cambridge: Harvard University Press.

Pennock, J. Roland. 1979. *Democratic Political Theory.* Princeton: Princeton University Press.

Pessen, Edward. 1977. *The Many-Faceted Jacksonian Era: New Interpretations.* Westport, Conn.: Greenwood.

Pope, Whitney. 1986. *Alexis De Tocqueville: His Social and Political Theory.* Beverley Hills, Calif.: Sage Publications.

Portes, Alejandro. 1998. "Social Capital: Its Origins and Applications in Modern Sociology." *Annual Review of Sociology* 24: 1–24.

Powell, G. Bingham, Jr. 2000. *Elections as Instruments of Democracy: Majoritarian and Proportional Visions.* New Haven: Yale University Press.

Putnam, Robert. 1993. *Making Democracy Work.* Princeton: Princeton University Press.

———. 1995. "Bowling Alone: America's Declining Social Capital." *Journal of Democracy* 6: 65–78.

———. 1996. "The Strange Disappearance of Civic America." *The American Prospect* (Winter): 34–49.

———. 2000. *Bowling Alone: The Collapse and Revival of American Community.* New York: Simon & Schuster.

Rabushka, Alvin, and Kenneth Shepsle. 1972. *Politics in Plural Societies: A Theory of Democratic Instability.* Columbus, Ohio: Merrill.

Riesman, David, et al. 1953. *The Lonely Crowd: A Study of the Changing American Character.* Garden City, N.Y.: Doubleday.

Rosenblum, Nancy L. 1998. *Membership and Morals: The Personal Uses of Pluralism in America.* Princeton: Princeton University Press.

Rostow, W. W. 1971. *The Stages of Economic Growth.* Cambridge: Cambridge University Press.

Rustow, Dankwart A. 1968. "Modernization and Comparative Politics: Prospects in Research and Theory." *Comparative Politics* 1: 37–51.

Sartori, Giovanni. 1987. *The Theory of Democracy Revisited.* Chatham, N.J.: Chatham House.

Schattschneider, E. E. 1960. *The Semi-Sovereign People: A Realist's View of Democracy in America.* New York: Holt, Rinehart and Winston.

Schutz, Alfred. 1966. *Collected Papers, vol. 3.* The Hague, Netherlands: Martinus Nijhoff.

Schutz, Alfred, and Thomas Luckmann. 1973. *The Structures of the Life-World.* Evanston: Northwestern University Press.

Tarrow, Sidney. 1996. "Making Social Science Work Across Space and Time: A Critical Reflection on Robert Putnam's *Making Democracy Work.*" *American Political Science Review* 90: 389–98.

Tocqueville, Alexis de. 1960. *Democracy in America*. Trans. Henry Reeve. New York: Schocken Books.

Truman, David B. 1971. *The Governmental Process: Political Interests and Public Opinion*. New York: Knopf.

Warren, Mark A. 2001. *Democracy and Association*. Princeton: Princeton University Press.

Wittgenstein, Ludwig. 1968. *Philosophical Investigations*. New York: Macmillan.

Ziegler, Harmon. 1964. *Interest Groups in American Society*. Englewood Cliffs, N.J.: Prentice-Hall.

Chapter Four

Post-Liberal Civil Society and the Worlds of Neo-Tocquevillean Social Theory

Michael J. Shapiro

Reinstalling the Nineteenth-Century Gaze

Alexis de Tocqueville's treatise on America is undergoing a significant revival. Academicians and journalists, concerned with the contemporary state of civic life, are reaching back to find ideas in Tocqueville's *Democracy in America* that will help them explain what they describe as the current malaise, a retreat from the public to the private sphere, a growing passivity which they regard as threatening to American democracy.[1] Tocqueville was keenly sensitive to differences in spaces of association. In the "America" of the nineteenth century, he witnessed the result of a radical deterritorialization; he attributed the vibrancy of civic activity to America's departure from the ground plan of aristocracy, the estate-based society, under siege but still significant on the European Continent.[2] The democratic proclivities that Tocqueville ascribed to America were made possible by a more open model of space, an opportunity for circulation and place-making not afforded by the European system of social boundaries, land tenure, and inheritance structures. Tocqueville recognized that the new land entitlement practices contributed to a social egalitarianism (among Euro-Americans) that shaped American civic life. While he displayed significant failures of insight with respect to spaces of otherness (an issue treated below), he is justly credited with articulating important insights about the new spaces of sociability and their political implications.[3]

Tocqueville's insights are not wholly irrelevant for assessing contemporary forces that encourage or discourage practices of civic association and political engagement, but to apply them to the present, it is necessary to treat them in the context of contemporary territorial dynamics, to recognize, among other things, the significant alterations of social space and modes of association created by media and communication technologies. As in Tocqueville's time, altered territorialities are creating different modalities of civic engagement.[4] The traditional liberal discourse on politics, within which Tocqueville's insights are being appropriated, is largely insensitive to modernity's spatial alterations. This discourse tends to efface spaces of difference and aggregate the social domain with a unifying grammar. Those invoking Tocqueville of late, for example, inquire into the relationship of social solidarity and civic-mindedness to a nation's democratic performance (e.g., Putnam 1993b).

There are significant alternatives, which operate within different spatial and temporal imaginaries. Spatially, contemporary post-liberal discourses delineate spaces of difference and register rifts and disjunctures, aspects of dissociation engendered by forces emanating from the operations of power, surveillance, and exchange (Hardt 1995). Temporally, while the traditional liberal discourse tends to point to the past as a basis for a model of vibrant civic life, post-liberal discourses are occupied with the present forces of social and political containment and the counter-forces of resistance. Seeking to locate the present in an array of contending civic impulses rather than as an epoch of decline from a prior and exemplary mode of civic engagement, they construct civil society as both "the institutional infrastructure for political mediation and public exchange," and the arena for the deployment of "the functions of discipline and exploitation that are inherent in and inseparable from these same structures" (27).

The provocation for this essay is the recent resurgence of the liberal discourse's romantic engagement with its Tocquevillean roots. My purpose is both to stage a confrontation between neo-Tocquevillean and post-liberal thinking and to map some of the contemporary terrain of civic engagement within American society, much of which has resulted from the impact of new technologies. I want to demonstrate the blindnesses in the neo-Tocquevillean insights, which ignore the respatializing implications of new technologies and are predicated on the same spatial model that Tocqueville assumed. And I want, more specifically, to indicate what is unavailable to a perspective that treats new technologies as pacifying agents rather than recognizing the ways in which they alter the frame of social agency as they ambiguate traditional territorialities and subjectivities.

Before we examine the reorientations of social space and their implications for civic engagement, however, we must look more closely at both the neo-Tocquevillian reading of the decline of civic association and the initial Tocquevillean mode of reading civic engagement. The most elaborate analyses that purport to enact Tocqueville's treatment of civic engagement are Robert Putnam's recent writings on American democratic life. Employing a variety of creative metaphors—figuring himself as a sleuth and storyteller as well as a social scientist—he has aimed his investigations at finding the culprit, at isolating the cause of civic decline in America. He notes, for example:

> For the last year or so, I have been wrestling with a difficult mystery. It is a classic brainteaser, with a corpus delecti, a crime scene strewn with clues, and many potential suspects . . . The mystery concerns the strange disappearance of social capital and civic engagement . . . the features of social life—networks, norms and trust—that enable participants to act together much more effectively to pursue shared objectives. (1995a, 34)

Putnam offers some compelling observations; the data show significant attrition in membership in what are traditionally interpreted as civic associations. But the linguistically embedded presuppositions guiding his search have in some ways occluded rather than disclosed "civic association." Instead of mapping the plurality of social spaces, Putnam's rhetoric of space and grammar of inquiry aggregate "America" into a molar social unit. What he calls the corpus delecti is a complex social body that a Tocquevillean gaze cannot adequately discern.

The particular economies of the Tocquevillean gaze—the imposed structures of recognition/nonrecognition—occupy much of what follows, but to appreciate the implications of Putnam's gesture of both revealing and concealing, we must first consider the gesture of commentary itself, the invocation of Tocqueville, which is more than merely a search for timeless or relevant ideas. As Michel Foucault has noted, "commentary" is, among other things, a strategy for controlling discourse; it "exorcizes its chance element" (1984, 116). More specifically, the Tocquevillean commentary repeats traditional terms of political inquiry rather than contesting them. As William Connolly has put it, the "desire to expunge contestability from the terms of political inquiry embodies "a wish to escape politics" by "placing a set of ambiguities and contestable orientations under the control of a settled system of understandings and priorities" (1984, 139).

Rather than providing a robust political discourse to confront the rapidly changing social and political orders and to treat confrontations between radically different interpretations of the present, Putnam rehearses a nineteenth-century discourse. By invoking Tocqueville's "settled system of understandings and priorities," he contains politics within a narrow sovereignty problematic, which assumes a unitary social order from which citizen action is provoked, and he restricts political action to influence on governmental decision makers. This sovereignty-oriented approach to social and political space (i.e., a focus that treats the nation as a whole and presumes the existence of a unitary national society) constitutes an aggressive nonrecognition of the variety of incommensurate social spaces constitutive of the "society" and the variety of different kinds of political enactment within different social venues.[5]

The dimensions of nonrecognition are not simply a result of misapplying the past to the present. Tocqueville's sociological work was an ambiguous achievement. His terms are also as notable for what they conceal as they are for what they reveal. What will emerge as we pursue a critique of both Tocqueville's and Putnam's sociological perspectives are their respective impoverishments of the idea of political action. To appreciate what Tocqueville said, however, it is necessary first to focus on what he saw and, at the same time, to focus on the reigning episteme within which he was able to credit what was available to his direct vision.

Tocqueville's Gaze

Two epistemic presuppositions directed Tocqueville's gaze. First was a narrative of modernity that incorporated a discourse on value. He shared John Stuart Mill's narrative of the inevitable advance of civilization, but "civilization," for both Mill and Tocqueville, was understood in terms of particular value-enhancing practices, specifically, practices of place that turn land and "natural resources" into finished, exchangeable goods.[6] Both are based on a mythic narrative in which modernity has emerged from the condition of the savage society, wandering in a wilderness and lacking cooperative orientations and technologies. In an essay on America, in which he "observes" the social, economic, and cultural practices of Native Americans, Mill is struck by how asocial they are: "In savage communities, each person shifts for himself; except in war . . . we seldom see any joint operations carried on by a union of many; nor do savages find pleasure in each other's society" (1962, 52). Not surprisingly, therefore, in his review of *Democracy in America,* Mill recognized that Tocqueville's argument is narrative in structure: Democracy is the political form of the future and the

American democracy is emblematic of an inevitable historical tendency, the direction in which society is "irresistibly tending" (1874, 85).

Given this story, along with Tocqueville's Millian assumption that the value of a place is produced by the manufactures (or "improvements") it yields, he was unable to recognize the ways in which Native American landscapes reflected the extensive cultural modifications enacted by organized Native American societies. As Matthew Dennis has noted: "Many Europeans . . . failed to recognize or acknowledge America as the product of centuries of cultural modification, as a 'landscape' shaped by the desires of its denizens to provide themselves a prosperous, secure, and fulfilling existence" (1993, 17).

What Tocqueville regarded as a wild and untamed venue had been very extensively modified.[7] The Native Americans did not live in a "wilderness," and they were not disordered. They had a different mode of sociality, a different set of practices, both conceptual and material, for organizing civic life, and, in general, a mode of organization of personal life, collective life, intertribal relations, and land use that was not perceptible to those who saw "civilization" on the basis of different markers.

Why was Tocqueville so confident in the power of his vision? The answer is related to the second epistemic presupposition guiding his observations. As a nineteenth-century observer, Tocqueville functioned within an episteme that placed confidence in direct vision. Whereas subjective vision was suspect during the prior two centuries, the situation of the observer during the nineteenth "depended on the priority of models of subjective vision" (Crary 1991, 9). And, not insignificantly, this subjective observer was mobile, an "ambulatory observer" taking in the sights not only within the "new urban spaces" (20) but also (in Tocqueville's case) in various global venues.

This reliance on direct vision was especially evident in Tocqueville's observation, roughly a decade after his trip to America, that the Islamic society of the city of Algiers lacked a coherent public, political life. Imagining that the architecture of the city constituted an unambiguous representation of its modes of organization and enactment, and therefore that one could see city life in its entirety, Tocqueville asserted that "the architecture portrays their necessities and customs . . . it portrays extremely well the social and political state of the Muslim and Oriental populations . . . [including among other things] the complete absence of political life" (1958, 192).

In short, Tocqueville's reading of Algiers assumed that the meaning of the city was wholly visible (Mitchell 1988, 58). Timothy Mitchell points out that the particular objectifying vision that Tocqueville brought to Algiers was partly a result of the European assumption that a "building stands for an institution" and partly a result of Tocqueville's experience with the nineteenth-century structure of European capitals such as Paris, which "were deliberately constructed around the individual observer" (59).

A more locally attuned reading would recognize that Algiers, like other middle eastern cities in the nineteenth century, did not "offer an 'architecture' or external framework pretending to portray its interior life" (58) and, more significantly, that social and political life in Algiers were constituted out of mobile boundaries. For example, gates at times enclosed various areas and at other times were opened to permit transactions (56). One could not see the various aspects of an urban life organized on the basis of various functions deployed at different times. In Algiers, "the life of the city was understood in terms of the occurrence and reoccurrence of practices, rather than in terms of an 'architecture'—material or institutional— that stands apart from life itself, containing and representing the meaning of what was done" (59).

Non-Places and Uncivic Bodies

In addition to the overconfidence Tocqueville placed in his ability to see aspects of the social and political order, his readings of the spaces of civic action were burdened by another commitment. There is a markedly religious frame involved in the disqualification of Native Americans from civic respect. "Wilderness" has a decidedly biblical connotation. In the biblical story, it is the place where a people reside when they are unredeemed, not yet summoned to live a life under God's sanction. The temporal frame with which Tocqueville treats the European state system's migration to North America is parallel with his view of "wilderness" as a less divinely sanctioned epoch, a time during which a people has not yet acquired a right to a territorial settlement. The eventual place of collective fulfillment or recognition is a land that, according to Tocqueville, had not yet been properly occupied: "One could still properly call North America an empty continent, a deserted land waiting for inhabitants" (1990, 25). Tocqueville is therefore not speaking of mere inhabitants but of divinely sanctioned ones.

Ultimately, Tocqueville's failure to recognize and sanction the complex social and civic organization of Native Americans derives from his commitment to what Connolly has called a "civi-theo-territorial complex" (1993, 170), to a civil society organized as a territorial state, with Christian monotheism, providing the "cultural glue binding the civi-territorial complex together" (169).[8]

Tocqueville's view of the civic activity of African Americans was no more acute than his reading of Native Americans. While he construed the "Indian" as a fiercely proud and independent character type, whom the Europeans have not been able to change (1990, 334), he stated that "the Negro makes a thousand efforts to insinuate himself among men who repulse him; he conforms to the tastes of his oppressors, adopts their opinions, and hopes by imitating them to form a part of their community" (334). But again, what is available to the gaze is misleading. As is evident in the writings of slaves and former slaves, this imitative behavior was one among various modalities of black tactics; it was part of black survival and resistance, a "mask of obedience" (Wyatt-Brown 1988), not an essential aspect of "character."

Throughout the history of African Americans, from slavery through to the present, negotiating an existence in a white-dominated world has required a variety of kinds of role playing, and black society has been more or less continually constituted on the basis of survival and resistance practices. Certainly, the spaces of resistant civic association in which African Americans convened at the time Tocqueville made his observations were necessarily recalcitrant to the white, sociological gaze. As an extreme but well-known case, Nat Turner's rebellious band met in the woods to plot their insurrection, not only to escape white surveillance but also because it was the only space not controlled at all moments by their white owners.[9] And Turner's rebellion, which occurred during the summer of 1831, while Tocqueville was making his observations, was not an isolated incident. The bulk of slave testimony indicates that "the slaves were constantly resisting and rebelling" (Thelwell 1968, 87).

One need not address the more violent episodes to find an active, resistant black civic action while Tocqueville was in America. In Philadelphia, for example, black abolitionists staged numerous parades as they moved their opposition to slavery "from the pulpit to the street, inventing counter-Independence parades out of the familiar July fourth militia march and the fife and drum band of black popular culture" (Davis 1986, 46). It was precisely during the period of Tocqueville's observations that increasingly violent confrontations occurred as white mobs attacked black street demonstrators and civic authorities attempted to curtail the public expression of black community solidarity, aimed at protesting their demeaned social, economic, and political status. Of course, the resistances that could be observed during occasional episodes of demonstration were a small part of a more general resistance. Other forms continued in more fugitive locales—in cellars, back alleys, and separated communities. In the North as in the South, black civic association was often disguised within seemingly benign cultural activities. In the antebellum period, black "insurgent community building" proceeded with coded expressions in public venues while elsewhere, for example in churches, blacks "performed their political identity at prayer meetings" (Berlant 1995, 468).

Contemporary black civic association is also fugitive if one holds out as a model the familiar, white spaces of civic assembly (an issue treated below). An inadequate conception of the variety of contemporary social spaces constitutes the primary blindness in the insights of neo-Tocquevillean readings of American civic life. However, to appreciate the contribution of the Tocquevillean patrimony to the contemporary assemblage of neo-Tocquevillean discernments, it is necessary to pursue Tocqueville's nineteenth-century spatial imaginary. Among other things, it was implicated in the disjuncture between his compassion for individuals enslaved (even though he failed to record black civic resistance) and his condoning of the destruction of Native American culture.

The Tocquevillean Geographic Imaginary

Tocqueville's models of space, his global, national, and social mappings, provide justifications for the (undemocratic) Euro-American dominance in America. He came to America not only as one interested in prisons and other aspects of social policy but also as a humanist scholar. There, as reflected in his *Democracy in America,* his commitment to the territorial state is tempered by his humanitarian regrets about the fates of those not enabled by this historical necessity—specifically, slaves and Indians. However, writing about Algeria in connection with his decision-making duties as a member of the French Chamber of Deputies, the priority of his imperialist map of the world becomes evident. This map is animated by his identity as a French nationalist (1840). While Tocqueville could not condone slavery—it was immoral for one [man] to own another—it was perfectly reasonable for one people to own another people.[10] His report on the Algerian colony constitutes a firm justification for repressive colonial rule in the name of the glory of France: "For France works to create civilized societies, not hordes of savages" (1840, 360).

France's exemplary role as a dominant nation-state was at the center of Tocqueville's map. A peoples' eligibility for respect and control over their collective existence was secondary to the dominance of the European territorial state. But there is yet one more space, another "world" above that of the territorial state in which Tocqueville took up residence, "the world of philosophy." In a letter to John Stuart Mill, in which he refers to a French reviewer of Mill's critical essay on his *Democracy in America,* Tocqueville notes that the writer, M. Royer-Collard, "considered it not only a good review, but also an original work of great profundity," and added that Mill should take the review quite seriously because Royer-Collard "still exercises great power in the philosophical world" (Boesche, ed. 1985, 145).

Where is this "philosophical world" situated vis-à-vis the others arrayed in Tocqueville's geographic imaginary? Tocqueville occupied many worlds at once. On the one hand, he centered much of the civilized world in France, and as a nationalist, arrogated civilizational authority to his home country. On the other hand, America was the future, and the condition of possibility for its democratic institutions that Tocqueville so much admired was its distance from the aristocratic institutions of Europe. Yet, at the same time, Tocqueville was an aristocrat; in fact his letter was written from his family estate, "Tocqueville," the epitome of aristocratic or "estate space," which continued to exist even as the dynamics of republican governance and commercial society were making such spaces increasingly anachronistic.

Finally, there is another space, a world of philosophical exchange in which thinkers like Mill and Tocqueville are proprietors. Moreover, they presume that their proprietorship is organized around an objective pursuit of truth rather than an interpretive economy of recognition/nonrecognition. For them, their observations are objective insights, not readings situated in the practices of space that constitute their nineteenth-century European spatial imaginaries.[11] They are heedless of the way in which their narratives of modernity and moral geographies help construct the worlds they perceive, the societies they sanction, those they disparage, and those they discern not at all. In effect, Tocqueville helps to convene a world in which he imagines a disinterested objectivity. With Mill, he resides in a meta-space within which he conceptually organizes the space of the world, a world which is, however, imaginatively shaped by his nationalism, Euro-centered notions of race and culture, and ethnoscapes of worthy and unworthy characters.[12]

The Neo-Tocquevillean Gaze

The inattention to specific structures of space in favor of an emphasis on national territoriality and the focus on individual character are not peculiar to Tocqueville. They describe more generally the contemporary liberal political discourse that his treatment of the American "democracy" helped to shape. While Tocqueville often recognized the role of structure in producing conditions of possibility for action, his tendency, shared with many contemporary liberal thinkers, was to construct persons as individual actors whose resources consist primarily of a type of character. They choose to comply with domination (Tocqueville's "Negroes"), act defiantly (Tocqueville's "Indians"), or act civically to address their problems as well as those of the public at large.

This view of political actors provides no space for both specifically situated, historical bodies as sites of the investment of power and the ground plan, the organization of social and political space that enables some and disenables others. Among other things, the civic order is structured by legal and political partitions of social space, by capital accumulations and flows that produce various kinds of like- and other-mindedness, and by the resulting opportunity spaces within which one can act and in which acts take on various kinds of significance. But the neo-Tocquevillean discourse is relatively silent about the political, economic, and technological forces shaping social space and, as a result, social subjects. And it is obtuse to the way modes of resistance revise subjectivities and reshape space. Its emphasis is instead on autonomous actors.

While neo-Tocquevilleans share Tocqueville's methodological individualism, they do not have his confidence in the epistemic status of direct vision. They operate instead within the modern episteme in which the all-seeing gaze has been displaced by technologies of data collection. However, as in the case of Tocqueville's, the neo-Tocquevillean discourse constructs the analyst as a disinterested observer, occupying neutral space, unrelated to the spaces and objects of analysis. Analysts share their observations on the "data" in an intellectual meta-space, outside of the spaces of civic action. Thus, for example, Putnam can ponder about how to solve "the problem of South Central Los Angeles" (1993a, 36), as if how he lives is wholly unrelated to this exogenous situation, worthy of contemplation and investigation. If we heed the forces structuring both national and global economies, the levels of poverty and drug trafficking in South Central Los Angeles are not unrelated to how academic liberals live (in places like Cambridge, Massachusetts). Income inequality and career choice are produced in relation to the interdependencies involved in national and global political economy. They cannot be understood simply as sets of "data" about various individuals.

The neo-Tocquevillean pursuit of an individualistic rather than structural interdependence model results in a focus on mentalities rather than material forces. Emphasizing mindedness, both for themselves and their subjects, neo-Tocquevilleans assume that intellectual resources are what are needed and that they are produced spontaneously by an urge toward civic-mindedness coupled with an inheritance of enabling ideas.[13] Putnam wants to know why this urge is gone. Like Tocqueville, his inquiry emerges from a story. He posits an edenic model of America's democratic history, arguing that until recently, a substantial amount of "social capital"—high levels of interpersonal trust and robust civic association—provided the basis for the American democracy (1995b).

In addition, and not incidently, Putnam's story of America is accompanied by a commitment to rigorous scientific analysis. Putnam's embrace of Tocqueville, like J. S. Mill's, is predicated on an admiration of Tocquevillean analysis as disinterested and rigorous: "Ever since the publication of Alexis de Tocqueville's *Democracy in America* the United States has played a central role in systematic studies of the links between democracy and civil society" (65). Not irrelevant to Putnam's valorization of rigor is the archeological metaphor he applies to his quest for sociological knowledge. Finding an answer is a matter of digging up data, not of reflecting on how social life and political engagement are framed: "Recently," he states, "American social scientists of a neo-Tocquevillean bent have unearthed a wide range of empirical evidence that the quality of public life and the performance of social institutions are indeed powerfully influenced by norms and networks of civic engagement" (66).

Let us look at the "data" on association in the United States that prompt Putnam's concern. He is certainly correct that memberships in bowling leagues and church organizations have declined, union membership is down, and fraternal organizations are losing members. At a minimum the venues of white male sociability are steadily losing their ability to hold members. What can account for this? After a lot of sleuthing, Putnam selects television as the culprit, based on data that show an increase in viewing hours as attendance at public meetings declines.[14] But what if we deal with the vagaries possible in the development of a sociological imagination—if instead of digging up data, we reconceive the terrain? The democratic imaginary for which Putnam seeks civic support reproduces the liberal imagination; it constructs a society of abstract individuals, having no significant embodiment and existing in neutral social space. They decide to leave home and be civic or slouch in front of a television set.

If, instead of constructing civic engagement as a movement from neutral to political space, we recognize an aspect of civic engagement in persistent struggles to maintain workable identities, it becomes difficult to quarantine the idea of political space within the boundaries of particular assembly halls. We can think instead of civic engagement as more pervasive and differentiated with respect to locale; it arises in connection with many aspects of everyday life, as part of differentiated sets of social ontology.[15]

Once we shift our attention from liberalism's homogenized space of encounter and from the abstract potential civic actor to locally situated subjects, we are able to recognize a broader range of civic engagement and avoid Putnam's tendency to erase the local spatial configurations within a rhetoric of national political culture. For Putnam, people simply have or do not have "a propensity to form civil and political organizations." There is no registering of the forces at work shaping social spaces or the mediascapes, television included, which reflect a significant degree of social agonism and create the force vectors driving people toward particular forms of civic association and away from others. There is no indication of how technological alterations in the structures of association construct barriers for some forms of civic activity and provide incentives and resources for others.

How can we view the social order if we reject Putnam's sociological gaze, narrowed by an empiricist reliance on poll data and a white middle-class model of spaces and organizations? Resisting the neo-Tocquevillean view that communication technologies are mere diversions from civic life, we can recognize how television and other mass media are used within different social spaces and most significantly are implicated in constituting the spaces within which association takes place. Two dimensions of inquiry recommend themselves. First, to highlight the homology between the Tocquevillean and neo-Tocquevillean sociological gaze, we can focus on the contemporary black public sphere. Second, in order to recognize the forces shaping the social spaces and therefore creating differential conditions of possibility for civic engagement by African Americans and other Americans, we can elaborate a critical view of social space. Within this view, what must emerge is not a homogeneous field of social space that can yield important civic activity if individuals were less passive, but a series of pressures that facilitate some kinds of action and impede others.

A Critical Model of Social Space

As a first approach, it is important to recognize that rather than the "society" unified grammatically within the histories of dominant forms of liberal thinking, what has emerged is a series of fortified enclaves, social spaces differentiated by both their physical barriers and modes of surveillance, each of which has differential forms of civic engagement.[16] Their modalities of action are affected by the forms of authority and control, which differentiate them.

The very South Central Los Angeles for which Putnam wishes to provide a solution is a case in point; it is revelatory of the contemporary spatialized mode of control. The state and powerful controls over capital investment play important roles in shaping the terrain within which the black public sphere is constituted. Increasingly, social theorists have recognized that contemporary racism is less a matter of social attitude and explicit legal separation of public services and accommodations and more a system of geographic and economic enclosure.

Among the reconfigurations of social space that should attract our attention, then, are what Michael Hardt calls the enclosures that "define the striae of social space" (1995, 34); they are a major aspect of modernity's spatial arrangements to which Gilles Deleuze addressed himself: "The individual never ceases passing from one enclosed environment to another, each having its own laws: first the family; then the school . . . ; then the barracks; then the factory; from time to time the hospital; possibly the prison, the preeminent instance of the enclosed environment" (1991, 3). A focus on the spaces of difference, the contemporary "striae" of social space, formed by forces of domination and control and by modalities of resistance, opens up a possibility for a sustained analysis of new forms of civic engagement. The new techniques of social control should provoke inquiry into new possibilities for contestation and freedom emerging from them. As Hardt puts it, there are "networks of sociality and forms of cooperation embedded in contemporary social practices" which "constitute the germs for new movements, with new forms of contestation and new conceptions of liberation" (1995, 41).

At a most general level, we can read our epoch in terms of the way it has surpassed the traditional liberal politics of sovereignty. In Deleuze's terms, the modern society of control has displaced the traditional society of sovereignty, and as a result, civic life must be recognized on the basis of a new pattern of shifting spaces and oppositional activities involved within them. At a more specific level, we can inquire into the various dimensions of the black public sphere, which offers a paradigm of civic association that cannot be appreciated by taking polls on rates of church attendance, and by counting bowling league, PTA, and labor organization memberships. Within the traditional models of liberal civil society, recycled by contemporary neo-Tocquevilleans, it operates as an "invisible public" (Baker 1994, 10). It is unmapped in the mainstream, liberal model of American civic space.

Ironically, the chief culprit in Putnam's neo-Tocquevillean lament—television—is a central element in the "sociality"[17] of one public sphere which is rendered invisible by his unitary assumptions about society and civic space. Grammatically—and thus analytically—television is not something that a society has as a medium with which to be attuned. Like other forms of technology—writing, paper and electronic money, telephones, virtual communication and interaction—television participates in the constitution of civic association. It inflects the patterns of remote versus local, helping to produce various patterns of use and interaction, and it is, in turn, shaped by those who use it. Television is part of the structure of association; it has reconfigured the social landscape and thus domains of association.[18]

The black urban experience is a case in point. Like any effective mode of sociality, black practices of association require an effective imaginary, a recognition of the forces constituting the spaces within which one functions and a language that suggests ways to both provoke solidarity within one space and contest the authoritative forces distributing privileges among social segments. Black music television, for example, has been supplying that recognition, and it has been enabled by the very commercial forces that are responsible for producing much of the separateness of black living spaces. Although until recently, television programming gave relatively little coverage to black music, it is an increasing feature of music television (MTV), especially rap.

Since the late 1980s, rap music has created a relay between television and the black ghetto. As Tricia Rose notes, "Nothing is more central to rap's music video narratives than situating the rapper in his or her milieu and among one's crew or posse" (1994, 10). Unlike, for example, the heavy metal features, which usually locate the singers in a concert hall, "rap music videos are set on buses, subways, in abandoned buildings, and almost always in black urban inner-city locations" (10). Rap's emphasis on "posses" and on the "hood" involves an explicit recognition of the terrain of black habitation (11). While only some of rap evokes aspects of civic engagement, much of it speaks to the situation of a significant portion of the contemporary black urban experience in a politically reflective way.

Certainly, there is not a single black public sphere, and some aspects of black civic association are subject to the neo-Tocquevillean lament, for example the diminution of what was once a significant oppositional, black counter-public in neighborhoods and churches (Dawson 1994, 197). But there are new configurations of oppositional civic engagement in black communities. If we resist restricting our attention to the traditional assembly halls as the paradigms of civic involvement, there is an increasingly robust modality of black civic action—the street. The street is a venue not only of defiant looks and styles but also of mass protest (hooks 1992). The street protests in reaction to the Rodney King verdict, for example, were concerted responses to the more general history of police brutality in black urban space. They helped to foreground an especially important part of black civic action, "bearing witness," and they foreground an important aspect of political enactment, intervening with the body.

As Elizabeth Alexander noted in her analysis of the Rodney King beating, witnessing, not only through seeing but also through subsequent stories about violence, constitutes an important part of black civic engagement (1994). Moreover, this engagement is unified through its more or less continuous aim of constructing an alternate national narrative because "the white-authored national narrative deliberately contradicts the histories our bodies know," as Alexander puts it (80). In sum, "the riot was more than an emphatic rejection of a single verdict; it was a protest against the systematic aggressions to which poor and nonwhite residents of Los Angeles are routinely subjected, especially if they are black" (Omi and Winant 1994, 107–8). Rather than a reactive episode, it was a more active part of the bearing witness that African Americans have practiced, both to share their experiences of specific bodily forms of brutality and to resist the violence of representation conveyed by mainstream narratives of American political history.

It is not necessary, however, to point to the more obtrusive forms of black resistance to disclose a significant civic sphere. If we resist the conceptual tendency to separate social life from civic action, it is possible to recognize that black habitation, for example, the social use of the home, neighborhood, and city, is a form of political action. Given the discriminatory pressures against the creation of black civil society—through legal manipulation, gentrification, discriminatory criminalization, and various forms of exclusion from mortgage funds, political office, and bureaucracy—"the territorial maintenance and integrity of black settlements" has been a form of "civic association" (Haymes 1995, 70).

In addition to constituting a civic sphere through the mere fact of managing to continue to live together, the black public sphere has been constituted in part out of distinctive modalities of expression. While liberal political analysts continue to look for civic action—within their homogenizing grammar of "we" Americans—many genres of African American expression represent the disjunctures between white and black American experience. For example, rap musicians acknowledge that black public action is often in the streets and point out the extent to which the streets are made mean not because of the character of the residents but because of the geographic and economic enclosures to which they are subjected.

Moreover, songs such as Goodie Mob's "Cell Therapy" (1995) evoke another increasingly important venue of black civic action, the prison. It is not incidental, for example, that the most prosperous and well-known rap music label is entitled "Death Row Records." Black Americans are disproportionately sent to death row. And, more generally, at a rapidly increasing rate, young urban black males are shuttled between the streets and the prison. The economic incarceration of the ghetto is paralleled by the exemplar of the carceral structure, the prison. For example, in California at present, "almost 40 percent of young black men are under the control of the criminal justice system" (Butterfield 1996, A-8). James Q. Wilson notes that "most crimes nationwide are committed by young people" and he concludes that "The system is more or less putting people in prison at the rate at which they commit crimes" (Butterfield 1996, A-8). The hollowing out of the economic opportunities for urban black males coupled with the disproportionate criminalizing of their end of drug sales and use (the heavier penalties for affordable crack versus those for cocaine powder), have rearranged the imagery of the two-tiered society. It is less a distinction of level than it is of enclosure. Black America is increasingly behind bars.

As in the case of analyzing the locus of television viewing, it is misleading to separate the prison from other spheres of civic action. Given the numbers of black prisoners—and their disproportionate sentencing that sends them to death row—black civic space comprises the prison as well as the street, among other venues. And the prison is linked increasingly to other parts of civic space. Just as television is not wholly isolated from civic association, the prison is increasingly a venue of black civic action. It is not only figured in various media—rap music, MTV rap videos, black talk radio, and the films of black directors—but various black organizations, Islamic and "gang" among others, maintain their structures within as well as outside prisons, with relays between the two spaces. And, increasingly, voices from prison—such as that of Mumia Abul-Jamal—are an important aspect of black civic engagement.

Various contemporary technologies aid and abet the formation of a prison-centered black public sphere. Recently, for example, controversy developed over a death row inmate's "Internet page" (Brandon 1996, 1, 4). Although this prisoner is white, it recalls the increasing use of the Internet as a link from the prison to the outside and as a space within which political activism against disproportionate incarceration of blacks and against capital punishment exists within virtual space. Among other things, it is a space within which the free Mumia campaign was promoted.

Conclusion: Toward a Post-Liberal Political Imaginary

Where does this leave us vis-à-vis the lamentations of the neo-Tocquevilleans? By discerning counter-publics or, more specifically, the spaces of black political action that are unmapped within the model of civic association drawn by neo-Tocquevilleans, we must arrive at a different view of contemporary American politics. As the reactions to the Rodney King beating and to the Simi valley and O. J. Simpson trials attest, much of white and black America occupies radically different terrains of sociality. Given the division, the issue cannot be quarantined within the frame of "solving problems" such as that of South Central Los Angeles as, for example, Putnam frames it.

From Tocqueville through the neo-Tocquevilleans, African Americans have been lodged within discourses that cannot register much of what has constituted their civic structures and enactments. Tocqueville's evocation of the discourse on race (where he writes of "The Three Races in the United States") served nationalist and neo-colonial perspectives within which the African Americans were a problem for Euro-Americans as they attempted to consolidate their democratic polity. In framing the issue as the "problem of South Central Los Angeles," Putnam reproduces the traditional, depoliticizing, American "race problem" and serves a similar political agenda. He focuses on the national civic society, figured in terms that reference white structures of civic engagement. Like Tocqueville's, his discourse erases significant spaces of civic difference.

If we heed the spatial metaphor and recognize the existence of separate, albeit overlapping, public spheres, we can point toward the need for a political discourse that does not dissolve boundaries and erase politically active bodies. Within a different economy of recognition than that offered by Tocqueville and neo-Tocquevilleans, there would be a discourse on politics that would facilitate a negotiation between groups occupying different spaces rather than one that homogenizes the social domain and seeks a generalized increase in civic engagement.

That economy of recognition would also have to avoid homogenizing, civic bodies as well as the social domain. Like most traditional liberal democratic theory, Putnam's version is based on an arithmetic view of social equality. He counts people's levels of engagement rather than dealing with encounters between incommensurately situated bodies. Putnam's (or unpolitical) lives are constituted as a group of autonomous individuals, enclosed within the boundaries of the static territories to which he refers as "communities." What is the alternative?

One radically different model is supplied by Jacques Ranciere, for whom discerning political engagement is not simply a matter of counting memberships. For Ranciere, "politics exists when the natural order of domination is interrupted by the institution of a part of those who have no part" (Ranciere 1998, 11), and "political activity is whatever shifts a body from the place assigned to it or changes a place's destination" (30). Resisting liberal democratic approaches to a universality applied to political communities such as "the reign of law" or "the process of governing," Ranciere rejects the traditional metapolitics within which "man and citizen are the same liberal individual enjoying the universal values of human rights embodied in the constitutions of our democracies" (63).

Recognizing the history of wrong involved in the founding violence of the law (e.g., constitution making) and in the preservation of the law, a form of policing or "policy" that functions within a traditional meta-politics, Ranciere evokes the distinction between "a logic of subjectivization and a logic of identification" (63). In contrast to "the arithmetic of shopkeepers and barterers," Ranciere speaks of "a magnitude that escapes ordinary measurement," a "paradoxical magnitude" that escapes a logic that equates "the equality of anyone at all with anyone else" (15).

As a case in point, we can focus on a set of historically wronged indigenous bodies, those now referred to as Native Americans. Prior to the mid-nineteenth century, official U.S. culture treated white relations with Native Americans as part of "foreign policy." Indeed, in 1831, while Tocqueville was constructing Native Americans as "noble savages," Justice John Marshall was recognizing the Cherokees, whose lands were within the state of Georgia, as a politically coherent and effective nation (even though he did not take the step that would have given them ultimate sovereignty within their territory).[19] However, after 1849, "The power to define and administer the Indian gradually shifted . . . from the War Department to the Department of the Interior (Borneman 1995, 667). Whereas the Indian had been a foreigner in the period in which war and trade were the dominant modes of interaction with white America, after 1849 they were symbolically as well as politically domesticated; the politics of identity/difference was repressed in the subsequent development of a national political discourse.

What were the spaces of encounter prior to this domestication? In their analysis of America's western past, William Cronon et al. refer to a period in the West in which Native and Euro-Americans met at a "frontier" (Cronon et al. 1992). They employ the concept of the frontier to suggest that the cultural confrontation involved a negotiation of relationships between the different groups in an ambiguous, nonproprietary space. The relationship was fluid, noninstitutionalized, precarious, and uncertain. Certainly there was considerable violence, but there was also a sense that co-existence required a resistance to fixity on both sides of the encounter.

Cronon et al. go on to note that the frontier moment was quite brief; relationships ceased being invented in the process of confrontation as fluidity gave way to hierarchy, as the engines of state power and the interests they vehiculated turned the frontier or place of invention and negotiation into a series of "regions," proprietary and juridical in structure and administrative rather than inventive in practice. Henceforth peoples, however different their interests, cultural practices, and inclinations, were to meet on a space already marked out with subjectivities no longer contingent on the effects of the encounter.

If we recognize that the current regionalization is based on control rather than negotiation and that it is also carceral rather than political, it is inappropriate to speak of solving the problem of one sphere within the liberal (and even tolerant) conceits of the other. Increasingly, mass media, popular culture, and black "specific intellectuals" are providing frames for recognizing not simply that the disproportionate incarceration of African Americans, particularly young men, is counter-productive—that it is simply worth filing under policy effectiveness—but also that there is more than one set of civic cultures, and that it is time to renegotiate the relationships among them. Rather than a generalized grammar of civil society, a discourse of encounter and negotiation would be more appropriate. What is implied by this reorientation toward politicizing the issue of civic engagement is not the encouragement of a general increase in civic engagement but a return to the spirit of the frontier. What is to be lamented is not the time spent in front of television sets instead of in town meetings, but a failure of creative encounter between different groups. Without denying the vast range of difference within white and black civic cultures, it is nevertheless important to recognize some form of aggregated difference, to point to tendencies to use media differently, derive different significance from mass and popular culture, experience events differently, and have different understandings of the significance of the contemporary "society of control," ranging from the commercialization and valuing of places to the surveillance and incarceration of people. When these differences provoke an encounter—for example an indigenous claim for reparations or the return of tribal lands—"the political" become manifest. Ultimately, then, in contrast with the political arithmetic of Putnam's neo-Tocquevillean (and empiricist) liberalism, an approach to political engagement must accommodate modes of difference that cannot be simply added up. "The political" manifests itself as events of encounter between differently situated bodies that do not necessarily share a community.

NOTES

1. Among the academic commentaries are Jean Bethke Elshtain (1995), Robert Putnam's various essays and books: 1993a, 1993b, 1995a, 1995b, 1996, and 2000.

2. As Donald Lowe notes, the estate-based society was organized on the basis of

a set of formal prerogatives, authorized by God. Estate society was thus ascriptive; statuses were hierarchically fixed, and "the major concerns within that formalized hierarchy were precedence, honor, and territoriality" (1982, 63).

3. The expression "spaces of otherness" is a rendering of Michel Foucault's analysis of what he calls "heterotopias" (1986).

4. To cite an example, one of the contemporary spaces of encounter is what some have called "prosthetic territories" (Brahm, Jr., and Driscoll 1995).

5. For an analysis of the conceptual deficits involved in referring in an undifferentiated way to "society" and an analysis of the political implications of aggregating into a whole what is unstable and precarious and in many ways dissociated, see Ernesto Laclau (1983).

6. I turn here to Mill because he articulated elaborately the nineteenth-century image of Native American societies that is rearticulated in Tocqueville's writings and because Mill's writing influenced, more generally, Tocqueville's perspective on the relationship between place and value. Mill's discourse on the structures of sociability was predicated on the same civilizational discourse as Adam Smith's political economy a century earlier.

7. The cultivation of the landscape was most dramatically in evidence in the case of the Iroquois, whose many modifications took place in the areas closest to villages, their huge corn fields for example (Dennis 1993, 27). In addition to a complex horticulture, Iroquois practices of space reflected gender distinctions, e.g., separating the feminized space of the village from the masculine spaces outside of it, spaces for the practices of hunting, warfare, and diplomacy. But, as Dennis notes, "Europeans interpreted the lack of rectilinearity in their fields as disorder and the absence of livestock as backwardness" (30). Nevertheless, through a variety of techniques, e.g., burning, the Iroquois (and others such as the Montaignais), used fire to shape and maintain their landscapes, and they managed game resources systematically. And, of course, as the ethnographic evidence shows, they had complex social structures and processes within their tribe as well as an elaborate system of exchanges for dealing with other tribes and peoples.

8. Tocqueville was not a simplistic moralizer, however. Allowing in his model of cultural encounter a degree of cultural pluralism, he lamented the demise of the "noble savage," feeling that Native Americans were undeserving of the destruction of their way of life that the European invasion had wrought. Nevertheless, as Connolly puts it, "the historical consolidation of the civi-territorial complex requires the elimination of the Indian" (1984, 170). Tocqueville, despite his qualms, is able to "come to terms with violence that is undeserved" (171). The European habitation is a form of justice sanctioned by history. In comparison, the "injustice in justice" (171) cannot be as telling for Tocqueville as was, for example, the injustice of slavery. And, most essentially, contrary to the many readings which locate Tocqueville as a sophisticated sociologist, the myopic gaze he trained on Native American social organization constituted a continuation of European violence by other

means, what Jacques Derrida has called a "violence of representation" (1982, 79–153).

9. Tocqueville did, however, recognize the potential violence that both slavery and its abolition promised, particularly because of the resentments that must ensue from the way that African Americans had been enslaved, oppressed, and excluded. See his chapter "The Three Races in the United States" in *Democracy in America* (1990, 331–34).

10. This observation I owe to Tzvetan Todorov's reading of Tocqueville's report on Algeria (1990).

11. Mill thought that Tocqueville's reading of the American democracy had achieved an exemplary level of scientific disinterest. He saw Tocqueville's book as part of a trend (which certainly included Comte). For Mill, contributions to knowledge by wise thinkers were a matter of strictly scientific evidence. As he noted, thinkers in "the more cultivated nations" were generating a "Philosophy of History" that was "directed and controlled by . . . the nature of sociological evidence," so that he anticipated a time in which "the circle of human knowledge will be complete" for it would no longer be abandoned to "empiricism and unscientific surmise" (1892, 565).

12. Certainly the perspicacity of Tocqueville's sociological inferences, observant though they may have been of norms of individuation and decision making, did not protect him from his nonrecognition of much of the structure of dominance in American society. While he recognized and abjured the institution of slavery, for example, he failed to see other egregious inequalities. In addition to condoning a male dominant society—women were less civically important than men for Tocqueville—he had no inkling of an America that had begun an epoch of racist discrimination that paralleled and extended beyond the end of the institution of slavery. From the period within which Tocqueville made his observations, and ever since, American social space has been a system of inclusions and exclusions, dominated, among other things, by the way that new immigrant groups have compromised with white power structures, accepting a piece of prosperity in exchange for collaborating in systems of racist exclusion (Saxton 1990). And, more generally, as Anne Norton has noted, as a result of his emphasis on classlessness, Tocqueville neglected "the intensity of class conflict generated by the industrial revolution" (1986, 47). Tocqueville also missed the increasingly political activity of women who had more power on the farms than in the new, more industrialized spaces in which their prerogatives were severely restricted (Ryan 1992).

13. These abstractions constitute the profile of Bellah et al. (1986) Their *Habits of the Heart*, which has been a much-read, college class-assigned analysis for over a decade, is more of a sermon than an investigation, for it imposes a view of civic responsibility on each interview and then judges the respondent on their scale of civic achievement. Although it is based on numerous interviews—with white middle-class Americans—it is dominated by two narratives. The first is the familiar

sociopolitical one about how civicness declines when modernity fragments societies, breaks up neighborhoods and, in general, introduces increasingly complex mediations into interpersonal associations. The other is an idealist story. The ideal American is one through whom "biblical and republican traditions in American politics" are ventriloquated (28).

14. Blaming television as the primary culprit was Putnam's tendency in his various articles in the mid-1990s. In his book-length treatment (2000), he moderates his attack on television, regarding it as one among many of the contributions to civic decline.

15. For a view of civic action that resists simplistic identification of civic action with participation in articulated political disagreements, see John Shotter (1989).

16. The well-known version of this model of social space applied to Los Angeles is of course Mike Davis's (1990). More recently, Teresa Caldeira has applied the model in a comparison of Los Angeles and Sao Paulo, Brazil (1996).

17. "Sociality," as opposed to "socialization," can be characterized as counterstructural, as Zigmunt Bauman has argued (1993, 143). While systems of sovereignty construct models of eligible citizenship and authorized forms of civic action, modalities of sociality emerge outside of the sovereignty system. While socialization involves the management of authoritative identities (120), sociality operates outside of such plans—the blueprints of the "democratic polity."

18. See for example John Fiske's analysis (1987), which, in contrast with simplistic treatments of television as a social narcotic, treats the many ways it is implicated in sociality.

19. On March 18, 1831, Chief Justice John Marshall claimed that the Cherokee nation was "a distinct political society separated from others, [and was] capable of managing its own affairs and governing itself." But because he felt that the court would compromise its authority if it ruled in the Cherokee's favor, he ultimately called them a "domestically dependent nation" and therefore a ward of the federal government. However, in *Worcester v. Georgia*, a year later, the Court reversed itself, stating that Indian nations are capable of making treaties and that such treaties are the supreme law of the land. Georgia refused to abide by the decision and President Jackson refused to execute it. He is alleged to have remarked, "John Marshall made his law; now let him enforce it (Mankiller and Wallis 1993, 89).

References

Alexander, Elizabeth. 1994. "Reading the Rodney King Video(s)," *Public Culture* 7: 1 (Fall): 77–94.

Baker, Houston A., Jr. 1994. "Critical Memory and the Black Public Sphere," *Public Culture* 7: 1 (Fall): 3–33.

Bauman, Zigmunt. 1993. *Postmodern Ethics*. Cambridge: Blackwell.

Bellah, Robert, et al. 1986. *Habits of the Heart*. New York: Harper and Row.

Berlant, Lauren. 1995. "The Queen of America Goes to Washington City: Harriet Jacobs, Frances Harper, Anita Hill." In Michael Moon and Cathy N. Davidson, eds. *Subjects and Citizens*. Durham: Duke University Press.

Boesche, Roger, ed. 1985. *Tocqueville: Selected Letters on Politics and Society*. Berkeley: University of California Press.

Borneman, John. 1995. "American Anthropology as Foreign Policy," *American Anthropologist* 97:4 (December): 665–69.

Brahm, Gabriel, Jr., and Driscoll, Mark. 1995. *Prosthetic Territories: Politics and Hypertechnologies*. Boulder, Colo.: Westview.

Brandon, Karen. 1996. "Death Row Inmate's Internet Page Stirs Debate," *Chicago Tribune* (February 18): Section 1: 4.

Butterfield, Fox. 1996. "Study Finds a Disparity in Justice for Blacks," *New York Times* (February 13): A-8.

Caldeira, Teresa P. R. 1996. "Fortified Enclaves: The New Urban Segregation," *Public Culture* 8: 2 (Winter): 303–28.

Connolly, William E. 1984. "The Politics of Discourse." In Michael J. Shapiro, ed. *Language and Politics*. New York: NYU Press: 139–67.

———. 1993. *The Ethos of Pluralization*. Minneapolis: University of Minnesota Press.

Crary, Jonathan. 1991. *Techniques of the Observer*. Cambridge: MIT Press.

Cronon, William, Miles, George, and Gitlin, Jay. 1992. "Becoming West." In William Cronon, George Miles, and Jay Gitlin, eds. *Under an Open Sky: Rethinking America's Western Past*. New York: Norton: 3–27.

Davis, Mike. 1990. *City of Quartz: Excavating the Future in Los Angeles*. New York: Verso.

Davis, Susan G. 1986. *Parades and Power: Street Theater in Nineteenth-Century Philadelphia*. Berkeley: University of California Press.

Dawson, Michael C. 1994. "A Black Counter-Public?: Economic Earthquakes, Racial Agenda(s), and Black Politics." *Public Culture* 7: 1 (Fall): 195–223.

Deleuze, Gilles. 1991. "Postscript on the Societies of Control," *October* 59 (Winter).

Dennis, Matthew. 1993. *Cultivating a Landscape of Peace: Iroquois-European Encounters in Seventeenth Century America*. Ithaca: Cornell University Press.

Derrida, Jacques. 1982. "Violence and Metaphysics." In *Writing and Difference*, Alan Bass, trans. Chicago: University of Chicago Press): 79–153.

Elshtain, Jean. 1995. *Democracy on Trial*. New York: Basic.

Fiske, John. 1987. *Television Culture*. New York: Routledge.

Foucault, Michel. 1984. "The Order of Discourse." Ian McLeod, trans. In Michael J. Shapiro, ed. *Language and Politics*. New York: NYU Press, 1984: 108–38.

———. 1986. "Of Other Spaces." Jay Miscowiec, trans. *Diacritics* 16 (Spring): 21–31.

Hardt, Michael. 1995. "The Withering of Civil Society," *Social Text* 14 (Winter).

Haymes, Stephen. 1995. *Race, Culture, and the City.* Albany: SUNY Press.

hooks, bell. 1992. "The Oppositional Gaze." In *Black Looks: Race and Representation.* Boston: South End Press: 115–31.

Laclau, Ernesto. 1983. "The Impossibility of Society." *Canadian Journal of Political and Social Theory* 7: 1 (Winter): 24–27.

Lowe, Donald. 1982. *History of Bourgeois Perception.* Chicago: University of Chicago Press.

Mankiller, Wilma, and Wallis, Michael. 1993. *A Chief and Her People.* New York: St. Martins.

Mill, John Stuart. 1874. "M. de Tocqueville on Democracy in America," (first published in 1840). In *Dissertations and Discussion,* Vol. II. New York: Henry Holt, 85.

———. 1892. *A System of Logic, Ratiocinative and Inductive, Being a Connected View of the Principles of Evidence and the Methods of Scientific Investigation.* London: Routledge.

———. 1962. *Essays in Politics and Culture.* Gertrude Himmelfarb, ed. New York: Doubleday.

Mitchell, Timothy. 1988. *Colonizing Egypt.* New York: Cambridge University Press.

Norton, Anne. 1986. *Alternative Americas.* Chicago: University of Chicago Press.

Omi, Michael, and Winant, Howard. 1994. "The L.A. Race Riot and U.S. Politics." In Robert Gooding-Williams, ed. *Reading Rodney King.* New York: Routledge.

Putnam, Robert D. 1993a. "The Prosperous Community: Social Capital and Public Life," *The American Prospect* 13 (Spring): 35–42.

———. 1993b. *Making Democracy Work.* Princeton: Princeton University Press.

———. 1995a. "Tuning In, Turning Out: The Strange Disappearance of Social Capital in America," *PS: Political Science and Politics* 28: 4 (December): 664–83.

———. 1995b. "Bowling Alone: America's Declining Social Capital," *Journal of Democracy* 6: 1 (January): 65–78.

———. 1996. "The Strange Disappearance of Civic America," *The American Prospect* No. 24 (Winter): 34–57.

———. 2000. *Bowling Alone.* New York: Simon & Schuster.

Ranciere, Jacques. 1998. *Disagreement.* Julie Rose, trans. Minneapolis: University of Minnesota Press.

Rose, Tricia. 1994. *Black Noise: Rap Music and Black Culture in Contemporary America.* Hanover: Wesleyan University Press.

Ryan, Mary P. 1992. "Gender and Public Access: Women's Politics in Nineteenth Century America." In Craig Calhoun, ed. *Habermas and the Public Sphere.* Cambridge: MIT Press: 258–88.

Saxton, Alexander. 1990. *The Rise and Fall of the White Republic: Class Politics and Mass Culture in Nineteenth Century America.* New York: Verso.

Shotter, John. 1989. "Rhetoric and the Recovery of Civil Society," *Economy and Society* 18:2 (May): 149–66.

Thelwell, Mike. 1968. "Back with the Wind: Mr. Styron and the Reverend Turner." In John Henrik Clarke, ed. *William Styron's Nat Turner: The Black Writers Respond*. Boston: Beacon.

Tocqueville, Alexis de. 1840. *Report on Abolition of Slavery in French Colonies.* Boston: James Monroe and Co.

———. 1958. "Notes du Voyage en Algerie de 1841." In J. P. Mayer and Andre Jardin, eds. *Oeuvre Complete*. Paris: Gallimard.

———. 1990. *Democracy in America.* 2 Vols. New York: Vintage.

Todorov, Tzvetan. 1990. "Tocqueville's Nationalism," *History and Anthropology* 4: 2 (April): 357–71.

Wyatt-Brown, Bertram. 1988. "The Mask of Obedience: Male Slave Psychology in the Old South," *The American Historical Review* 93:5 (December): 1228–252.

DISCOGRAPHY

Goodie Mob. 1995. "Cell Therapy." New York: LaFace Records.

Part II

Historical Perspectives on Social Capital

Chapter Five

Liberty, Equality, and . . . Social Capital?

Stephen Samuel Smith and Jessica Kulynych

> *On the banners of the French Revolution was inscribed a triad of ideals—liberty, equality, and fraternity. Fraternity, as the French democrats intended it, was another name for what I term "social capital."*
>
> —Putnam (2000, 351)

Although *Bowling Alone* is replete with statements about the wondrous qualities of social capital, few are as grandiose as the claim linking it to one of the most famous, lofty, and inspiring slogans in Western political history. Given the grandiosity of the claim, it is made with surprising nonchalance. No evidence, historical or otherwise, is offered for the putative equivalence of social capital and fraternity. Rather, it is presented as if self-evident.

We call attention to this nonchalance because it is our thesis that the term *social capital* is used much too casually, with little regard to the problems of using the language of capitalism to talk about civic engagement and community, many of whose presumed virtues are exemplified by the historic meaning of fraternity. This nonchalance is more than a little ironic because the use of words and the choice of names was anything but casual during the French Revolution. As Lynn Hunt points out, names identified with the Old Regime were replaced by revolutionary appellations, numerous provinces and towns were also renamed, and babies were consciously named after classical heroes. At the height of the concern with names in 1793, Hunt continues (1984, 21), some Parisian deputies urged the National Convention to systematically rename streets and public squares after "all the virtues necessary to the Republic" so as to give the people "a silent course in ethics" and, we would add, politics, given the conflation of the two during the Revolution. The seriousness with which the French revolutionaries took names was part of the seriousness with which they took language. "Words came in torrents," Hunt comments (1984, 20), had a "unique, magical quality," and "became increasingly invested with emotional, even life-and-death, significance." As a result, political language:

> was not merely an expression of an ideological position that was determined by underlying social or political interests. The language itself helped shape the perception of interests and hence the development of ideologies. In other words, revolutionary political discourse was rhetorical; it was a means of persuasion, a way of reconstituting the social and political world. (Hunt 1984, 24)

In those parts of the planet where the term "social capital" has recently become a staple of academic and policy discourse, there has, of course, been much greater political stability than there was in France during the Revolution. In such tranquil times and places, language is typically less subject to political debate and more likely taken for granted than during political upheavals. But the very fact that language is more likely to be taken for granted during tranquil times facilitates the way in which it helps constitute our understanding of the social and political world.[1]

Our concern in this chapter, we emphasize, is not with the way the empirical referents of the term social capital are conceptualized, theorized, and studied. Others are very ably discussing these issues. Rather, our concern is with the problems of using the term social capital to discuss community and civic engagement. These concerns can be previewed by noting that according to Putnam, social capital "refers to connections among individuals—social networks and the norms of reciprocity and trustworthiness that arise from them" (2000, 19). Such networks and their concomitant norms of reciprocity are exemplified most famously by bowling leagues and other aspects of local community involvement, as indicated by the full title of Putnam's book: *Bowling Alone: The Collapse and Revival of American Community.* However, the term social capital arises from an explicit analogy with the way the word capital has figured in economic analysis for hundreds of years. The primary meaning of the word capital thus comes from the way it has been used in economic analysis. This meaning is irretrievably linked to capitalism, individualism, competition, the market, and the acquisition of wealth, things that most political discourse views as opposed to those aspects of community that discussions of social capital typically value. The tension, conflict, and contradiction between capital and community are obscured by the term social capital because it strongly suggests that it, financial capital, and human capital are merely different species of the same genus, capital. Moreover, given the historic and primary meaning of the word capital, to use the term *social capital* to describe the virtues of community and the prerequisites of democracy is to facilitate a view of civic engagement and democratic participation as a kind of economic transaction, thus further obscuring important distinctions. Finally, to urge all of us to be social capitalists, as the last chapter of *Bowling Alone* so unabashedly does, is to becloud the historic meaning of the word capitalist. Such beclouding euphemizes many of the longstanding meanings of the word capitalist, helps legitimize capitalism, and impedes thinking about noncapitalist ways of organizing society.

We develop these claims in four stages. The first is an historical investigation that begins by showing that any claim of the synonymy of fraternity and social capital conflates what the French revolutionaries considered two very different worlds of meaning—one associated with community and the other associated with the pursuit of economic gain. The second stage shows how the conflation of community and capital undermines many of the conceptual distinctions that are crucial to the seminal influences on contemporary political and social thought. In the third stage, we develop our assertions about the problems arising from the use of the term social capital by a close reading of *Bowling Alone* that focuses on what the book says, and does not say, about economic inequality and democracy. In the final stage we compare the way that the term social capital obscures the conflict between capital and community with the advertising industry's attempt to make capital appear more neighborly.

Another Name for Fraternity?

Contrary to the conventional wisdom exemplified by *Bowling Alone's* statement that liberty, equality, and fraternity were inscribed on the banners of the French Revolution, that slogan—in, of, and by itself—was not all that common during the Revolution.[2] Especially in the Revolution's early stages, Ozouf points out, other triads were much more common: "the nation, the law, and the king in the first civic oaths" and after the king's unsuccessful flight "the nation, liberty, and equality" (Ozouf 1989, 695). As the Revolution became more radical, the word *fraternité* became increasingly common. According to the most comprehensive history of the slogan *Liberté, Egalité, Fraternité*, the last of the three "is more a word of the 'left' than *liberté* or *egalité*" (Roberts 1976, 336). It is far from accidental, Roberts continues, that *fraternité* "is used more as the Revolution itself becomes more radical for, chronologically, there can be no doubt the idea of fraternity can be found at the very roots of the radicalization: it was the self-designated sociétés fraternelles . . . which were the cradle of *sans-culotterie*" (336).

A full discussion of the *sans-culottes* is well beyond the scope of this chapter. But little in their history suggests they would be happy with *fraternité* being called a form of capital. "Without being truly in favor of equal distribution," Higonnet writes, "[the *sans-culotte*] scorned money. Gold was for him an object of suspicion" (1998, 395). Similarly, Palmer has emphasized how the *sans-culottes* "burned with a new sense of equality" (1964, 47) and "objected to business men, big merchants, financiers, commercial capital, and stock companies" (48). Thus, to view the *sans-culottes'* cherished ideal of fraternity as a form of capital is to ignore their opposition to all that capital, in the traditional meaning of the term, represents.

Even if the *sans-culottes'* antipathy to capital in the traditional meaning of the term is set aside, *fraternité* had a meaning for them that simply cannot be comprehended by the term social capital. In those years of the Revolution, *fraternité* connoted, as Roberts notes, a "relationship which ought to exist between all Frenchmen as members of a national and egalitarian community, and its realisation is both demanded and praised" (Roberts 1976, 334). That demand and praise had a profoundly emotional aspect. The stakes of the Revolution, as many saw them, could be summarized in the slogan urged on Parisians by their local government: "*Unité indivisibilité de la Loi: Liberté, Egalité, Fraternité, ou la Mort*" (1976, 338). But it is difficult to imagine even the most ardent social capitalist keeping a straight face if that slogan were "Liberty, Equality, Social Capital, or Death."

In addition to what Roberts considers *fraternité's* most characteristic meaning during the Revolution, the word has a broader meaning—brotherhood—the one word translation that typically appears in French-English dictionaries (Larousse 1993, 395). This meaning also informed Revolutionary discourse. Thus, the person responsible for drawing up Paris's jury lists chose Catholics, Protestants, and Jews in order to illustrate "the fraternity of men regardless of religion" and got hold of the one person of color he knew in order to "consecrate the fraternity of colors" (as quoted in Ozouf 1989, 696). To apply the term social capital to brotherhood is to obliterate the difference between the universal and communal denotations of the word brotherhood and the competitive, individualist ones inherent in the terms capital and capitalism.

Fraternité also has a much narrower meaning than either of the two previously discussed. Although this narrower meaning may have been less prevalent during the Revolution, it plays a role in many other contexts in French history. A few words about one of these other contexts are also appropriate since it has been the topic of a recent and careful study. In *Fraternity Among the French Peasantry,* Alan Baker documents the importance of voluntary associations in the Loire Valley in the nineteenth century. Insofar as voluntary associations are often seen as the stuff of social capital, that book might seem to provide some justification for applying the term social capital to *fraternité,* albeit not during the French Revolution. However, any such application faces two problems. First, Baker views sociability as an expression of the concept of fraternity (1999, 32). While there is presumably some positive relationship between sociability and the more expansive meaning that *fraternité* had during the French Revolution, that more expansive meaning is very different from sociability. Moreover, the fraternity of which Baker writes was expressed "as association or co-operation, as opposed to capitalist exploitation" (1999, 32). Thus, to view even fraternity-as-sociability as a form of capital would be to bring together in one term what were considered polar opposites in the discourse of nineteenth-century rural France.

Social Capital, Tawdry Commerce, and Liberalism

Just as the term social capital is at variance with the French understanding of *fraternité* during the Revolution and in the nineteenth century, so, too, does it jibe poorly with the understanding of the Frenchman whose observations about the United States of the early nineteenth century make him, in Putnam's view, the "patron saint of contemporary social capitalists" (2000, 292). Tocqueville is ambivalent about the rise of both democracy and industrial capitalism. While he sees a subtle and complex relationship between political association and commercial activity, he certainly does not diminish the differences between the two. In an essay exploring Tocqueville's contradictory positions on democracy and commerce, Holmes notes that from Tocqueville's perspective, "Commerce may not be the worst thing one person can do to another; but it is selfish, petty, tawdry, and low" (Holmes 1993, 39). Although democratic politics can be dangerous, it "rescues modern individuals from the degrading focus on their own well-being encouraged by commercial society" (1993, 39). Given the frequency with which discussions of social capital are rooted in Tocqueville's work, it is ironic that the vital associational life so valued by Tocqueville as a "machine for awakening, stretching, and enlivening the mind . . . [which] lifts individuals above themselves and engages them in the concerns of others, in the problems of the whole community," is now being described in the "tawdry" language of commerce.

Nor does the term *social capital* jibe well with classical liberalism. From such a perspective, the idea of "social capital" is both superficially appropriate and theoretically baffling. As a concept that applies economic terminology to political life, social capital seems—initially at least—to fit perfectly within the classical liberal tradition. One of the hallmarks of classical liberal thinking is the attempt to explain social and political activity in market terms. Hobbes initiates this trend by devising a theory of civil government based entirely on self-interest. As economic thinkers of the seventeenth century are also moving toward an exclusive theory of self-interest, there is a logical connection here between economic and political thought. Locke justifies the creation of government as a means of protecting private property. Madison develops a theory of democratic government grounded in self-interest and based on the principle that government can control, coordinate, and aggregate private interest for the public good. At first glance all of these theories seem to leave behind the fear— rooted in the classical Greek understanding—that politics or public life is somehow corrupted if private interests are allowed to influence it. The use of economic terminology, that is, *social capital,* to describe important aspects of political life and its preconditions would not seem to be that different from expanding the economic concept of self-interest to explain the political world.

However, the assumption that all of human behavior can be explained by economistic or self-interested motives is a quite simplified view of the classical liberal tradition. Madison, for example, sees self-interest as a primary human motivator, but it is not necessarily an objective or rational motivation. As he states in Federalist 10, "so strong is this propensity of

mankind to fall into mutual animosities that where no substantial occasion presents itself, the most frivolous and fanciful distinctions have been
sufficient to kindle their unfriendly passions and excite their most violent
conflicts" (1961 [1787], 79). For Madison, reason is influenced and sometimes subsumed by passion, making self-interest frequently synonymous
with the pursuit of power, glory, and ambition. Holmes similarly gives a
compelling description of the various human motivations described by
liberal thinkers such as Adam Smith and David Hume. Both Smith and
Hume chronicle a variety of human motives specifically distinguished
from self-interest. Smith, for example, distinguishes among what he calls
the unsocial, selfish, and social passions. Included in the last category are
"generosity, humanity, kindness, compassion, mutual friendship and es-
teem" (Smith 1966 [1759], 52). Such sentiments are reminiscent of the
French revolutionaries' conception of *fraternité*, and for Smith are as different from self-interest as *fraternité* was different in the minds of the
French revolutionaries from the pursuit of wealth. In other words, as
Holmes notes, self-interest "is merely one motive among others" in much
of classical liberal thought (1990, 268). Human behavior was understood
as exceedingly complex, and it was characterized by fundamentally different motivations. Economistic motives could not be understood without
the contrasting motives that gave them definition.

One conclusion (or caution) we can draw from the variety of classical
liberal thought is that any apparent liberal satisfaction with the use of
purely economistic descriptions of human behavior represents a simplified version of a very rich classical liberal tradition. Indeed, thinking about
the appropriateness of using economic terminology to describe human
behavior in the liberal tradition forces us to confront the unfortunate narrowing of this invaluable intellectual tradition, which today tends to emphasize only one side of the human motivational coin. It is primarily the
twentieth-century desire to quantify and measure human behavior that
has resulted in this simplification. If the concept of social capital is appropriate from the perspective of classical liberalism, it is only appropriate
from our narrowly redefined understanding of that intellectual tradition.

There is also a more basic sense in which using the concept of social
capital to describe political activity undermines the classical liberal intellectual tradition. This terminology conflates two of the most crucial distinctions in the classical liberal tradition: the separation of public and private, and the distinction between the individual and society. While similar
human motivations (such as self-interest) might prevail in both politics

and economics, the classical liberal tradition is clear in its desire to separate the realm of political activity from the realm of economic activity. For classical liberals, "politics is regarded as a distinct and separate sphere in society, a sphere set apart from economy, culture and family life" (Held 1996, 98). Liberal thinkers define a separate sphere of economic activity distinct from the realm of government and protect that sphere against democratic incursions by the public. We suspect that classical liberals might rightly be suspicious of language that talks about political participation and democracy as if it were a subset of economic transaction. Indeed, the idea that private differences such as those of wealth and privilege should not hold sway in the public sphere of consensual authority is the key democratic impulse in the classical liberal tradition.

It is also substantively outside the liberal tradition to focus on a "social" type of capital that explains the political activity of an individual or group. For classical liberals, individuals are presumed to be prior to society. Their activity is based, at least in part, on rational calculation based on their assumed interests. The entire focus on networks of relationships that facilitate action flattens the individual/society distinction that is so crucial to classical liberalism. Indeed, the movement to begin thinking about public goods and public power as social and structural is a modern-day critique of the classical liberal tradition. In that respect, the term *social capital* may seem more congenial to modern liberalism than to classical liberalism, but even with modern liberalism there are major problems.

While the classical liberal tradition has a somewhat schizophrenic relationship with the economistic language of social capital, such language is unambiguously at odds with the modern liberal tradition. Modern liberalism, as it develops in the United States in the first part of the twentieth century, redefines key concepts of classical liberalism. While still concerned with the freedom and dignity of the individual, modern liberal thinkers expand their understanding of both power and freedom. While classical liberals are primarily concerned with excessive state power, modern liberals have come to recognize the dangers to freedom from other forms of concentrated power, specifically economic power. They also reinterpret individual freedom in a more positive way. Freedom is not only the right to be left alone, free from government interference: it is also the real practice of exercising control over your life, and the ability to develop your unique capacities as an individual (all of which may be stunted by concentrated economic power). John Dewey, who played a major role in shaping modern liberalism, criticizes an intellectual tradition that has come to define individuality in terms of economic self-seeking. Dewey advocates an expanded understanding of public power where the power of government can be put to the use of liberty, enabling all to develop their inherent capacities as individuals. He decries the prevalent theory of competitive individualism, and seeks to replace that theory with a greater focus on social cooperation, conscience, and social responsibility.

Modern liberalism's concern with the overly economistic interpretation of individuality and social life is incompatible with Putnam's categorization of cooperative activity that enables democracy as a form of capital. Dewey explicitly raises his concern with the cultural connotations of industrial capitalism, forcefully advocating "genuine industrial freedom":

> It is absurd to conceive liberty as that of the business entrepreneur and ignore the immense regimentation to which workers are subjected, intellectual as well as manual workers. . . . the full freedom of the human spirit and of individuality can be achieved only as there is effective opportunity to share in the cultural resources of civilization. No economic state of affairs is merely economic. It has a profound effect upon the presence or absence of cultural freedom. Any liberalism that does not make full cultural freedom supreme and that does not see the relation between it and genuine industrial freedom as a way of life is a degenerate and delusive liberalism. (Dewey 1972 [1935], 500)

The economistic terminology of social capital makes it very difficult to see the impediments to freedom operating within the modern industrial state. Modern liberalism's critique of capitalism—virtually by definition—is neither as systematic nor as comprehensive as that rooted in the Marxist tradition. Still, those who have called themselves liberals in the twentieth century have generally paid considerable attention to capitalism's adverse effects on various groups (e.g., blue-collar workers and the aged). And liberals in practice put considerable effort into developing policies to address these adverse effects. From this perspective, the celebration of the term *social capital* serves to obscure potentially damaging features of modern life.

Indeed, to the extent that social capital celebrates market forces in forging a democratic community, it implies that the answer to democracy's ills is "privatization" or "market reforms," rather than a stronger role for the public sector in creating legal-institutional supports for greater grassroots participation in the community. As Skocpol observes, in fact it is the active promotion by the state of participation and communal norms of solidarity that contributed to the development of community associations embodying social capital (Skocpol 1999). The widespread use of the term *social capital* is part of a worldview that conceptualizes social and political processes in terms of the language of business and commerce, as well as one that sees the market as better able than government to provide services that have historically been the latter's responsibility. That worldview has led to a host of initiatives for the privatization of services—such as education, public safety, prisons, and garbage collection—about which modern liberals are typically skeptical. We return to this assault upon the public as an autonomous sphere in our discussion of how the term *social capital* affects thinking about democracy.

From Past to Present

The discourse of the French Revolution, Tocqueville's reflections on the United States, classical liberalism, and modern liberalism are some of the major sources of contemporary thinking. In all of these cases, we have argued, the term social capital creates an unacceptably universal category that disguises crucial conceptual distinctions, vitiates important historical critiques, and unnecessarily simplifies complex issues. In principle, of course, there is nothing wrong with a term not fitting well into the categories of established intellectual traditions. Frequently, a term can advance understanding precisely because it transcends existing conceptual frameworks, and that has clearly been the goal of the scholarly use of the term social capital. However, rather than transcend existing categories in a way that facilitates inquiry, the term *social capital* conflates them in a way that narrows the range of thought and retards the analytic, empirical, and normative aspects of a critical analysis of actually existing society. We develop this assertion by discussing *Bowling Alone's* discussion of economic inequality and democracy.

Economic Inequality and the Agenda for Social Capitalists

We can begin to see how the term *social capital* interferes with effective thinking about the contemporary political world by discussing economic inequality and *Bowling Alone's* policy recommendations and exhortations. In *Bowling Alone*, Putnam (2000, 359) fully acknowledges the declining economic equality of the last third of the twentieth century, viewing it along with declining civic engagement as "the twin master trends of our time" and saying that "there is every reason to think" that the two trends "reinforce one another." However, virtually nothing about economic inequality appears in the book's concluding chapter, "Toward an Agenda for Social Capitalists." Master-trend though it may be, declining economic equality, for example, is absent from the list of the profound changes that Putnam lists, early in the chapter, as affecting the possibility of "replenishing our stocks of social capital"[3] (2000, 403). And in sketching the six areas that "deserve special attention from aspiring social capitalists: youth and schools; the workplace; urban and metropolitan design; religion; arts and culture; and politics and government" (404), the book does not discuss how economic inequality affects prescriptions in any of the areas, except for a brief mention in the discussion of politics and government.

Given that *Bowling Alone* is about civic engagement, not economic inequality, to note this omission may appear the most facile kind of criticism: taking a book to task for what is not said, rather than for what is said. But the omission is a crucial one because the scant attention paid to economic issues in the agenda for social capitalists reflects an approach to current social problems *including* civic engagement that is so one-sided as to be deeply misleading, if not wrong. The attempt to describe the workings of community life and civic engagement in the language of capital muddles both the extent to which the workings of financial capital have undermined community and civic engagement as well as the extent to which the rejuvenation of community and civic engagement has involved challenges to the operation of capitalism.

An example of this muddling is *Bowling Alone*'s failure to pursue fully the analogy it draws between the last decades of the nineteenth century and the last decades of the twentieth. The last decades of the nineteenth century—the Gilded Age—saw, in Putnam's view, "dramatic technological, economic, and social change that rendered obsolete a significant stock of social capital" (2000, 368). However, in the wake of the Gilded Age came the Progressive Era, "the most fecund period of civic innovation in American history" (368) that created entirely new stocks of social capital. Similarly, in Putnam's view, the last decades of the twentieth century also have "rendered obsolete a significant stock of America's social capital" (367), with the result that the time is ripe for a twenty-first century analog of the Progressive Era: "The specific reforms of the Progressive Era are no longer appropriate for our time, but the practical, enthusiastic idealism of that era—and its achievements—should inspire us" (401). Yet for all the diversity, lack of cohesion, and frequent self-contradictoriness of Progressivism, surely an important aspect of that era's idealism and achievements were fueled by "anger over the excesses of industrial capitalism" (Faragher et al. 2000, 612). In its account of Progressivism, *Bowling Alone* acknowledges many aspects of this anger, for example, muckraking and trust-busting. But despite the book's exhortation to draw inspiration from the Progressivism, virtually nothing in the agenda for social capitalists reflects any concern with the excesses of late-twentieth century capitalism, including growing economic inequality. Nor does the agenda for social capitalists include anything even vaguely reminiscent of the trust—busting, muckraking, and anger over the excesses of capitalism that were an important aspect of Progressivism.

Moreover, although *Bowling Alone* views declining economic equality and civic engagement as two reinforcing master trends, the book pays scant attention to the way in which civic engagement is stratified by income, wealth, and social class, even though, as Schlozman, Verba, and Brady note, the "inequality of civic engagement is unambiguous" (1999, 457).[4] Indicative of this scant attention are the book's ninety-six figures which highlight a wide range of data and findings. But not one of the figures provides any breakdown of individuals' civic engagement by their income, wealth, or social class. Rather, one has to read the text carefully for observations such as one, drawing on Wilson's work on Chicago's black ghetto, that "social networks are absent in precisely the places where they are needed most" (Putnam 2000, 321).

However, *Bowling Alone's* discussion of Wilson's work further illustrates the one-sidedness of *Bowling Alone's* emphasis on social capital. Calling Wilson "the nation's leading urban sociologist" and his book *The Truly Disadvantaged* a "classic," Putnam cites it as part of a discussion of how the "decline in neighborhood social capital—community monitoring, socializing, mentoring, and organizing—is one important feature of the inner-city crisis, in addition to purely economic factors" (Putnam 2000, 312). The words "in addition to" are deceptive because they put the decline in social capital on a par with "purely economic factors" and imply that the two are largely independent of each other. But while *The Truly Disadvantaged* repeatedly emphasizes that the problems of inner-city black ghettoes have a range of inter-related causes, it also makes clear that economic factors have played a decisive role within this multi-causal web. For example, prior to summing up the chapter on "Social Change and Social Dislocations in the Inner City," Wilson writes:

The increasing social isolation of the inner city is a product of the class transformation of the inner city, including the growing concentration of poverty in inner-city neighborhoods. And the class transformation of the inner city cannot be understood without considering the effects of fundamental changes in the urban economy on the lower-income minorities, effects that include joblessness and that thereby increase the chances of long-term residence in highly concentrated poverty areas. (1987, 61–62)

In keeping with its analysis of the causes of the problem of inner-city black ghettoes, *The Truly Disadvantaged's* policy recommendations are weighted heavily toward economic measures, as indicated by the opening paragraph of the conclusion to the book's last chapter:

In this chapter I have argued that the problems of the ghetto underclass can be most meaningfully addressed by a comprehensive program that combines employment policies with social welfare policies and features universal as opposed to race- or group-specific strategies. On the one hand, this program highlights macroeconomic policy to generate a tight labor market and economic growth; fiscal and monetary policy not only to stimulate noninflationary growth, but also to increase the competitiveness of American goods on both the domestic and international markets; and a national labor-market strategy to make the labor force more adaptable to changing economic opportunities. On the other hand, this program highlights a child support assurance program, a family allowance program, and a child care strategy. (Wilson 1987, 163)

In sum: (i) stocks of what Putnam calls social capital are extremely low in inner-city ghettoes, (ii) economic measures are the centerpiece of Wilson's recommendations to improve inner-city ghettoes including stocks of social capital, and (iii) *Bowling Alone* lavishly praises Wilson's work. Nonetheless, the policy recommendations of the agenda for social capitalists do not reflect any of the importance that Wilson attaches to alleviating economic inequality. At a time when the quotidian operation of the world capitalist system is exacerbating economic inequalities within most countries as well as among them, there is something profoundly disquieting about an agenda for social capitalists that pays virtually no attention to the relationship between economic inequality and social capital. The discrepancy between the policy recommendations of *Bowling Alone* and *The Truly Disadvantaged* only makes the omission more disquieting.

The scant attention given economic inequality in the agenda for social capitalists reflects what we consider an even more fundamental problem with the term social capital; it suggests that its empirical referents are fungible with other forms of capital and that large stocks of one kind of capital can offset smaller stocks of another kind. Thus, in talking about the problems facing inner-city residents, *Bowling Alone* says:

> Precisely because poor people (by definition) have little economic capital and face formidable obstacles in acquiring human capital (that is, education), *social* capital is disproportionately important to their welfare. Thus, while our evidence . . . makes clear that the erosion of social capital and community has affected Grosse Pointe in essentially the same degree as inner-city Detroit, the *impact* of that development has so far been greater in the inner city, which lacks the cushioning of other forms of capital. (2000, 318)

But surely, there are profound limits in the extent of exchangeability and fungibility, especially in the extent to which any "investments"—however great—in social capital can make up for staggering differences in access to financial capital. These limits arise from the fact that whatever social capital might be embodied in most citizens' organizations, it plays a role in society that is fundamentally different from the role played by financial capital. That difference is rooted in how the operation of the economy constitutes many other aspects of social life. As Ehrenberg says:

> The economy is not just another sphere of association like a book group, bowling league, or block association. It is an extraordinarily powerful set of social relations whose imperatives are penetrating and organizing ever-wider areas of public and private life. No conceivable combination of PTAs, soup kitchens, choral societies, or Girl Scout troops can resist it. It is no longer possible to theorize civil society as a site of democratic activity and counterpoise it to an inherently coercive state without considering how capitalism's structural inequities constitute everyday life. (1999, 248)

Applying the term social capital to these bowling leagues, block associations, churches, and Girl Scout troops serves to preempt the consideration of how capitalism's inequities constitute everyday life precisely because the word *capital* in the term *social capital* obscures the crucial distinction that the economy is "not just another sphere of association."

Moreover, to encourage people who have scant access to financial capital to think of themselves as social capitalists is to facilitate their applying the language of capitalism—investing, owning, profit, the bottom line—to activities that historically have been viewed as different from economic pursuits. The spread of this language to these other activities serves ideological functions in that it helps make the relations of capitalism appear a widespread and perhaps inherent part of the human experience to which there are minimal feasible alternatives.

Democracy and Social Capital

One form of activity historically seen as distinct from economic activity is democratic political participation, especially the thick, participatory, and deliberative form of democracy that Putnam ostensibly advocates. The chapter on democracy in *Bowling Alone* begins with praise for the participatory versions of democracy espoused by Jefferson, Tocqueville, Mill, and Dewey, as well as with disdain for the twentieth-century equation of good citizenship with merely "choosing among competing teams of politicians at the ballot box, as one might choose among competing brands of toothpaste" (2000, 336). It is clear that Putnam situates his work within the former tradition and fears the trend toward consumerist democracy and the "citizenship by proxy" fostered by TV-based politics and the "hiring" of interest groups to defend our interests (Putnam 2000, 343). Given these preferences and concerns, it is indeed ironic that *Bowling Alone* would rely on a market metaphor to describe the very resources that supposedly make market-oriented democracy less likely.

The economic terminology of social capital trivializes the world of meaning that surrounds the cherished concepts of citizenship, democracy, and the public good. One of the beneficial effects of the voluntary associations and networks that Putnam calls social capital is to instill "habits of cooperation and public spiritedness" (2000, 338). *Bowling Alone* offers Tocqueville's observation that "feelings and ideas are renewed, the heart enlarged, and the understanding developed by the reciprocal action of men one upon another" as evidence that these associations and networks create an emotional commitment to public life (2000, 338). Democracy and citizenship are concepts, like fraternity, that evoke a host of feelings, emotions, and commitments that go beyond an objective appraisal of constitutional design and that transcend the kinds of cost-benefit analyses that define the market. As Benjamin Barber observes, Americans use "the fierce attachments of patriotic sentiment to bond a people to high ideals" (Barber 1996, 32). The term social capital, which comes from the linguistic tradition of economics, simply cannot convey the depth of meaning associated with the ideals of democracy and civic virtue. Putnam has taken the heart of democratic public life, the daily civic activities that create these connections between people and commitments to public goods, and labeled them *social capital*—putting the whole of public life on par with an economic transaction. Just as we cannot imagine eighteenth-century Parisians putting their lives on the line for *social capital,* as they did for *fraternité,* in the contemporary United States, the historic meaning of the word *capital* is very much at variance with the emotional attachment to the community that is an essential aspect of the civic involvement and civic virtue that *Bowling Alone* seeks to promote.

If Putnam is serious about his preference for participatory, deliberative democracy, it is hard to see how using language inconsistent with, and contradictory to, that tradition furthers his goal. The virtue of social networks and associations is the relationships they foster among people, combating modern tendencies toward anonymity and citizenship by proxy, which Putnam sees as "anathema to deliberation" (Putnam 2000, 342). *Bowling Alone* argues that communities "where people know one another, interact with one another . . . and trust one another to behave honorably, . . . have a model and a moral foundation upon which to base further cooperative enterprises" (2000, 346). Yet, the virtue of the market is precisely its anonymity, which, according to market enthusiasts such as Milton Friedman, makes it the perfect antidote to racism and sexism. The cooperative interactions Putnam desires are very different from an economic transaction. The marketplace does not demand that we act honorably or virtuously, or that we care for those with whom we interact; it only demands that our transactions be, in Friedman's own words, "bi-laterally voluntary and informed" (Friedman 1962, 13).

Furthermore, the very type of interaction fostered by civic engagement—genuine public deliberation and practical reasoning—is distinctly different from the strategic communication necessary for and expected in market transactions. In other words our attitude must be very different when we approach one another in the arena of public decision making than when we seek to maximize profit in the marketplace. *Bowling Alone* provides evidence that social capital discourages "free-riding," by showing that in states with high levels of social capital people are less likely to ignore civic duties or to let others pay for public goods (Putnam 2000, 348–49). Yet, the free rider problem is the classic example of the application of economic reasoning to politics. It does not make sense from an economic standpoint to pay or play when others will do so for you. How can we describe the very resources that lessen this sort of self-interested calculation in the economistic language that defines the problem in the first place?

Friendly and Neighborly Capital?

This chapter began by comparing the attention lavished by the French revolutionaries on names to the nonchalance with which *Bowling Alone* asserts that fraternity is just another name for social capital. In keeping with that nonchalance, the book ignores the problems of using the language of capital to talk about community and civic engagement. Nor has the vast majority of scholars theorizing and studying social capital paid much attention to these problems.

This lack of attention makes for a useful comparison with the public relations efforts of U.S. corporations during the twentieth century. As exquisitely detailed by Roland Marchand in *Creating the Corporate Soul,* the first half of the twentieth century saw a sustained public relations effort to persuade the public that the giant corporations which dominated the U.S. economy had a soul. By the mid-1940s, however, the word *soul* "had come to seem archaic, both to assailants and to defenders of the giant corporation" (Marchand 1998, 360). The search for a different corporate image led Bruce Barton, one of the seminal figures in twentieth-century advertising, to urge United States Steel "to present itself to the public in explicit language as a 'good neighbor'" (361). Of many possible compliments, "good neighbor," Barton pointed out, was "one of the simplest, and yet one of the most profound" (362). Barton's point resonated with the director of public relations for U.S. Steel; his recollections of the job were titled *And Be Neighborly* (Marchand 1998, 360). A half-century after Barton stressed the importance of neighborliness to U.S. Steel, it remains a staple of corporate imagery, as attested by the slogan "Like a good neighbor, State Farm is there." The metaphor of the good neighbor is effective, Marchand continues (1998, 361), because it places the giant corporation "within the ambience of that social formation most redolent of comfortable, friendly, and agreeable relationships among individuals and groups—the local community."

As this discussion of corporate imagery indicates, public relations experts consciously sought to obscure the distinction between the concentrations of capital represented by corporate behemoths and the friendly and agreeable relationships among individuals and groups that historically constitute valued aspects of local communities. Seeking to study those very same community-based relationships, scholars, we have argued in this chapter, have used a vocabulary—that of social capital—that also conflates this distinction. To be sure, these scholarly inquiries have been largely motivated by an attempt to understand the world and promote civic engagement, while public relations experts sought largely to improve corporate images and protect corporate profits. Yet the force of that distinction compounds the irony of our penultimate observation: the hired guns of the advertising world have paid much greater attention to the marketing advantages of a vocabulary that conflates capital and community than some of the academy's most distinguished social scientists have paid to this vocabulary's conceptual and normative disadvantages.

Like corporate hucksters, but motivated by very different concerns, the French revolutionaries also attempted to use the many connotations of words to shape people's understanding. Perhaps in their zeal to instill ethical and political values, these revolutionaries paid too much attention to what names mean, signify, and imply. But in claiming that the French revolutionaries' cherished and lofty ideal of fraternity is another name for social capital, *Bowling Alone* is surely paying too little.

Notes

1. For additional discussion of how the term social capital both affects and reflects the intellectual and political milieu of the United States at the start of the twenty-first century, see Smith and Kulynych (2002). That article also argues that given the many problems of the term *social capital,* both lay and scholarly discourse would benefit from replacing the term *social capital* with the term *social capacity.*

2. As Ozouf points out, "Not until 1848 was the threefold principle of liberty, equality, and fraternity embodied" in a French Constitution (1989, 695). Ironically, it was the Batavian Republic—one of the Republics created under the auspices of Revolutionary France—that in 1795 was the first Republic to use "Liberty, Equality, Fraternity" as an official motto (Palmer 1964, 180).

3. The changes *Bowling Alone* lists—"most women are employed, markets global, individuals and firms mobile, entertainment electronic, technology accelerating, and major war (thankfully) absent" (2000, 403)—only makes the omission of economic inequality more striking since globalization and the increased mobility of capital are generally considered two of the reasons why economic inequality has increased.

4. Although Schlozman, Verba, and Brady focus primarily on political participation, they also note that the "well educated and well heeled" are also "more likely to be affiliated with voluntary organizations. Data collected in 1967 indicate that those on the highest rung of the income ladder were three times as likely to be active members of organizations as those at the bottom. In 1990, the ratio was exactly the same" (Schlozman, Verba, and Brady 1999, 451).

References

Baker, Alan R. H. 1999. *Fraternity Among the French Peasantry.* New York: Cambridge University Press.

Barber, Benjamin. 1996. "Constitutional Faith." In Joshua Cohen, ed. *For Love of Country,* 30–37. Boston: Beacon.

Dewey, John. 1972 [1935]. "The Future of Liberalism." *Journal of Philosophy* 32 (9), April 25, 1935. Reprinted in Carl Cohen, ed. *Communism, Fascism, and Democracy,* second ed. 496–501. New York: Random House.

Ehrenberg, John. 1999. *Civil Society: The Critical History of an Idea.* New York: NYU Press.

Faragher, John Mack, Mari Jo Buhle, Daniel Czitrom, and Susan H. Armitage. 2000. *Out of Many: A History of the American People,* vol. II: since 1865 (3rd ed). Upper Saddle River, N.J.: Prentice Hall.

Friedman, Milton, 1962. *Capitalism and Freedom.* Chicago: University of Chicago Press.

Held, David. 1996. *Models of Democracy,* second ed. Stanford: Stanford University Press.

Higonnet, Patrice. 1998. "Sans-culottes." In François Furet and Mona Ozouf, eds. *A Critical Dictionary of the French Revolution,* 393–99. Cambridge: Harvard University Press.

Holmes, Stephen. 1990. "The Secret History of Self-Interest." In Jane Mansbridge, ed. *Beyond Self-Interest,* 267–86. Chicago: University of Chicago Press.

———. 1993. "Tocqueville and Democracy." In David Copp, Jean Hampton, and John E. Roemer, eds. *The Idea of Democracy,* 23–63. New York: Cambridge University Press.

Hunt, Lynn. 1984. *Politics, Culture, and Class in the French Revolution.* Berkeley: University of California Press.

Larousse Grand Dictionnaire. 1993. Paris: Larousse.

Madison, James. 1961 [1787]. Federalist No. 10. In Clinton Rossiter, ed. New York: Penguin.

Marchand, Roland. 1998. *Creating the Corporate Soul.* Berkeley: University of California Press.

Ozouf, Mona. 1989. "Fraternity." In François Furet and Mona Ozouf, eds. *A Critical Dictionary of the French Revolution,* 694–703. Cambridge: Harvard University Press.

Palmer, R. R. 1964. *The Age of the Democratic Revolution*, vol. 2. Princeton: Princeton University Press.

Putnam, Robert. 2000. *Bowling Alone: The Collapse and Revival of American Community.* New York: Simon & Schuster.

Roberts, J. M. 1976. "Liberté, Egalité, Fraternité: Sources and Development of a Slogan." *Tijdschrift voor de Studie Van de Verlichting* 4 (no. 3–4): 329–69.

Schlozman, Kay Lehman, Sidney Verba, and Henry E. Brady. 1999. "Civic Participation and the Equality Problem." In Theda Skocpol and Morris P. Fiorina, eds. *Civic Engagement in American Democracy,* 427–60. Washington, D.C.: Brookings.

Skocpol, Theda. 1999. "How Americans Became Civic." In Theda Skocpol and Morris Fiorina, eds. *Civic Engagement In American Democracy,* 27–80. Washington, D.C.: Brookings.

Smith, Adam. 1966 [1759]. *The Theory of Moral Sentiments.* New York: Augustus M. Kelley.

Smith, Stephen Samuel, and Jessica Kulynych. 2002. "It May Be *Social,* But Why Is It *Capital?* The Social Construction of Social Capital and the Politics of Language." *Politics and Society* 30 (no. 1): 149–86.

Wilson, William Julius. 1987. *The Truly Disadvantaged.* Chicago: University of Chicago Press.

Chapter Six

Patriotism, Generational Change, and the Politics of Sacrifice

Scott L. McLean

Samuel Stoughton in his 1668 Election Day sermon in Boston lamented the failure of his generation to live up to the achievements and standards of their Puritan fathers. "The first generation have been ripened time after time," Stoughton preached, "But we who rise up to tread out the footsteps of them that are gone before us, alas! What are we? . . . O New England, thy God expected better things of thee and thy children" (quoted in Bercovitch 1974, 48–49). Stoughton's Jeremiad echoed an ancient warning that a society cannot endure unless each generation inherits the memories of the past while creating its own future. So too, Robert Putnam's social scientific Jeremiad in *Bowling Alone* (2000) warns us that people born after 1945 are not taking over the civic responsibilities of their elders, the "civic generation" born between 1910 and 1940. Older age cohorts have higher levels of civic connectedness than younger ones, and as younger citizens take the place of older ones, the civic character of the nation changes.

Putnam describes this trend as "generational replacement" and says it is a "new formulation of the mystery" of why social capital has declined in America. But it is more than a new formulation of the old mystery. It virtually eclipses the role of television, which in previous renditions of his argument (Putnam 1995a; 1995b; 1996) was the "main culprit" behind civic decline. Putnam's earlier work noted that the age cohort born between 1925 and 1930 is exceptionally civic (1995a; 1995b; 1996) but he rejected generational factors as "the main culprit" because he could not find a link between "crisis" events after World War II and the more-or-less steady decline of civic engagement in postwar age cohorts (1996).[1] Thus his new focus on generational replacement is a significant amendment of his ideas. In his book (Putnam 2000), he estimates that between 65 and 70 percent of social capital depletion since 1945 is accounted for by the "slow, steady and ineluctable replacement of the long civic generation by their less involved children and grandchildren" (283).[2] He speculates that this is because the civic generation came of age during the nationally galvanizing experiences of the Great Depression and World War II, while in stark contrast the younger generations had the civically alienating experiences of Vietnam, Watergate, and being raised watching television. Though he lacks any direct evidence to support the claim, he says that these events, and the *zeitgeist* they inspire, have a systematic impact on each generation's civic activities as they age.

Oddly, the emergence of generational change as the main culprit has received very little critical scrutiny, and Putnam makes very little effort to elaborate or substantiate it, much less incorporate its insights into his recommendations for reform. Perhaps the generational replacement theory has not been seriously challenged because the title "Bowling Alone" already implied a nostalgic look back to the 1950s lifestyles of the greatest generation. His previous indictment of television as the main culprit for civic decline already depicted a "TV generation" which spends more time watching the boob tube than socializing or joining associations. In addition, it is attractive and seemingly unassailable because it appears to be supported by evidence Putnam gleans from an analysis of birth cohorts.

This chapter will analyze in a critical way Putnam's use of the concept of "generations." If one is interested in understanding why civil society changes, then generational replacement is the best place to start, because it is different than practically any other kind of explanation. Other explanations, especially the others in *Bowling Alone*, start with the assumption that people are changing their minds or their habits over time. But generational replacement provides for a mechanism in which civil society can change in the aggregate without any change occurring in individuals at all. Even if no individuals change their minds or activities, when younger people with less civic capacity replace their more civic elders, gradually civil society in the aggregate has less social capital. Thus, as civic Americans die off and are replaced by uncivic, the task of explaining civic disengagement gets transformed into a mere matter of actuarial calculation.

Putnam deserves credit for identifying the differences in associational activity between age cohorts. However, we should be cautious in accepting his description of the trend as an "explanation" for the nation's declining social capital. A description of a trend is hardly an explanation for it. For example, he speculates that the cohorts roughly correspond to "generations" defined by major events that people experienced when they reach young adulthood, but he gives no reason and no data to support his claim that every birth cohort is a "generation" with a unique identity and style of associating. Some critical questions remain. What are the deeper causes of the trend? Is there evidence that the explanation is correct? What exactly is a "generation"? What sociological conditions distinguish a "generation" from a group of people who happen to be born at about the same time, and were these conditions present for each of the age cohorts Putnam calls "generations"? How does a memory of a national crisis reinforce "civic-mindedness" in a citizen (Putnam 2000, 267)? If the generational differences account for the majority of social capital decline, Putnam must also shoulder the burden of supporting his account of the origins of the generations and why they exhibit different levels of civic capacity (or incapacity).

Most important, while for Putnam the generational replacement theory represents a new and fundamental diagnosis of the nation's civic ills, it makes no corresponding difference in the content of his familiar recommendations for building new stores of social capital. Putnam rightly recoils from the idea that we should re-create the conditions of the wartime *zeitgeist* through jingoistic foreign policies. But how can service learning initiatives for young people (Putnam 2000, 405), while meritorious in many ways, substitute for a national crusade? How can promoting more commonplace experiences in picnics, volunteerism, and recreational leagues today substitute for the sense of community generated by major national crisis? It is as if Putnam is uncomfortable wrestling with the implication that the "greatest generation" was created by accident and there may be no way to deliberately create a new civic generation. It is easy to tell people to turn off their televisions, but much harder to discover a moral equivalent of war.

My critique of Putnam's generational explanation is that he is making unsupported assumptions, which conceal more or less arbitrary choices of age cohorts, without making an attempt to verify any of the causal links he makes about the power of historical events. Although it is hard to argue against the idea that there was a sense of national crisis in the Depression and a wave of patriotic fervor during World War II, we need to make a distinction between the events themselves, how they are interpreted and remembered, and how they are played out as resources for living a civic life in a diverse society.

Background: Generations and Politics

Is it realistic to expect that we should reach the high standards of civic activity set by the "civic generation"? Or should we give thanks for the fact that their efforts freed us from the necessity of taking on the same kind of civic burdens, and look for new styles of association consistent with social justice and democracy? Putnam's discussion of generations is part of a surge in popular fascination with the achievements of the "greatest generation" and a related disappointment with younger age cohorts. For many years, careful social scientists have analyzed the political activities and views of age cohorts. Scholars who study political generations have found that generational differences can account for different views of social and cultural issues such as abortion, pre-marital sex, drug use, and yes, television viewing—though not foreign policy or the economy (Mayer 1993; Schuman and Rieger 1992; Schuman and Scott 1989). In addition, the "generation gap" in social attitudes also shifts, with differences in attitudes and activities virtually disappearing on some issues over time.

But every few years a "new generation" is invented in the popular media, and most of the time these accounts extend a minor cohort difference or a current trend into the future, and turn it into a war between generations (Ladd 1994). Starting in the early 1990s, this occurred with the age cohort called "Gen X." Writers like Neil Howe and William Strauss dubbed the new group coming of age the "thirteeners," but Neil Howe's novel *Generation X: Tales of an Accelerated Culture* (1991) gave them the name that stuck. The latest "generation" to be mythologized are the "millenials," sometimes referred to as "the Echo Boom" or "GenY" (Strauss and Howe 1994). This is the age cohort Putnam hopes to make more civic with his educational proposals (Putnam 2000, 405).

Usually these types of discussion on generations are full of pop psychology reactions to horrifying incidents involving youth. Youth riots at the reincarnated Woodstock as well as tragic school shootings in Jonesboro, Arkansas, Paducah, Kentucky, and Columbine High School in Colorado led to increased public fears of youth violence. Politicians called for greater use of police against young people, as well as setting precedents for trying juvenile delinquents as adults. Paradoxically, along with this tougher attitude toward young adults came a subtle turn toward "protect-ing children" from whatever social ills may have corrupted Gen X and Gen Y—drugs, pornography, TV violence, and tobacco.

This round of generational worry also seems based on the increasing ethnic diversity among young Americans. The large age cohort born be-tween 1977 and the present are children of the Baby Boomers but also of the 1970s wave of "new immigrants" who came from Asia, Latin America, and Africa. This group has fewer members that identify themselves as white than older adults, and they are twice as likely as other age cohorts to identify themselves as "multiracial" (Takahashi 2001).

At the same time as youth took center stage in cultural politics at the beginning of the decade, the end of the 1990s saw the rise of a veritable cottage industry built on the praise of "the greatest generation" and con-current deprecation of the not-so-great baby boom generation. Swing music is back on the pop charts and the dance step "the Lindy" is in vogue. Books like Tom Brokaw's *The Greatest Generation* celebrate the achieve-ments of the birth cohort that battled the Depression as well as the Japan-ese and Germans. Political leaders like former Senator Bob Dole, who push for a World War II memorial, remind us that veterans of that war pass away at a rate of roughly 1,000 per day (Marin 2001). Films like *Sav-ing Private Ryan* and *Pearl Harbor* give postwar generations vicarious thrills with realistic battle scenes as well as opportunities for retroactive expression of patriotism.

The focus on the very youngest and oldest Americans is driven by the anxious middle—the Baby Boomers. Senator Robert Dole in 1996 said that President Bill Clinton epitomized a generation that "never sacrificed." While that charge had little impact on the 1996 election, it seems more salient after Clinton's impeachment, when a wave of fascination with the "greatest generation" began. It is ironic, to say the least, that Americans would become fascinated by the generation that saw the Depression and World War II, just at the very era when the New Deal state that emerged to respond to these crises is being dismantled. Welfare reform in 1996 ended the New Deal promise of poverty relief as a national entitlement, while the young are beginning to accept the idea that Social Security, as we know it now, will not be available to them.

Putnam is not guilty of wild exaggeration. He attempts to avoid embell-ishment and alarmism about the future of the sort associated with the Sunday newspaper supplement. In good social scientific fashion, he wishes to avoid confusing a short-term effect with a major long-term factor. His

discussion of generations is built on empirical differences between generations. Still, as we will see in the next section, sometimes he speculates beyond limitations of his data in order to make sense of what he sees.

Putnam's Generational Theory

No doubt *Bowling Alone* will add fodder to the next round of battles over
generations and American identity. In his analysis of trends in social trust
and civic engagement over the past forty years, Putnam noticed that older
Americans were more involved with community than younger Americans.
People born between 1920 and 1940 have led lives of greater civic involvement than people born between 1945 and 1964, and people born between
1965 and 1980. Although social capital declined first in the 1960s, "the
roots of our lonely bowling probably date to the 1940s and 1950s," when it
seemed like "an anticivic X-ray" rendered the postwar generations less
likely to connect with the community (Putnam 2000, 255). Something
happened (or did not happen) to people growing up immediately after
World War II that began America's civic downward spiral. Putnam stresses
with the generational theory that the main cause of civic decline is something other than people becoming "turned off" to community. Rather, it is
caused by each successive generation never getting "turned on" to civic engagement in the first place. The cohort analysis shows that the key factor is
how involved in associations Americans were when they began their adult
civic lives. Each cohort was as trusting and active as it ever was over time,
but there are dramatic differences between each cohort. He notes that high
levels of social capital are concentrated among the age cohorts born and
raised before World War II and low social capital is concentrated in the
age cohorts born and raised after the war. Associational membership, voting, social trust, and other measures of social capital are lower for postwar
cohorts. Shifts from "schmoozing" activities like card playing and inviting
friends over for supper toward solitary television viewing are occurring
across cohorts, however (Putnam 2000, 265–66).

Putnam notes that there are two possible explanations for these trends:
life cycle and socialization. First, consider the life cycle theory. Generally,
Americans tend to become more and more involved in civic associations
until their fifties and then gradually decrease their civic activity as they
age. By comparing age cohorts at their peak years of involvement, Putnam
tested whether the generational differences are attributable merely to the

fact that young people move from low to high levels of involvement as they age. If life cycle is the best explanation, Putnam writes, "America should have experienced waves of rising community involvement as the boomers ascended the normal life cycle of rising community involvement" (2000, 250). He found that the expected life cycle upswings have been swamped by unexpected generational downswings. In other words, people do increase their involvement as they age, yet every age cohort that has reached adulthood since the 1950s has been less engaged in community affairs than its immediate predecessor, and the more recent the cohort, the more dramatic its disengagement from community life (Putnam 2000, 251, 254). Hence, Putnam eliminates the life cycle explanation and embraces the idea that these age cohorts are "generations."

Using this information on cohorts, Putnam theorizes the existence of a "long civic generation" (born between 1910 and 1940), which even to this day shoulders the burdens of community involvement and social trust. Their "children," the "baby boom generation" (born between 1945 and 1964) are less involved and trusting, and "Generation X" (born between 1965 and 1980) are now adults and exhibiting far less community involvement and social trust than their baby-boomer "parent" and their civic "grandparents."

It is important to point out here that Putnam's use of terms like "children," "parents," and "grandparents" is only figurative. Putnam's analysis compares cohorts over time, not parents and children. A major problem with his analysis of the role of family changes in generational differences is that his data do not allow a direct test over time. His data simply do not permit a direct analysis of whether there is a link between the level of civic activity of parents and the activity of their children. Putnam is able only to look at the timing of trends in family structure and compare them to the timing of civic decline between the different samples of each age cohort he defines. The problem with this method is that it is quite a blunt instrument, lumping together the civic activity level of everyone from an age cohort and therefore missing the intracohort differences—like family environments or differences in how public events are actually experienced by different segments of the cohort. These other factors might account for the higher aggregate level of civic activity in the cohort over time and perhaps isolate the experiences that most strongly affect people's civic capacity. He also neglects to consider that there might be a time lag between the appearance of an event and its subsequent impact on a generation.

In other words, a more plausible generational theory would require the support of a direct analysis of the same children and their parents over time.[3] Putnam's data only allow him to employ an indirect approach, which compares a randomly selected sample of adults with children at one point in time with a different sample at another point in time. Such an approach is liable to miss key differences between groups within a generation that would more effectively pinpoint the sources of generational differences. I will discuss some of these potential sources of generational difference below.

First, Putnam asks whether these generations are defined and influenced by their early upbringing or by the way the structure of family relationships has changed from the 1920s to the 1980s. He wants to know if generational differences are rooted in the socialization process—how family structure and early environment shape the civic habits we adopt later in life. If Putnam is correct that "face to face" associations are necessary for a vibrant civil society, then shouldn't the family—the first and most powerful of all face-to-face associations—be the logical place to look for the source of civic decline? After all, the percentage of households made up of a married couple with children has been dropping to its historic low of below 25 percent in 2000 (Schmitt 2000).

Moreover, Putnam demonstrates that "family connectedness" is changing, and he points the disappearance of the customary family evening meal as the starkest example (2000, 100). Family attendance at religious services and even families watching TV together has declined, as households increasingly have multiple television sets (2000, 101).

Keep in mind that Putnam's analysis of "generations" should be distinguished from the rhetoric of politicos from Bill Clinton to Bill Bennett who say that the nuclear family is under siege and must be protected if civic revival is to occur. Putnam's evidence does not support the idea that changes in families are the key to civic decline across generations. Changes in the family are relatively continuous, whereas generational analysis presumes a sharp break between one generation and another. After analyzing his evidence, Putnam says "family instability . . . seems to have an ironclad alibi for what we have now identified as the critical period, for the generational decline in civic engagement began with the children of the maritally stable 1940s and 1950s. . . . Similarly, working mothers are exonerated by this respecification of our problem, for the plunge in civicness among children of the 1940s, 1950s and 1960s happened while mom was still at home" (Putnam 2000, 267). In fact, Putnam points out that people who

are married, with children, attend fewer club meetings than demographi-
cally similar unmarried people (2000, 278). "Apart from youth and church
related engagement, *none* of the major declines in social capital and civic
engagement that we need to explain can be accounted for by the decline of
traditional family structure" (2000, 277, 279, emphasis in original).

Even if Putnam did have evidence of strong correlations between
changes in family life and changes in civic engagement, it would run
counter to the basic assumptions of his social capital concept. For him, we
join groups and informally socialize with friends in order to "benefit our
own interests" (Putnam 2000, 20). Emotional bonds or loyalties are often
treated with suspicion or relegated to the private realm. Putnam thinks social capital best applies to a range of formal and informal associations,
from political parties to poker nights. While these kinds of associations
can plausibly be described in instrumental terms as "bridging" social capital, Putnam has difficulty with associations typical of "bonding" social
capital. There, instrumental interests seem to disappear, and group identities play a greater role in behavior. Sometimes, such groups are so powerful in reshaping and defining identities of the members that it becomes
nearly impossible to say that people belong to them out of "interest." Putnam barely considers such groups "civic" at all, since their members see
their membership less as something chosen and more as something they
are "born into." Similarly, Putnam sees the family bound together by affection and identity rather than by interest, more so than other types of association, and thus he sees it as fundamentally a private institution. Hence
for Putnam the family, while a powerful institution shaping moral life, and
a prime example of "bonding" social capital, simply lacks sufficient power
to revitalize civil society in the direction he thinks is necessary (Beem
1999). What is most desperately needed, he says, is not more "bonding"
social capital—of the sort seen in "identity" groups and families—but instead much more social capital of the "bridging" sort, which occurs outside the family.

Having set aside life cycle explanations and the changes in the nuclear
family as the reasons for age cohort differences in civic activity, Putnam
argues that the only remaining explanation is that the age cohorts are
actually "generations." The idea of political generations is at least as old
as Plato's discussion of the decline of the ideal regime in *The Republic*.
However, the more relevant framework for Putnam's speculation on
generations is laid out in Karl Mannheim's classic 1928 essay "The Problem of Generations" (Mannheim 1952). Mannheim argued that political

generations coalesce around the collective experience of a major historical situation. "Youth experiencing the same concrete historical problems," Mannheim said, "may be said to be part of the same actual generation" (304). It is therefore helpful to return to Mannheim's essay as a foundation for a critique of Putnam.

Mannheim said that generations possess qualitative as well as quantitative differences in their orientations toward engagement in civil society, based on their having personally experienced in common major historical events as they reached young adulthood. But Mannheim's essay makes several key points that can be used to illustrate the weaknesses of Putnam's use of generational replacement as an explanation for social capital decline. First, Mannheim asked: Is a generation a collection of people born in the same span of years? No, he argued, that is an age cohort, only potentially a generation. Putnam, however, reverses the logic, and simply assumes in a mechanical way that because he is seeing empirical differences between age cohorts roughly divided in twenty-year increments, they therefore must be "generations." He assumes that the only remaining task is to identify some historical events that presumably must have made them into generations. Lo and behold, since Putnam conveniently divides his cohorts according to the events of World War II, Vietnam, and the start of the Reagan administration, he declares that it must be these events that defined the generations. How conveniently it fits together—but Putnam hopes that his readers do not notice how he used his dependent variable to define his independent variable, thus assuring the result he assumed from the start.

The generational thesis basically holds that the events experienced by youth during their formative years will have an enduring impact that is manifested in the political process (Jennings 1987, 386). Putnam implies that different formative events lead to different levels of involvement between age cohorts. One such event, World War II, touched almost every family on the home front, as about 80 percent of the men born in the 1920s served in the military (Putnam 2000, 168).

This "raises the possibility that the wartime zeitgeist of national unity and patriotism that culminated in 1945 reinforced civic-mindedness" (Putnam 2000, 267). Putnam also notes that the civil rights movement, the Kennedy and King assassinations, Vietnam, and Watergate somehow led the Baby Boomers to be more alienated from politics and less trusting of neighbors and hence also less involved in their communities (2000, 257). Putnam characterizes the "GenX'ers" as even more crudely materialistic "than their parents" because they were raised on a steady diet of TV, are insecure about their futures, thrust into a cutthroat job market, and all without the benefit of any collective experiences of public achievement or public sacrifice. "Collective action—and especially politics—is even more foreign to the X'ers than to the boomers" says Putnam (2000, 61).

Thus, Putnam asserts that the experience of these great events (or the lack of such experiences) at the point of first political awareness and activity somehow produced substantial differences in social trust, church membership, partisan political activity, and associational membership from one generation to another. But how do these specific events affect a lifetime worth of civic activity? Could other events play a role? Could the memories and experiences be more powerful for certain demographic groups than for others?

Another problem with Putnam's cohort analysis is that it begins with an assumption that roughly every twenty years a new generation emerges. Mannheim pointed out that such assumptions are the main problem of most generational theories. Mannheim attacked generational theories like Putnam's that start from the mechanistic "naturalism" of cohort analysis and abruptly land in the most extreme kind of "spiritualism" which vaguely sees generations shaped by a *zeitgeist* during young adulthood (Mannheim 1952, 311).

> Such theories try to establish a direct correlation between waves of decisive year classes of birth—set at intervals of thirty years, and conceived in a purely naturalistic, quantifying spirit—on one hand, and waves of cultural changes on the other . . . [Yet] whether a new *generation style* emerges every year, every thirty, every hundred years, or whether it emerges rhythmically at all, depends entirely on the trigger action of the social and cultural process. (Mannheim 1957, 310; emphasis in original)

One cannot mechanically reduce a generation to a collection of individuals who happen to be born about the same time; cohorts can be born, come of age, and die without ever becoming a generation, in Mannheim's sense of the term.

Most disappointing is the way Putnam leaves out the basic element of Mannheim's framework for analyzing the politics of generations: the idea of "generation units." Mannheim stressed that while members of a generation experience the same historical problems, there are differing "generation units" within the generation "which work up the materials of their common experiences in different specific ways" (Mannheim 1952, 304).

Generation units are parts of generations that respond to historical events in ways that shape the political landscape and set the terms of political discourse for decades. For Mannheim, it is the generation unit, not the generation, on which political processes turn.

To see what Mannheim meant by a generation unit, consider the biographies of George W. Bush and Al Gore. Both would be considered part of a "Vietnam generation" that experienced the Vietnam War, yet we see that they drew different lessons from it and came to terms with it in different political ways. Bush became involved in socializing, but avoided protests and serious study while a student at Yale, and joined the Texas Air National Guard. Gore was an introspective overachiever actively opposing the war, but eventually serving in Vietnam. Both Gore and Bush were part of the same generation yet represented differing ideological and political responses to the major historical event they both experienced when they reached maturity. Their socialization and upbringing influenced their responses, at least as much as the fact that they reached adulthood at about the same time.

Thus, to make claims about generational civic characteristics without checking the intervening factors such as ideology, race, gender, region, and most importantly, partisan identifications and loyalties, is a major shortcoming in *Bowling Alone*.[4] Putnam assumes that the events of history have a systematic and direct impact on the civic activities of entire age cohorts. He sees an aggregate difference in civic activity between age cohorts and speaks of an entire generation behaving differently than the others. He does not consider the possibility, as Mannheim did, that one or two generational units may account for the bulk of the civic difference. And he does not analyze, as other political scientists have, the fact that subgroups within age cohorts, such as conservatives, women, blacks, or the poor take different lessons from their experiences of great events like wars, protests, and major elections than men, whites, or the wealthy do (Jennings 1987; Mayer 1993). Mannheim's idea of generation unit has been supported again and again by political scientists (Bodnar 1996; Funkenstein 1989; Holsti and Rosenau 1980; Jennings 1987; Ladd 1994; Mayer 1993; Roberts and Lang 1985). For example, Mueller (1973) and Mayer (1993) as well as Jennings (1987) have demonstrated strong evidence that actually, only a small fraction of the "Vietnam generation" were actively opposed to the war. This seems to be a pattern that holds for previous major U.S. wars: older Americans are more likely to oppose U.S. entry into wars than younger Americans (Erskine 1972). The difference is that in the Vietnam era opposition was especially vocal and politically organized.

Related to this problem are Putnam's two debatable assumptions that historical events experienced when coming of age affect all future forms of civic engagement in pretty much the same way, and that every cohort reaches the age of political awareness at pretty much the same age. As attractive as this idea is, there is not much evidence that generational differences in attitudes or memories play a significant role in affecting future activity in a systematic way. It appears that a more demonstrably powerful cause of a person's political activism is the support and ideology of a person's parents (Roberts and Lang 1985, 470). The only exception are the studies of voting behavior which find strong connections between the electoral choices facing people in the first presidential election in which they voted and their party identification during their lifetimes (Jennings 1987; Ladd 1994; Miller and Shanks 1996). Should Putnam not extend the insights of generational voting studies to the very different forms of social engagement he looks at in *Bowling Alone?* Probably not, because law sets the age of voting eligibility, but the age at which people become "politically aware and active" may be very different, and may be affected by historical events. At what age did World War II or Vietnam traumatize people? Age eleven? Thirteen? Eighteen? Twenty-five? What age groups will be most critically affected by the terrorist attacks of September 11, 2001?

Only a very small group of college-age Americans in the baby boomer cohort were involved in protests, and even they became more conservative and developed a tendency to vote for Reagan in the 1980s, along with the majority of the cohort (Jennings 1987). In fact, higher percentages of supposedly "apathetic" college freshmen of the 1990s reported actually acting on their objectives by participating in organized demonstrations than the freshmen of the 1960s (Warden 1994).

Another issue is how Putnam focuses on the way a single major event can reinforce certain civic or uncivic attitudes over the long haul, without looking at any ongoing processes where past and present interact. My point is that generational identity is probably not formed by a single event or even a series of separate occurrences, but constructed over time in a social process of remembering, acting, and defining one's moral values. The impact of the past is modified or defined by how groups of people interpret it in terms of present problems. Did the events of 1930 to 1945 simply launch the activities of the Civic Generation, or is it the subsequent process of remembering and memorializing those events over the years that continually drove their activity? While a major event can transform an age cohort into a generation, how that event is remembered and what "lessons of history" are taken from it by different parts of that generation is the stuff of politics (Robinson 2000; Schuman and Rieger 1992).

At the time of the major event, people's personal experiences and immediate reactions may predominate, with collective representations of the event and the "lessons of history" only sinking in years later after interpretations by historians, teachers, media, and political elites (Holsti and Rosenau 1980). Events need not be directly experienced to have an impact. People have their own personal memories that are not identical to collective memory (Funkenstein 1989, 7).

The point I am making here is that while all personal memories are dependent on social context, collective memory is even moreso emerging from later interpretation by political elites and media—or what Durkheim called "collective representations" (Halbwachs 1980; Holsti and Rosenau 1980; Robinson 2000). Indeed, the most politically significant meaning of an event is likely to be taken more by those who were not even alive at the time it happened. For example, the Vietnam generation is more likely to "remember" World War II as "the good war" or "a victorious war" than those who actually lived through it (Holsti and Rosenau 1980; Mayer 1993). All cohorts grew dissatisfied with the Vietnam War between 1964 and 1972 and there is evidence that the Baby Boom cohort was more supportive of the war than their elders (Mayer 1993, 168).

Finally, we should note that the "solidarity" during World War II was much more complex than Putnam portrays it in his discussion of generations. Putnam says that while the mobilization efforts "sputtered to a stop by 1944," they had nevertheless "demonstrated the mobilizing power of shared adversity." Putnam reiterates the civic myth that during World War II a public-spirited citizenry unconditionally sacrificed their selfish desires, went all out and pulled together in the name of defeating the Axis powers. Everyone did their part for the war effort through a wide variety of civic associations (Putnam 2000, 267–69). Putnam argues that these activities generated "social solidarity" which affected the subsequent lives of the greatest generation.

Historians of the home front in World War II are showing that sacrifice and solidarity indeed existed on the home front during the war, but it was a very different nationalism than that seen in Japan, Germany, or even Great Britain (Bodnar 1996; Leff 1991). Most Americans said they were not making the "real" sacrifices like the soldiers on the frontlines were. On the contrary, during the war years, in fact, about half of Americans felt that people were not "taking the war seriously enough" (Cantril 1951, 483). And at the time, staffers of American mobilization agencies commonly complained of the difficulties of transforming people's "willingness" into "action" and of cracking the shell of half-hearted sacrifice and unwillingness to forgo ordinary pleasures and comforts of life. President Roosevelt attempted to scold the public into greater cooperation but was disgusted at the "whining demands of pressure groups" that continued to seek government support of their interests during the crisis (Leff 1991, 1297).

Solidarity can take a number of different forms regarding how governmental or economic institutions relate to civic institutions. As Rogers Smith has pointed out, American national identity is a complex mixture of liberal universalism and ethnocultural traditionalism (Smith 1988; 1997). While government propaganda in wartime used liberal ideas that Americans should sacrifice in the name of universal values such as freedom and equality, it also called for sacrifices in order to defend one's own family and private life. In the 1940s, like never before, the separate spheres of loyalty in families, workplaces, and congregations began to overlap, and the interconnection of these spheres extended into the early parts of the Cold War era (Bodnar 1996, 297).

Conclusion

Putnam's generational hypothesis has a number of shortcomings that highlight the limitations of his social capital concept. He defines generations according to events of his own choosing, without substantiating his decision with evidence that these events really did affect their future behavior. He assumes that the events affected all members of the cohort in the same way, and neglects to consider that perhaps the cohort differences are accounted for by key groups within each cohort. He does not examine the extent to which gender, race, or class differences play a role in the cohort differences in civic activity or political memories. Nor does he consider that collective memories are distinct from individual recollection and constructed through a political process involving social elites, mass media, and how both apply the "lessons of history" to subsequent events.

Crucially, though, the generational analysis in *Bowling Alone* implies we should reconsider Putnam's initial definition of social capital as a private good that is pursued because of self-interest. The creation of generalized trust and the capacity to interact with members of the groups we are less "comfortable" with requires something other than mere repetition of these social contacts (Uslaner 2000). Patriotism, Putnam suggests, can summon people's capacity for self-sacrifice in ways that self-interest and social clubs cannot. It points us toward thinking about communal sentiments and identities not enlightened self-interest as the things that most strengthen civic life.

The problem is that Putnam does not explore the power of communal memories and identities in leading people toward social and political engagement. While he argues that the practical implication of his analysis of generations is to embark on a search for the moral equivalent of war (Putnam 2000, 276), unfortunately, his "agenda for social capitalists" at the end of *Bowling Alone* offers no insight on how his research might help us find it. He only offers what he calls "old-fashioned" ideas for reforming how we have been preparing young people for active civic lives: civics classes that get youth involved in politics; community service learning; spending more money on public education and extracurricular activities; hiring more teachers; reducing classroom size; and a civic equivalent for 4-H or Boy Scouts that would combine civic values and fun (Putnam 2000, 405–6).

These are meritorious ideas, but they are based on dealing with the "minor" causes of civic decline, and not really grappling with the issues Putnam raises when he talks about generational differences. Perhaps this is because Putnam argues that the events happen more or less spontaneously and are contingent on circumstance. Collective memories, for him, are little more than a mental record of individuals' past experiences. You can't change the past, and you cannot recreate the experiences of the civic generation. Or can you? Benedict Anderson (1991), for example, argued that collective memories situate individuals in time and play a role in constructing an "imagined community," which provides a powerful source of identity and values that give meaning to many activities in civil society. A wave of nostalgia for a time of simplicity and achievement has its dangers, but drawing the right lessons from history can also inspire us to inherit a civic past and construct a civic future.

The individualistic elements of social capital concepts should be radically revised in light of Putnam's ideas on generations, patriotism, and memory. Key collective interpretations of the past, as well as individual experiences of civic sacrifice and action, define citizens' identities and launch them onto a civic trajectory in their life paths, giving their future civic memberships a meaning and persistence that goes beyond the pursuit of self-interest.

My argument in this chapter should not be understood as a call for militarism or nationalist chauvinism in America, but rather that we should conceive of civic engagement as part of a "politics of sacrifice" in civil society. As Putnam correctly points out, the revival of community can bring out the dark side of participation too. Nationalism in a liberal civil society is too often content with vicarious patriotism and empty rituals of citizenship rather than practical participation in the community. But by the same token, the social capital concept too often tends to see civil society as a collection of self-interested individuals involved in a series of disconnected groups. Michael Walzer argues that we need to see civil society not merely as an arena for the pursuit of interests but as a kind of negotiation between interests and sacrifices, between national identity and group membership, between personal memories and collective memories.

We stand at a turning point in the question of American identity. Although troubled by society's moral values at century's end, Americans' pride and optimism about their country is high by historical standards (Chambers 2000). The end of the Cold War has lifted the burden of defining the American identity as anti-communism but the new war on terrorism has presented the new challenge of how to promote democracy and human rights under conditions of globalization. The aging of the large Baby Boom age cohort will present further challenges to the welfare state, which for decades has defined the rights of the citizen. Finally, the increasing multiculturalism of the U.S. population—increasingly expressed in youth culture—will make American identity even more difficult to pin down.

These circumstances offer new opportunities as well as challenges for redefining American identity and communal belonging in ways that extend democratic participation. The direction American community will take in the next decades will depend upon which symbols of American identity and national memory will prevail. It will depend on the moral and political purposes to which they are put. The task for normative theorists, then, is not to encourage xenophobia, nativism, or militarism, but to construct normative arguments for more inclusive civic identities and memories that do not neglect people's desires for meaning, distinctness, accountability, and enduring value in their memberships. The quest for a moral equivalent of war continues.

NOTES

1. Putnam announced in his *American Prospect* article (Putnam 1996) that he found generational differences that show civic decline is more than a momentary slide and is likely to continue well into the next century.

2. Putnam guesses that 10 percent of civic disengagement is contributed by "pressures of time and money," 10 percent is contributed by suburban sprawl, 25 percent by television. This leaves 55 percent remaining for generational change but he adds another 10 to 15 percent from television-related generational difference. Thus, Putnam is guessing that 65 to 70 percent of the decline in social capital is caused by generational change (2000, 283–84).

3. Jennings and Niemi (1981) used this type of analysis for Baby Boomers and their parents, and found significant differences in their civic orientations, including generational differences in expressing civic obligations like voting and community service.

4. Nie et al. (1976) stress that the most important political characteristic of age cohorts is party identification. The cohort coming of age during the Depression and World War II have a large majority of Democratic voters, while the cohort coming of age in the late 1970s are the backbone of the Republican coalition.

REFERENCES

Anderson, Benedict. 1991. *Imagined Communities: Reflections on the Origin and Spread of Nationalism.* London: Verso.

Axelrod, Robert. 1984. *The Evolution of Cooperation.* New York: Basic.

Beem, Christopher. 1999. *The Necessity of Politics: Reclaiming American Public Life.* Chicago: University of Chicago Press.

Bellelli, Guglielmo, and Amatulli, Mirella. 1997. "Nostalgia, Immigration and Collective Memory." In *Collective Memory of Political Events,* ed. by James W. Pennebaker, Dario Paez, and Bernard Rime. Mahwah, N.J.: Lawrence Erlbaum Associates.

Bercovitch, Sacvan. 1974. "Introduction." In *The American Puritan Imagination Essays in Revaluation,* ed. by Sacvan Bercovitch. Cambridge: Cambridge University Press.

Bodnar, John. 1992. *Remaking America: Public Memory, Commemoration and Patriotism.* Princeton: Princeton University Press.

———, ed. 1996. *Bonds of Affection: Americans Define Their Patriotism.* Princeton: Princeton University Press.

Cantril, Hadley, ed. 1951. *Public Opinion, 1935–1946.* Princeton: Princeton University Press.

Chambers, Chris. 2000. "Americans Generally Satisfied with State of Nation This

July 4th." Gallup Organization Poll Release, July 3. <www.gallup.com/poll/re-leases/pr000703.asp>.

Erskine, Hazel. 1972. "The Polls: Pacifism and the Generation Gap." *Public Opinion Quarterly* 36.4: 616–27.

Funkenstein, Amos. 1989. "Collective Memory and Historical Consciousness." *History and Memory* 1(Fall): 3–13.

Halbwachs, Maurice. 1980. *The Collective Memory.* Trans. by Francis J. Ditter and Vida Yazdi Ditter. New York: Harper and Row.

Holsti, Ole, and Rosenau, James N. 1980. "Does Where You Stand Depend on When Your Were Born? The Impact of Generation on Post-Vietnam Foreign Policy Beliefs," *Public Opinion Quarterly* 44: 1–22.

Jennings, M. Kent. 1987. "Residues of a Movement: The Aging of the American Protest Generation." *American Political Science Review* 81.2 (June): 367–82.

Jennings, M. Kent, and Niemi, Richard G. 1981. *Generations and Politics: A Panel Study of Young Adults and Their Parents.* Princeton: Princeton University Press.

Ladd, Everett Carll. 1994. "The Twentysomethings: 'Generation Myths' Revisited." *The Public Perspective* 5.2 (January/February): 14–15.

———. 1999. *The Ladd Report.* New York: Free Press.

Leff, Mark H. 1991. "The Politics of Sacrifice on the American Home Front in World War II." *Journal of American History* (March): 1296–1318.

Mannheim, Karl. 1952. "The Problem of Generations." In *Essays in the Sociology of Knowledge,* ed. by Paul Kegskemeti. London: Routledge and Kegan Paul.

Marin, Rick. 2001. "Raising a Flag for Generation WWII." *New York Times* (April 22): Section 9, p. 1.

Mayer, William G. 1993. *The Changing American Mind.* Ann Arbor: University of Michigan Press.

Miller, Warren E., and Shanks, Merrill J. 1996. *The New American Voter.* Cambridge: Harvard University Press.

Mueller, John E. 1973. *War, Presidents and Public Opinion.* New York: Wiley & Sons.

Nie, Norman, Verba, Sydney, and John R. Petrocik. 1976. *The Changing American Voter.* Cambridge: Harvard University Press.

Putnam, Robert D. 1995a. "Bowling Alone: America's Declining Social Capital." *Journal of Democracy* 6: 65–78.

———. 1995b. "Tuning In, Tuning Out: The Strange Disappearance of Social Capital in America." *PS: Political Science and Politics* 28: 664–83.

———. 1996. "The Strange Disappearance of Civic America." *The American Prospect* (Winter): 34–49.

———. 2000. *Bowling Alone: The Collapse and Revival of American Community.* New York: Simon & Schuster.

Roberts, Carl W., and Lang, Kurt. 1985. "Generations and Ideological Change: Some Observations." *Public Opinion Quarterly* 49.4 (Winter): 460–73.

Robinson, Michael. 2000. "Collective Memory: From the 20s Through the 90s." *The Public Perspective* 11.1 (January): 14–15.

Schmitt, Eric. 2000. "For First Time, Nuclear Families Drop Below 25% of Households." *New York Times,* May 15, A1.

Schuman, Howard and Scott, Jacqueline. 1989. "Generations and Collective Memories." *American Sociological Review* 54.3 (June): 359–81.

Schuman, Howard, and Rieger, Cheryl. 1992. "Historical Analogies, Generational Effects and Attitudes Toward War." *American Sociological Review* 57.3 (June): 315–26.

Skocpol, Theda. 1999. "How Americans Became Civic." In *Civic Engagement in American Democracy,* ed. by Theda Skocpol and Morris Fiorina. Washington, D.C.: Brookings.

Skocpol, Theda, Munson, Ziad, Karch, Andrew, and Camp, Bayliss. 2001. "Patriotic Partnerships: Why Great Wars Nourished American Civic Voluntarism." In *Shaped by War and Trade: International Influences on American Political Development,* ed. by Ira Katznelson and Martin Sehfter. Princeton: Princeton University Press.

Smith, Rogers M. 1988. "The 'American Creed' and American Identity: The Limits of Liberal Citizenship in the United States." *Western Political Quarterly* 41: 225–51.

———. 1997. *Civic Ideals: Conflicting Visions of Citizenship in U.S. History.* New Haven: Yale University Press.

Smith, Tom W. 1995. "Remembering the War: World War II and the Lessons of History." *The Public Perspective* 6.5 (August/September): 51–52.

———. 2000. "Changes in the Generation Gap, 1972–1998." *GSS Social Change Report* No. 43, October.

Strauss, William A., and Howe, Neil. 1994. "Generational Perspectives on Society: The Millennial Generation." In *Building a Community of Citizens,* ed. by Don Eberly. Lanham: University Press of America.

Takahashi, Corey. 2001. "Selling to Gen Y: A Far Cry From Betty Crocker." *New York Times,* April 8: Wk 3.

Uslaner, Eric. 2000. "Producing and Consuming Trust." *Political Science Quarterly* 115.4: 569–90.

Verba, Sydney, Schlozman, Kay Lehman, and Brady, Henry E. 1995. *Voice and Equality: Civic Voluntarism in American Politics.* Cambridge: Harvard University Press.

Warden, Sharon. 1994. "Culture: What's Happened to Youth Culture Since Woodstock?" *The Public Perspective* 5.4 (May/June): 19–20.

Chapter Seven

Social Capital
The Politics of Race and Gender

R. Claire Snyder

In the third section of *Bowling Alone: The Collapse and Revival of American Community* (2000), Robert Putnam addresses the key question raised by his research: "Why, beginning in the 1960s and 1970s and accelerating in the 1980s and 1990s, did the fabric of American community life begin to unravel" (184)? In attempting to solve this "intriguing mystery," Putnam considers a wide array of evidence, yet in the end he ultimately fails to assemble the clues in a way that reveals the primary culprit. The trail gets hotter when Putnam mentions the politics of the 1960s. Certainly, important connections exist between "Vietnam, Watergate, and the disillusion with public life." However, the primary villain will not be apprehended by searching the American Left, as Putnam does when he singles out the "cultural revolt against authority (sex, drugs, and so on)" for interrogation (187). To the contrary, the main perpetrators in the story of the mysterious destruction of social capital reside within the American Right in the ideological duo of social and fiscal conservatism. More specifically, in this essay I accept Putnam's contention that civic engagement has been declining in America, but I make the case that it was the reactionary backlash of social conservatism against democratic social movements for racial and gender equality, beginning in the 1960s, joined by the concomitant attack on progressive government and economic justice perpetrated during the 1980s, that should be held responsible for fueling the flames of distrust within society, rendering citizens suspicious of their own public institutions, and consequently weakening America's civic fabric.

Putnam's Analysis of America's Civic Decline

When exactly did America's well-documented civic decline actually begin? By all accounts, sometime around 1964. Putnam argues that the best evidence suggests that social trust rose from the mid-1940s to the mid-1960s, peaking in 1964 just as many other measures of social capital did. . . . In the mid-1960s, however, this beneficent trend was reversed, initiating a long-term decline in social trust" (139–40). At the same time, civic engagement also declined precipitously. For example, "nearly half of all Americans in the 1960s invested some time each week in clubs and local associations, as compared to less than one-quarter in the 1990s" (62). Americans have become simultaneously less trusting of, and less engaged with, each other since the mid-1960s.

While social capital deteriorated, so did trust in government. "The greatest drop in [political] confidence occurred from 1964 to 1974" (Nye 1997, 11). That is to say, in 1964, 75 percent of people said "they trusted the federal government to do the right thing most of the time," compared to 25 percent in the late 1990s (Nye 1997, 1; Putnam 2000, 47). Similarly, in 1966, 66 percent of Americans "*rejected* the view that 'the people running the country don't really care what happens to you,'" whereas in 1997 57 percent "*endorsed* that same view" (Putnam 2000, 47). And as mistrust of government grew, so did political disengagement. In 1966, 57.8 percent of people thought it was important to keep up with public affairs, compared to 26.7 percent in 1997 (Boggs 2000, 12). In 1960, 62.8 percent of people voted in the presidential election as opposed to 48.9 percent in 1996, despite the fact that many more people are now allowed to vote (Putnam 2000, 47).

American citizens became disconnected from and mistrustful of each other starting around 1964, the same time at which they became alienated from and suspicious of government, yet for some reason Putnam downplays the connection between the social and the political: "Our subject here is social trust, *not* trust in government or other social institutions. Trust in other people is logically quite different from trust in institutions and political authorities" (137). Consequently, Putnam's analysis of America's civic decline focuses primarily on the problems of civil society, which he views largely in isolation from the ideological battles simultaneously raging in the political sphere. However, while distinctions can certainly be made between social and political trust, Putnam's choice to restrict his investigation to the former alone ends up circumscribing his analysis in a way that obscures important explanatory variables.

Moreover, despite definitional distinctions, an important theoretical relationship exists between social and political trust. Social trust is a vitally important ingredient within democracies not only because it improves the quality of civil society but also because it provides the necessary foundation for a citizenry's commitment to public institutions and policies aimed at serving the common good rather than just individual interests. It is my contention that not only is there a positive correlation between declines in social capital and civic engagement on the one hand and the rise of anti-government sentiments and attacks on public institutions on the other, but that the latter phenomenon, which constitutes the ideology of the New Right, has directly contributed to declines in social capital, civic engagement, support for public institutions, and trust in government.

Generational Change, Political Backlash, and the Culture Wars

Despite the impressive length of his study and the massive amount of social scientific data he examines, Putnam never actually explains *why* social capital has eroded so precipitously. However, he does establish that the two most obvious suspects, "pressures of time and money, including the special pressures on two-career families" and "suburbanization, commuting, and sprawl," probably account for only about 10 percent of the answer each. Citing a correlation between exposure to television and civic decline, Putnam speculates that the "effect of electronic entertainment—above all, television—in privatizing our leisure time" bears about 25 percent of the blame. The remaining 50 percent of the explanation falls to "generational change—the slow, steady, and ineluctable replacement of the long civic generation by their less involved children and grandchildren" (283). And here he marshals impressive data. More specifically, while the generation that came of age during World War II represents a paragon of civic engagement, even to this day, its Baby Boomer children (born between 1945 and 1964) are significantly less involved, and their Generation X grandchildren (born between 1965 and 1980) are even less so. This means that "at century's end, a generation with a trust quotient of nearly 80 percent was being rapidly replaced by one with a trust quotient of barely half that. The inevitable result is steadily declining social trust, *even though each individual cohort is almost as trusting as it ever was*" (141). But what explains this generational decline?

The tenacity of trust within each particular cohort implies that levels of trust are fixed sometime during its childhood or adolescence and then continue mostly unchanged throughout adulthood. Hence, the political culture in which a generation comes of age must play a critical role in determining its political and social attitudes. Putnam briefly discusses changes in political culture but does not explore this variable in more than a superficial way. He emphasizes the powerful role played by World War II in the formation of "the long civic generation." He suggests that the Baby Boomers were so "indelibly marked by the events of the sixties—the civil rights movement (which happened while most of them were still in elementary school), the Kennedy and King assassinations, the trauma of Vietnam, and Watergate"—that they have reason to be "distrusting of institutions, alienated from politics," and consequently "less involved in civic life" (257). Their Gen X children, he continues, simply "accelerated the tendencies to individualism found among boomers": They have "an extremely personal and individualistic view of politics" probably because "they came of age in an era that celebrated personal goods and private initiative over shared public concerns." However, "unlike boomers, who were once engaged, X'ers have never made the connection to politics, so they emphasize the personal and private over the public and collective" (259).

Interestingly, for some reason which he never articulates, Putnam views the "60s activism of the Baby Boomers—their campus flings"—as simply an anomaly (257). In other words, he does not believe that something happened that caused an extremely engaged generation to disengage. To the contrary, despite the fact that American civic decline began sharply in 1964, Putnam inexplicably insists, "the roots of our lonely bowling probably date to the 1940s and 1950s, rather than to the 1960s, 1970s, and 1980s" (266). Deviating from his social scientific methodology momentarily, he opines "it is as though the post-war generations were exposed to some anticivic X-ray that permanently and increasingly rendered them less likely to connect with the community. Whatever that force might have been, *it*—rather than anything that happened during the 1970s and 1980s—accounts for most of the civic disengagement that lies at the core of our mystery" (255).

But couldn't the anti-democratic backlash against the attempts of the '60s generation to extend the American dream by allowing African Americans to participate fully in civic life have caused the Baby Boomers to lose trust in their fellow citizens? Couldn't the right-wing outrage at the federal government's support for civil rights and extension of social welfare benefits to minorities have contributed to a loss of trust in the government among conservatives? And couldn't the racist backlash against the civil rights movement have irreparably damaged the American social fabric, thus preventing the formation of relationships across difference that would comprise social capital in contemporary America?

Likewise, the increasing hegemony of social and fiscal conservatism that arose during the 1970s and 1980s, in direct reaction to attempts at creating a truly democratic civil society, could be responsible for the extreme individualism, mistrust of others, and disengagement from civic life among the children of the Baby Boomers. It is not enough to mention that Generation X grew up in "an era that celebrated personal goods and private initiative over shared public concerns" (259), nor is it sufficient to mention the "uncertainty" of 1970s economic malaise or hint at the "insecurity" caused by "divorce explosion" (259). Instead, I would argue, a primary cause of the isolated individualism, self-serving materialism, and solipsistic disengagement among Generation X—and Generation Y—stems from the fact that they came of age hearing a constant barrage of right-wing vitriol against a wide array of different groups— from the anti-democratic and inflammatory attacks on equal rights for women to the mean-spirited diatribes against the poor to thinly veiled appeals to racist fears and resentments to the ridiculing of progressive politics as "political correctness" to the demonization of homosexuals. Given this context, the real question is how the children and grandchildren of the Baby Boomer generation could possibly trust or connect with anyone at all?

Democratic Theory and Its Misdirects

To the extent that Putnam even hints at the ideological conflicts of American politics, he remains circumspect, not only because he writes as a social scientist, but also because he locates himself firmly within the confines of contemporary democratic theory. This school of thought constitutes a trans-ideological project that strives to move beyond the historical Left/Right impasse by finding common ground across political difference via inclusive democratic practices (Barber 1998), common traditions

(Sandel 1996), and/or shared public work (Boyte and Kari 1996). Consequently, even if Putnam had addressed the impact of ideological struggles on social capital, he would have most likely followed the strategy taken by other democratic theorists who generally strive for balance in judging Left and Right, seeking the truth in both sides. For example, Michael Sandel argues that social and political trust began to evaporate in the 1960s because of "a growing sense that events were spinning out of control and that government lacked the moral or political authority to respond. . . . Americans began to think of themselves less as agents than as instruments of larger forces that defied their understanding and control" (1996, 296). He portrays George Wallace as an early mouthpiece of America's discontent: "Beyond the undeniable element of racism in Wallace's appeal lay a broader protest against the powerlessness many Americans felt toward a distant federal government that regulated their lives but seemed helpless to stem the social turmoil and lawlessness that troubled them most" (298).

While Sandel has a point, however, it is not completely accurate to say that the government was unable to respond to the conflicts of the 1960s. Quite the contrary, the federal government *did* in fact respond, by intervening in the business of local communities in a way that advanced the progress of democracy against reactionary white supremacists who stood opposed to citizenship for African Americans—not to mention basic human dignity. Wallace may have "voiced the resentments of white working-class voters," but the fact that they felt "victimized by forced busing to integrate public schools, angered by student protests and antiwar demonstrations, and disempowered by permissive courts and arrogant federal bureaucrats," should not be viewed neutrally by political theorists committed to democracy.

E. J. Dionne takes a similar approach in evaluating the state of American civic life. He argues that the American people have lost faith in their democratic institutions because voices on both the Left and the Right have succeeded in "framing political issues as a series of false choices," and that "the cause of this false polarization is the cultural civil war that broke out in the 1960s" (Dionne 1991, 13). American citizens have little interest in these conflicts, he argues, yet political elites in both parties—and their upper-middle class constituencies—continue this warfare in order to advance their own interests at the expense of the general public (12–13). This struggle between Left and Right has alienated increasing numbers of

American citizens and caused "the abandonment of public life" (10). Thus, both sides must share the blame for the decline of citizenship and social capital.

Despite these valiant attempts at understanding and evenhandedness, a commitment to fairness, tolerance, and pluralism should not obscure the empirical fact that both historically and contemporaneously the Left has worked to extend democratic values, such as political inclusiveness, social equality, economic justice, and personal autonomy, while the Right has generally stood directly opposed to that endeavor. Criticizing democratic theory along these lines, Stephen Bronner argues that an overemphasis on the utopian goal of finding "common ground" in the face of differences can actually obscure political analysis and undermine its incisiveness. "Terms like *left* and *right* . . . remain essential," Bronner argues, "in order to distinguish between" the wide variety of oppositional social movements that organize within "civil society" (1999, 312). And John Ehrenberg concurs: "The White Citizens Council was different from the Student non-Violent Coordinating Committee," he tells us, "and it makes no theoretical or political sense to lump the Christian Coalition together with the American Civil Liberties Union. Qualitative distinctions and political choices must be made" (Ehrenberg 1999, 249). In short, a neo-Tocquevillian analysis of civil society that fails to distinguish between democratic and anti-democratic organizations does not produce an adequate theory of democracy (1999, 231–32).

Thus, if we really want to explain why "we have been pulled apart from one another and from our communities over the last third of the century" (Putnam 2000, 27), we need to review the history of the 1960s using a lens that will allow us to identify which forces have worked to bring us together and which to pull us apart. Who fought for voting rights for African Americans, the end of segregation, and the creation of gender-blind laws, and who fought to maintain race and gender privilege? Who wanted all sectors of society to participate in political decision making, and who wanted to shore up the power political elites and their corporate patrons? Who insisted that the political agenda be expanded to include issues of concern to African Americans, women, and the economically disadvantaged, and who deems those issues simply "divisive"? Who struggled for economic justice for all citizens and who labels every progressive policy "communism"? Did our civic life really deteriorate "silently, without warning" (Putnam 2000, 27)?

Civic Engagement and Civic Decline: The Paradox of the 1960s

It's ironic that social capital began to decline precisely at the moment when African Americans officially achieved legal and political equality via the Civil Rights Act of 1964 and the Voting Rights Act of 1965. The extension of the franchise, the right to serve on juries, and the lifting of Jim Crow laws eliminated formal barriers to civic participation, constrained the coercive power of police and prosecutors, and undermined the ability of racist whites to terrorize blacks within the realm of civil society via lynch mobs and Klan networks (Piven and Cloward 1979, 181–82). With these long-standing methods of exclusion undermined, African Americans were optimistic that "the mantra of 'freedom'—universally invoked as the purpose of both World War II and the Cold War—might finally benefit them" (Isserman and Kazin 2000, 45).

The high levels of social capital that existed in American civil society in the early 1960s also existed within black communities, and this underwrote the ability of African Americans to act together for social change. Experience in voluntary organizations within civil society, such as black churches, provided them with the skills necessary for participatory citizenship—a clear illustration of the importance of social capital (Boyte and Evans 1992). African Americans wanted not only formal equality but also citizenship in the fullest sense of the term. They wanted freedom to "participate and contribute as full, independent, and powerful citizens in public affairs: to engage in the substantial work of citizenship. It was precisely this public participation—in rallies, sit-ins, demonstrations, voter registration drives, and public problem-solving—that generated the movement spirit, despite violent opposition and great danger" (Boyte and Kari 1996, 137–38). However, high levels of social capital also benefited white supremacists that used voluntary organizations, like the Klan and the white citizens councils, to attack African Americans. "As the white caste system came under assault, traditional southern white leaders rose up in outrage," denouncing "the courts, the federal government, and civil rights organizers of unwarranted infringements upon states' rights" (Piven and Cloward 1979, 211). High levels of social capital can be used to advance democracy or oppose it. Thus, the presence of social capital per se is not an indicator of a vibrant democracy.

At first, right-wing resistance to civil rights seemed to be the last gasps of a dying order. When the general public became aware of the brutal treatment received by African American citizens struggling to achieve minimal standards of democratic citizenship in the South—in 1964 when ABC News interrupted their Sunday Night movie, *Judgement at Nuremberg,* "to show 15 minutes of raw and dramatic footage from the attack on the Edmund Pettus Bridge"—it created a "groundswell of northern support" for the black struggle, and young "volunteers poured into Selma" (Isserman and Kazin 2000, 136; Piven and Cloward 1979, 250). The prospects for an integrated civic life looked promising; Gallup polls conducted in the spring of 1965 "showed that 52 percent of Americans identified civil rights as the 'most important problem' confronting the nation, and an astonishing 75 percent of respondents favored federal voting rights legislation" (Isserman and Kazin 2000, 138). When President Johnson signed the Voting Rights Act into law, "the first of the South's 2.5 million previously disenfranchised eligible blacks were lining up to register to vote under the watchful eyes of federal officials" throughout "the Deep South" (Isserman and Kazin 2000, 139).

So what happened at this very moment that caused people to lose faith in government and in each other? The year 1965 marks the beginning of the rise of the New Right that mobilized in direct opposition to the democratic social movements of the 1960s (Hardisty 1999, 76). In fact a direct correlation exists between the rise of the New Right and the disintegration of social capital. With the landslide defeat of Barry Goldwater in 1964, right-wing leaders immediately began developing a more marketable message, "mainstreaming the ideological positions of the Old Right and developing winnable policies" that "highlighted a protest theme against a range of 'social issues'" (Hardisty 1999, 38). And they were quite successful. Followers of the Old Right and the New Right—racists, anti-Communists, fiscal conservatives, libertarians, anti-feminists, and Christian fundamentalists—made common cause in vehement opposition to democratic social movements. Not only did these conservative forces actively stymie the extension of democracy, but also their rhetoric deliberately and successfully contested the idea of positive government, eroded support for public institutions, and undermined the idea that American citizens owe each other anything at all. This strategy served the Right well politically, but it also exacerbated feelings of individualism and disconnection among citizens and consequently played a central role in the destruction of social capital over time.

As the Right began repackaging its agenda, democratic movements on the Left simultaneously became more radical. 1965 marks the beginning of increased anger among young African American citizens, who had become impatient with the slow pace of change and were concerned about the continued saliency of the movement in the face of its preliminary successes. As the bodies of murdered civil rights workers began to pile up—and with the assassinations of Malcolm X and James Meredith in particular—young activists became increasingly disillusioned with the prospect that African Americans would ever be fully integrated into American civic life, and they began to radicalize their struggle. "One bullet too many and one federal betrayal too many" led them to rethink their strategy of nonviolence, lose faith in racial cooperation, and raise their fists in Black Power (Piven and Cloward 1979, 253).

Young black leaders were also worried about the effects of integration on black social capital, which would continue to be necessary if African Americans were to move beyond mere formal equality. While minimum standards of democratic citizenship had been officially met, racism within civil society "appeared to be growing stronger and more widespread" (Isserman and Kazin 2000, 177). Would African Americans ever be allowed to participate fully in American democratic life? Would middle-class blacks continue struggling for justice now that they had achieved legal equality and economic opportunity for themselves? Would traditional customs of deference and dominance lead to the evolution of an all-white leadership structure within a civil rights movement that was becoming increasingly white? Shouldn't black people take responsibility for their own problems? Black Power seemed to make sense. According to Stokely Carmichael and Charles Hamilton, "the concept of black power rests on a fundamental premise: *Before a group can enter the open society,* it must first close ranks . . . solidarity is necessary before a group can operate effectively from a bargaining position of strength *in a pluralistic society*" (quoted in Piven and Cloward 1979, 253, my emphasis). According to this thinking, black citizens need to solidify their connections with each other—shore up their social capital—in preparation for full participation in the larger civic life of American society.

Also in 1965, the struggle for civic equality for African Americans moved from the political and legal arenas into the economic realm, and this threatened conservative whites in a new way. Cognizant of the fact that the suffrage would benefit the black middle class more than rural and urban poor, African American activists had already begun "to shift their emphasis to economic problems" by 1962 (Piven and Cloward 1979, 269). Pressure from the civil rights movement succeeded in opening up existing welfare programs to African Americans; it "forced states for the first time to relax the welfare eligibility requirements that had excluded Blacks for decades" (Roberts 1997, 206). In 1964, President Johnson began prioritizing anti-poverty programs in his speeches, and at first public opinion supported the elimination of poverty. "'Public awareness of poverty in the United States, virtually non-existent'" in 1963, became pervasive by 1964; President Johnson succeeded in elevating the war on poverty to the level of "national consensus" (Piven and Cloward 1979, 270). As a result, services to the poor were greatly expanded, including job training, educational assistance, and urban renewal programs, efforts aimed at nurturing self-sufficiency, integrating the economically disenfranchised into the larger economy, and building communities, rather than simply handing out cash (Isserman and Kazin 2000, 110–11).

Anti-poverty programs played a vitally important role in mobilizing African American citizens to participate fully in civic life. These programs created "a new leadership structure in the ghettos and . . . activated masses of black poor" (Piven and Cloward 1979, 271). A "grassroots movement composed of welfare mothers, joined forces with neighborhood welfare rights centers and legal services lawyers to agitate for major changes" that would help poor female citizens. By 1967, this civic engagement had produced significant results (Roberts 1997, 207). The Great Society would "give every citizen the full equality which God enjoins and the law requires," to use Johnson's words (quoted in Isserman and Kazin 2000, 112).

However, longstanding welfare programs began to lose legitimacy among the white majority as soon as they were extended to African Americans. "The fortunes of the war on poverty would remain in the ascendant" only "as long as the poor continued to be thought of as the great, great grandchildren of Daniel Boone—which is to say white and rural" (Isserman and Kazin 2000, 111). Once programs aimed at economic justice for American citizens were extended to African Americans, "the image of the welfare mother quickly changed from the worthy white widow to the immoral black welfare queen (Roberts 1997, 207)—an image later utilized to good effect by President Reagan in his attack on America's already minimalist welfare state. In the end, conservatives successfully spearheaded a "white backlash [that] decimated the War on Poverty programs within a decade" (Roberts 1997, 208). Indeed, by 1990 "78% of white Americans thought that Blacks preferred to live on welfare" (Roberts 1997, 17), and in 1996 Democratic President Bill Clinton ended "welfare as we know it."

The year 1965 also marks the escalation of the war in Vietnam and the rise of the anti-war movement. The purging of whites from the civil rights movement helped fill the ranks of Students for a Democratic Society (SDS), a New Left organization originally "dedicated to creating a genuinely 'participatory democracy' in which individual citizens could help make 'those social decisions determining the quality and direction' of their lives" (Isserman and Kazin 2000, 169). SDS wanted to "revitalize American politics, to give substance to the most progressive traditions, to broaden and democratize the public sphere." They favored a "rejuvenated citizenship grounded in distinctly American experiences, discourses, and traditions" and a "broadening of public discourse" (Boggs 2000, 125–26). Faced with the escalation of a war apparently aimed at overturning the will of the North Vietnamese people and inspired by the successes of the civil rights movement, young citizens began to "scrutinize political decisions in moral terms" (Isserman and Kazin 2000, 170). What resulted was a widespread movement within civil society that was highly participatory, beginning with teach-ins to educate citizens about the issues and expanding rapidly from there (Isserman and Kazin 2000, 170–71). As political analysis deepened, however, the New Left became more radical and began calling for a strategy of "common struggle with the liberation movements of the world"—which increasingly raised the ire of anti-Communists (Isserman and Kazin 2000, 172).

Second-wave feminism also developed during the 1960s, and it was in opposition to this movement that the New Right was finally able to consolidate its base (Mansbridge 1986, 110). Liberal feminists had begun working toward legal equality for women in 1961, when President Kennedy convened the Commission on the Status of Women. The struggle for formal equality continued during the 1960s, culminating in the fight for the ratification of the Equal Rights Amendment (ERA), which simply stated: "Equality of rights under the law shall not be denied or abridged by the United States or any State on account of sex" (Mansbridge 1986, 1). Old Right activist Phyllis Schlafly successfully mobilized conservative homemakers against equality before the law for women. Due to their "precarious social position," homemakers turned out to be "a natural resource for groups that wanted to turn back the clock on the sexual, legal, and labor-force trends that had undermined the patriarchal basis of the family in the decades before the ERA struggle" (Mansbridge 1986, 109–10). The conservative mobilization against legal equality for women combined with outrage over abortion and contempt for the more radical and participatory Women's Liberation Movement solidified the New Right during the 1970s and played a "very important" role its success: the election of Ronald Reagan in 1980 and the rightward shift of American politics (Hardisty 1999, 72).

The Reagan Revolution launched the ultimately successful attack on government that continues to this day.

> By refusing to view governments as responsible for their citizens and seeing individuals as responsible only for themselves, conservatives after 1979 effected a major realignment of political ideas. Conservatism no longer elevated the traditions and values of a broadly defined social unit. Instead, it was a libertarian-style defense of the right of achieving individuals to earn more, spend more, consume more, and pay less to support those who did not achieve in material terms. (Bashevkin 1998, 6)

This attack on the idea that Americans owe each other anything *as citizens* helped make American culture more selfish and individualistic. In addition, right-wing rhetoric, like Reagan's famous tale about the welfare queen picking up her check in a Cadillac, not only undermined support for social welfare programs but also rendered American citizens suspicious of the poor, who were erroneously imagined as predominantly African American. Such rhetorical strategies both appealed to and exaggerated racist resentments among whites and rendered American citizens more disconnected from and mistrustful of each other. Over time, individuals living in the United States lost interest in having a shared civic life, public institutions, or governmental policies aimed at the common good. This is the anti-civic culture in which Generations X and Y came of age.

Putnam's Conclusions about Race and Gender

Lack of attention to politics prevents Putnam from correctly identifying the key causal factors in the decline of social capital. Overlooking the history of the last thirty-five years, Putnam misses the significance of race in the story, even though he notes, "the decline in social connectedness and social trust began just after the greatest successes of the civil rights revolution of the 1960s" (Putnam 2000, 279–80). Although "it seems intuitively plausible" to him "that race might somehow have played a role in the erosion of social capital over the last generation" (279), his methodological approach leads him to dismiss race as an important factor for the following reasons: "First, racial differences in associational membership are not large. . . . Second, the erosion of social capital has affected all races. . . . Third, if civic disengagement represented white flight from integrated community life after the civil rights revolution, it is hard to reconcile with the generational differences described" previously (280). Taken out of context these facts tell us nothing. In order to explain them, we must examine the changes in American political culture that led to disengagement by both blacks and whites.

Putnam also misses the mark in his discussion of gender issues, which he conflates with "the transformation of American family structure and home life" (278). Here he *does* establish that the entry of women into the work force, the rising number of single women, and the increasing number of divorces did *not* cause the decline of social capital—a common contention of conservatives: The empirical "evidence is *not* consistent with the thesis that the *overall* decline in civic engagement and social connectedness is attributable to the decline in the traditional family. On the contrary, to some extent the decline in family obligations ought to have freed up time for more social and community involvement" (279). However, because Putnam centers his discussion of gender on the decline of the traditional family, he overlooks the anti-feminist attack on women's civic equality as a key factor in the decline of civic life.

Not surprisingly, Putnam also misses the critical importance of the right-wing attack on public institutions in explaining the generational change he documents in *Bowling Alone*. In fact, he misses the mark so much that he actually suggests, following the lead of right-wing ideologues, that "big government" and the so-called culture of dependency, rather than the discrediting of the entire public sector, might be responsible for eroding social capital: "Circumstantial evidence, particularly the timing of the downturn in social connectedness, has suggested to some observers that an important cause—perhaps even *the* cause—of civic disengagement is big government and the growth of the welfare state. By 'crowding out' private initiative, it is argued, state intervention has subverted civil society" (281). His empirical testing eliminates this possibility.

Because he chooses not to look for clues within American politics, Putnam ultimately fails to solve the mystery. He never recognizes that the American Right played a central role in the destruction of social capital. This group came to power by opposing the extension of democracy every step of the way—not only radical demands but also basic democratic principles, like voting rights and legal equality. The racist backlash against integrating black people into American civic life fed into attacks on the federal government and the welfare state, which were seen as disproportionately benefiting African Americans, and the anti-feminist backlash against women's civic equality galvanized the masses. The rhetorical strategies the New Right used in advancing its agenda ultimately undermined solidarity and trust among citizens. Thanks to the triumph of social and fiscal conservatism, young people who came of age during the 1980s grew up hearing about the "tyranny" of the federal government, the illegitimacy of "activist judges," the "reverse discrimination" against white men, the dysfunctional "culture of dependency" among poor blacks, the immorality of female "baby-killers," and the goodness of greed. While conservatives do not bear sole responsibility for the generational changes Putnam documented, the direct correlation between the rise of the New Right and the decline of American civic life certainly provides enough circumstantial evidence for an indictment on charges of maliciously destroying social capital. It's now time to begin preparations for the trial of empirical testing.

References

Barber, Benjamin R. 1998. *A Place for Us: How to Make Society Civil and Democracy Strong*. New York: Hill and Wang.

Bashevkin, Sylvia. 1998. *Women on the Defensive: Living Through Conservative Times*. Chicago: University of Chicago Press.

Boggs, Carl. 2000. *The End of Politics: Corporate Power and the Decline of the Public Sphere*. New York: Guilford Press.

Boyte, Harry C., and Sara M. Evans. 1992. *Free Spaces: The Sources of Democratic Change in America*. Chicago: University of Chicago Press.

Boyte, Harry C., and Nancy N. Kari. 1996. *Building America: The Democratic Promise of Public Work*. Philadelphia: Temple University Press.

Bronner, Stephen Eric. 1999. *Ideas in Action: Political Tradition in the Twentieth Century*. Lanham, Md.: Rowman and Littlefield.

Dionne, E. J., Jr. 1991. *Why Americans Hate Politics*. New York: Simon & Schuster.

Ehrenberg, John. 1999. *Civil Society: The Critical History of an Idea*. New York: NYU Press.

Hardisty, Jean. 1999. *Mobilizing Resentment: Conservative Resurgence from the John Birch Society to the Promise Keepers*. Boston: Beacon Press.

Isserman, Maurice, and Michael Kazin. 2000. *America Divided: The Civil War of the 1960s*. Oxford: Oxford University Press.

Mansbridge, Jane J. 1986. *Why We Lost the ERA.* Chicago: University of Chicago Press.

Nye, Joseph S., Jr. 1997. "Introduction: The Decline of Confidence in Government." In *Why People Don't Trust Government,* ed. Joseph S. Nye, Jr., Philip D. Zelikow, and David C. King. Cambridge: Harvard University Press.

Piven, Frances Fox, and Richard A. Cloward. 1979. *Poor People's Movements: Why They Succeed, How They Fail.* New York: Vintage Books.

Putnam, Robert. 2000. *Bowling Alone: The Collapse and Revival of American Community.* New York: Simon & Schuster.

Roberts, Dorothy. 1997. *Killing the Black Body: Race, Reproduction, and the Meaning of Liberty.* New York: Vintage Books.

Sandel, Michael J. 1996. *Democracy's Discontent: America in Search of a Public Philosophy.* Cambridge: Belknap Press of Harvard University Press.

Walzer, Michael 1998. "The Idea of Civil Society." In *Community Works: The Revival of Civil Society in America,* ed. by E. J. Dionne, Jr. Washington, D.C.: Brookings: 123–43.

Chapter Eight

Social Capital as Political Fantasy

Carl Boggs

Harvard political scientist Robert Putnam has achieved something akin to celebrity status—rare for any academic—by virtue of his compelling use of a metaphor, "bowling alone," to characterize the transformation of American social and political life during the postwar era (Putnam 2000). He argues that a pervading sense of civic malaise and disengagement has taken over a society in which the vast majority of people are materially satisfied but deeply alarmed about the political, cultural, and moral direction of the country. "During the first two-thirds of the century," Putnam writes, "Americans took a more and more active role in the social and political life of their communities—in churches and union halls, in bowling alleys and clubrooms, around committee tables and card tables and dinner tables . . . then, mysteriously and more or less simultaneously, we began to do all those things less often" (Putnam 2000, 183). Of course Putnam is not the first writer to call attention to the disintegration of civic culture in the United States, but what distinguishes his work is a focus on eroding "social capital"—the collapse of networks of interaction among individuals that imbue human life with qualities needed for community, collective action, and democratic participation along lines theorized by Jean Jacques Rousseau and later celebrated by Alexis de Tocqueville in his classic *Democracy in America.* Hence: "Weakened social capital is manifest in the things that have vanished almost unnoticed—neighborhood parties and get-togethers with friends, the unreflective kindness of strangers, the shared pursuit of the public good rather than a solitary quest for private good" (Putnam 2000, 403). In a word, Americans have abandoned en masse bowling leagues and are now, more often than ever, taking to the lanes alone as a sign of their social disconnectedness. When the article upon which this book was written first appeared in 1995 Putnam was, as he concedes, an obscure academic; now he is invited to Camp David, lionized by talk-show hosts, pictured with his wife on the pages of *People* magazine, and is generally the toast of both the Beltway and academia.

Putnam clearly has his fingers on the pulse of some critical long-term developments in twentieth-century U.S. history. There is abundant evidence to suggest that we do in fact live in a rather thoroughly depoliticized society, even if significant countertrends are becoming visible at the turn of the millennium. Virtually every indicator reveals a sharp falloff in political activity of all sorts, while the younger (post–World War II) generations—even with their considerably higher levels of education—turn out to be less knowledgeable about and less interested in public affairs, as each succeeding UCLA survey of entering college freshmen around the country shows. Putnam is quick to suggest, however, "declining electoral participation is merely the most visible symptom of a broader disengagement from community life" (2000, 35). Social capital (hereafter referred to as SC), which ostensibly energizes the public realm and sustains political democracy, is vanishing across every group and sector, across every ideological divide, across every geographical region, of the society. This deep, steady civic decline would seem to have dire consequences not only for political institutions but for the general state of health and happiness, education, family welfare, safety, culture, and economic prosperity. To bolster his thesis, Putnam has marshaled enormous bodies of data from an endless array of social science and public opinion surveys.

The author's iconic status does not prevent his book from being so conceptually flawed and historically misleading that it would seem to require yet another large tome just to give adequate space to the needed systemic critique. Despite its ambitious scope and careful empirical investigation into a whole catalogue of attitudinal and behavioral trends, *Bowling Alone* ultimately distorts or ignores so many vital issues that any thorough analysis of the American political morass is inconceivable within its framework. The book incorporates a prodigious amount of evidence in 400 pages of text, 30 pages of appendices, and more than 50 pages of notes, but the author faces the Sisyphean task of crawling out from beneath mountains of statistical data far enough to survey the public landscape with historical clarity.

Putnam contends that civic decline in the United States is best understood largely in *generational* terms: today middle-aged and older people whose formative years spanned the 1930s to 1950s remain comparatively active, while younger cohorts (the so-called Baby Boomers and Gen-Xers) have become increasingly disengaged, cut off from the political, social, and religious participation that was the lifeblood of American community and civic virtue throughout the century into the early 1960s. While all social groups experienced a weakening of SC, the various age cohorts remained a singular and outstanding exception (Putnam 2000, 247): to the extent important generational shifts are effectively traced we can observe how society as a whole can change dramatically (in this case measured by diminishing SC) while individuals or particular age cohorts exhibit continuity. Putnam concludes that the civic-minded generation shaped by World War II and its aftermath had higher levels of social and political involvement owing to its patriotism, sense of community, strong feelings of civic obligation, and more active social life as shown by indicators such as greater willingness to work for a political party, sign petitions, write letters to public officials, attend public meetings or rallies, join voluntary groups, and simply interact with friends and neighbors (Putnam 2000, 45). This "long civic generation" voted more often, kept itself more informed of public affairs, was more philanthropic, and in general had a more elevated concern for the public good. In contrast, the newer generations (coming of age after the early 1960s) were more passive, less philanthropic, less socially engaged, more inclined toward privatized lifestyles, and more likely to be alienated from the political system.

Putnam's thesis, in short, is that civic participation began its descent in the mid-1960s—paradoxically at just that historical moment when large-scale movements for social change ushered in a new era of civic involvement and political activism that would contrast starkly with the quiet, bland, conservative national consensus of the Eisenhower fifties. Could it be that we have actually witnessed a steady downward spiral in public engagement *since* the civil rights movement burst upon the stage, *since* the great upheavals of the 1960s, *since* the rapid spread of new social movements and related tendencies in the 1970s, and *since* the proliferation of diverse community groups that even today remain very much a part of the social terrain? Or is Putnam in touch with something most every other commentator on the political scene has missed? Can he really be arguing that this series of developments, which enlisted the participation of tens of millions, forced dramatic shifts in popular discourse and social policy, and reshaped the political terrain—bringing forth a legacy of grassroots protest and cultural renewal—coincide in fact with a steady deterioration of public life? Can he be insisting that Americans *after* 1965 became more disengaged, less aware, less politically active than they were at the height of the placid fifties, when McCarthyism filled the air, when social movements and third parties were nowhere to be seen, when racism, sexism, and homophobia were part of the taken-for-granted ideological discourse? Or is Putnam indeed coming from another planet?

Much of the problem stems from the limits of Putnam's methodology—namely, from his rather arbitrary choice of indicators to reflect declining SC. Joining the Rotary or Elks club, singing in choir ensembles, competing in sports leagues, and going to dinner parties may indeed have furnished some element of solidarity for many people, but these could be categorized as mostly safe, conformist, traditional community activities favored by the older generations and, within those generations, by largely middle-class or upper middle-class strata; "politics" scarcely entered into such forms of participation, or did so in only the most limited, conventional fashion. The old voluntary organizations Putnam cherishes went into decline precisely because they lost their *raison d'etre* as their goals became outdated, mostly reflective of a small-town America that itself was in the process of vanishing. Likewise, earlier cohorts may have been more willing to work for political parties, turn out for elections, sign petitions, and write letters to government officials or newspapers, but such expenditures of time and energy were viewed as peripheral, even wasteful, by newer generations that—for many justifiable reasons—became increasingly suspicious of a political system riddled with scandals, corruption, official deceit, and ideological convergence of the major parties and their candidates. Many of these civic activities, in any case, have relatively little to do with building SC, in contrast to what Putnam intimates. Declining church attendance and related functions no doubt mirrors both the secularization of American society and the growing pursuit of spiritual interests outside the realm of organized religion. As for eroding union membership, one need look no further than the transformation of the work force itself (marked by a shrinking industrial blue-collar sector and an expanding service sector) along with the impact of globalization and intensified corporate assault on organized labor. The reality is that none of these developments, alone or in tandem, ultimately reveal what Putnam contends they do—a steady, precipitous decline in SC over a period of forty years leading to a thorough collapse of civic life in postwar American society.

According to Putnam, "externally, voluntary associations, from churches to professional societies to Elks clubs and reading groups, allow individuals to express their interested demands on government and to protect themselves from abuses of power by their political leaders" (Putnam 2000, 338). This statement captures one of the central weaknesses of *Bowling Alone:* at no point does Putnam establish any connection between the social and political realms that would permit such far-fetched claims about the impact of SC. In reality, voluntary groups of the sort listed here have readily coexisted with a variety of authoritarian movements, parties, and governments, including both fascist and Communist; throughout the history of fascism, in fact, party leaders generally celebrated such groups. Putnam adds: "Political information flows through social networks and in these networks public life is discussed" (2000, 338). For some "networks" this is undoubtedly true, but again, the social/public linkage is merely assumed rather than investigated, thus blocking any genuine analysis of SC *content.* He further writes: "Internally, associations and less formal networks of civic engagement instill in their members habits of cooperation and public spiritedness, as well as the practical skills necessary to partake in public life" (338).

Putnam never makes the case for this generalization, for there is no truly substantial case to be made. It was surely never valid for conventional groups like the Rotary or Elks clubs, and it is emphatically less true of contemporary forms such as gangs, cults, self-help groups, militias, and even those social movements inclined toward "identity politics." What seems to escape Putnam's analysis is that both the functions and trajectory of community groups will always depend upon the cultural or ideological environment—not only internally but also *externally,* as part of the hegemonic system of ideas and beliefs.

What Putnam further ignores in his thesis of perpetually vanishing SC is the conspicuous growth of many forms of social participation and civic activity since the early 1960s that depart from, indeed call into question, the specific criteria for declining public life he privileges throughout *Bowling Alone.* The great popular movements spanning the sixties and seventies receive only scant attention in a brief discussion of "countertrends," which are dismissed with facile reference to their supposed ossification during the 1980s and 1990s. There is surely some validity to this contention, but the larger truth is probably closer to what David Meyer and Sidney Tarrow suggest in their anthology *The Social Movement Society:* In many ways social protest and popular movements have become an integral feature of contemporary civil society and, to a lesser extent, the institutional order (Meyer and Tarrow 1998). The civil rights, anti-war, women's, environmental, community, and gay rights movements mobilized constituencies that, separately and together, changed the world. Over a period of nearly four decades they brought new issues into the political arena, catalyzed the energies of millions of citizens, pressed (often successfully) for institutional change, and broadened the public sphere. Putnam invokes the trajectory of environmental groups as an example of movement sclerosis over time, but he greatly oversimplifies his case: environmentalism has often fallen victim to the D.C. lobby culture built around direct-mail fundraising, bureaucratic maneuvers, and minimalist reforms. Yet progressive, grassroots organizations with large memberships and broader agendas (for example, Friends of the Earth, Earth First!, Greenpeace, Earth Island Institute, various anti-nuclear groups, even the rejuvenated Sierra Club) have also proliferated during the 1980s and 1990s, keeping ecological concerns such as global warming, deforestation, resource depletion, toxic wastes, food contamination, and animal rights at the forefront of public awareness more than at any point in American history.

Fixated on the spurious notion that SC has continuously deteriorated since the early 1960s, Putnam fails to consider the spread of newer, in many ways more interesting, civic phenomena over exactly that same time span—not only social movements but thousands of self-help and new-age groups, religious movements, and community organizations (resource centers, clinics, bookstores, periodicals, public interest groups, tenants' associations, and so forth) often spawned by the larger movements. In *Bowling Alone,* the self-help revolution is located within the same "countertrend" category as social movements, but the cumulative impact of these groups with their millions of participants is never really explored. One might expect that such groups, intensely committed to personal transformation and cultural renewal, would be understood as the ideal embodiment of SC, but Putnam can never get beyond the Elks club, card games, and bowling leagues. Further working against the book's declensionist thesis is the flourishing of small, local groups overflowing with SC: urban gangs, cults, paramilitary militias, and assorted patriarchal movements like Promise Keepers, Brotherhood of Aryan Nations, and the Muslim Brotherhood, with a combined membership of perhaps several million, not counting additional millions of supporters. These more recent tendencies, spanning a wide ideological spectrum, are generally more communal and "participatory" than the kind of SC typical of Putnam's older, more established civic organizations. Leaving aside their goals, territorial claims, and modus operandi, these newer forms seem overwhelmingly preoccupied with recovering a sense of group identity and solidarity in a post-Fordist capitalist society that reproduces individualism, materialism, privatism, and passivity as part of its economic-political logic. Why *Bowling Alone* so completely ignores or devalues these dynamic expressions of social activity in favor of increasingly archaic older forms presents us with a mystery that no amount of statistical data contained here can help us unravel.

Whether groups of the sort mentioned above—or even well-established social movements—can translate abundant SC into viable *political* modes of engagement is of course an entirely different matter. There is no easy or necessary correspondence between the two, and much depends upon the ideological context. In fact, these groups typically either have no clear political orientation or they lean viscerally toward some form of anti-politics—that is, their SC does not especially contribute to the kind of civic virtues so highly regarded by Tocqueville and Putnam. Urban gangs, self-help groups, cults, and militias clearly fit this designation, which may explain why they receive practically no attention throughout the text. As we have seen, Putnam never gets around to making ideological or political distinctions of any sort, so we are provided with no means of determining the particular *content* or direction of SC, or even identifying variable types of SC.

Yet any discussion that identifies bowling leagues, choir ensembles, letter writing, self-help groups, and mass-based popular movements under the same rubric cries out for such conceptual differentiation. As even this relatively brief list of activities indicates, SC takes many forms, which means that its broader relevance to the public sphere and to politics cannot be established without the kind of contextual interpretation that, unfortunately, is largely missing from *Bowling Alone*. If certain modes of SC skirt the boundaries of politics, others (party activity, going to meetings or demonstrations, union work) can be emphatically political but remain within the institutional status quo, while still others (many grassroots movements) press for an alternative discourse and practice that might enlarge the whole field of politics. SC itself may have only the most refracted or indirect relationship to politics, if we understand politics to include such dimensions as statecraft, social governance, collective decision making, and citizenship. In the end, Putnam's work fails to establish criteria for determining the political effects of SC in its multiple forms. Elaborate lists of civic activities and social practices are thrown together in a single amorphous grouping, which illuminates little about SC and does even less to demonstrate how these activities and practices matter for the health of political democracy which, after all, constitutes the leitmotif of Putnam's book.

To be sure, something profound has been taking place in American society over the past few decades, but the historical process in question might more usefully be viewed as a downward *political* spiral associated with a variety of conditions Putnam barely recognizes in his study. While SC almost certainly has *not* fallen since the 1960s or even 1980s, and might even have surpassed previous levels in certain areas of daily life, there can be little doubt that the political system (especially as regards democratic citizenship) has steadily eroded, as a host of studies in the 1990s has conclusively shown (Boggs 2000; Ophuls 1997; Eliasoph 1998; Greider 1992; Dionne 1991). This is not a matter simply of reduced civic trust or philanthropy or club-joining or letter-writing—or even reduced voter turnouts. It is more a question of the narrowing public sphere in which political debates and election campaigns have become largely meaningless, the major parties have converged on vital issues of the day, and big money has hijacked virtually every realm of governmental activity, while urgent social problems go unsolved. Viewed in this light, it makes far more sense to argue that trends toward civic (more accurately political) disengagement have their origins in the late 1970s or early 1980s rather than the 1960s, since it was during this later period that large-scale disillusionment regarding political action as such began to fester. The historical dating of this process is crucial, since it allows for an analysis grounded in the dramatic growth in centralized economic and governmental power, the mounting impact of globalization, the simultaneous institutional expansion (and ideological narrowing) of media culture, and of course the ascent of the Reagan presidency.[1] The 1960s and 1970s gave rise to ample cynicism and distrust, much of it fueled by the Vietnam War and Watergate, but in those years alienation from the political system was channeled into dynamic movements built upon not only enlarged SC but widespread optimism and civic élan; the period in fact was one of *repoliticization*. With the 1980s, in contrast, American society experienced a marked trend toward *depoliticization*, as the social movements and groups began to turn inward, away from the public sphere, even where they may continue to embrace high levels of SC. It is precisely within this historical milieu that the question of disintegrating public trust in government must be understood. For the vast majority of citizens, withdrawal of trust made perfectly good sense in the wake of lies about the Vietnam War, several political assassinations, Watergate, COINTELPRO, revelations about the CIA, Iran-

Contra and other Washington scandals, and just corrupt political busi-
ness-as-usual.

In charting the entire flow of events and developments, it is possible to
find any number of causal variables at work (including Putnam's favorite
culprit, TV), but one dominant factor clearly stands above the others: the
massive growth of corporate power, with its colonization of the public
sphere and most every other area of social life.

If corporate power has indeed penetrated everyday life more deeply
than ever, meanwhile reshaping the very contours of SC, its reconfigura-
tion of the political terrain has been no less striking. All this extends well
beyond the corrosive influence of money, PACs, and lobbies on the conduct of election campaigns and legislation—a phenomenon familiar
enough to American political history. It engulfs the entire terrain of public
life, including social policy, education, technology, the mass media, and
popular culture, while its impact on public consciousness is hard to exag-
gerate. The crucial point here is that already oversized corporations have
grown dramatically in the resources and power they command over the
past two or three decades, a process given impetus by heightened globalization endowing transnational structures (financial and trade bodies,
communications, global agencies like the IMF, the World Bank, and WTO,
megacorporations) with the power to constrict national and local sover-
eignties. In the United States, an ideological shift beginning in the early
1980s that favored "free market" principles, deregulation, and privatization has strongly reinforced this development. It is within this historical
context that increasing depoliticization, above all the severe decline in citizenship and local decision making, must be situated.

Putnam, however, seems rather clueless regarding such far-reaching
structural and ideological transformations. Wedded to a generational
model that posits a sharp decline in SC over a four-decade period and
identifies the sixties as harbinger of a downturn in civic participation, he
cannot help but obscure the overall trajectory of *both* SC and politics
while missing the central factors behind *political* decline, which is the real
story. The author's explanation of civic disengagement turns out to be
highly impressionistic, devoid of the all-important conceptual distinction
between "social" and "political" dimensions of public life. Understandably,
therefore, when it comes to establishing causal relationships the study
abruptly loses its empirical veneer. We are told that the single most important factor in SC decline (accounting for roughly 50 percent) is the long-
term generational shift from supposedly "civic" World War II cohorts to

the more passive, self-interested, privatized Boomer and Xer cohorts. Electronic entertainment (mostly TV) accounts for some 25 percent of the trend, while pressures of time and money along with the impact of suburbanization and sprawl explain the rest. As for TV, Putnam writes: "Nothing—not low education, not full-time work, not long commutes in urban agglomerations, not poverty or financial distress—is more broadly associated with civic disengagement and social disconnection than is dependence on television for entertainment" (Putnam 2000, 231). But in a volume overflowing with data, Putnam offers no insight into how he arrives at this particular causal matrix or these percentages; why he chose to exclude some factors (the role of corporate power and globalization, for example) also remains a mystery. The explanatory framework contained in *Bowling Alone* ultimately rests upon a foundation of pseudo-empiricism, with all the assembled data, charts, and graphs telling us little about the *conditions* underlying historical change. This problem stems in part from Putnam's feeble guiding premise—that American society has experienced long-term erosion of SC—and from his misplaced emphasis on generalized "civic disengagement" rather than a more definitive (and accurate) focus on *political* decline.

Trends in citizen participation cannot be fully analyzed without taking into account the whole trajectory of economic and governmental power, yet *Bowling Alone* flies directly in the face of this imperative (Ehrenberg 1999). How does a presumably sophisticated observer of the American scene like Putnam manage to ignore the overwhelming influence of big business—not to mention its offshoot, globalization—on the workings of the political system? Putnam does refer to the "commercialization of politics" once or twice, but fails to elaborate in any way upon the theme and never integrates it into his explanatory schema. He cites the well-known argument that market capitalism is likely to have a destructive impact on SC (or at least on political democracy) but then quickly proceeds to dismiss that possibility with the observation that capitalism has been constant throughout U.S. history and thus could not account for significant *variations* in civic involvement (Putnam 2000, 282). But this sleight of hand ignores a crucial reality: the corporate domain has grown immensely more powerful since the 1970s, not only in its control of economic and institutional resources but, perhaps even more significantly, in its capacity to shape popular attitudes, beliefs, and values. The issue of unbridled corporate domination has elicited increasing great alarm from citizens' groups, journalists, academics, and even mainstream politicians who seem ready to battle against what appears to be runaway power—witness a series of huge mass protests first galvanized by the anti-WTO mobilizations in Seattle at the end of 1999. We do not need Aristotle (or Marx) to tell us that anything resembling democratic politics is unthinkable so long as un-accountable privileged interests are able to thoroughly colonize government and the public sphere. Even venerable *Time* magazine (January 1998) devoted a special issue to the corrosive effects of big business in politics. Yet nowhere in *Bowling Alone* does Putnam confront this reality, apparently believing that the vagaries of economic power have changed little since Tocqueville visited America in the mid-nineteenth century. Even where Putnam writes about the deleterious effects of TV on civic life, he ignores the decisive *corporate* domination of electronic entertainment.

Putnam rails against individualism, materialism, privatized retreat, and a plethora of beliefs and attitudes that subvert the requirements of community and democratic citizenship, but instead of narrowing his search for causes to TV and urban/suburban sprawl he could turn, with more compelling logic, to the systemic impact of an economic order designed to reproduce exactly such tendencies. This is an order that contributes mightily to the process of depoliticization, giving rise through its very workings to popular alienation from government, "politics," and politicians—though not necessarily to a decline in SC which, as I argue, has resurfaced in new (though often anti-political) forms over the past few decades. Putnam seems oblivious to such discourse, and to the manner in which an ideological tradition like liberal capitalism with deep roots in American history sustains those very attitudes, beliefs, and habits Putnam finds so destructive of civic virtue. As Michael Sandel (in *Democracy's Discontent*) and William Ophuls (in *Requiem for Modern Politics*) have recently argued, the modern liberal preoccupation with material self-interest, individual sovereignty, contractual social relations, and proceduralism winds up inherently and fundamentally at odds with any attempt to create a politics of common vision, public good, or community; Rousseau and Tocqueville are short-circuited by the continuing legacy of John Locke and Adam Smith. The liberal predicament has only been deepened with the expansion of corporate power. In Sandel's terms, the "procedural Republic" is nicely suited to a world of concentrated economic and political power but can scarcely give rise to a vibrant public sphere characterized by civic virtue, informed citizenship, and democratic participation.

As for the critical (and related) theme of globalization, Putnam writes: "I have no doubt that global economic transformations are having an important imprint on community life across America. The link is most direct, however, as regards larger philanthropic and civic activities. It is less clear why corporate de-localization should effect, for example, our readiness to attend a church social, or to have friends over for poker, or even to vote for President" (Putnam 2000, 283).

This rather strange passage actually turns out to be vintage Putnam. He refers to "larger civic activities" without, however, indicating how they might encompass something of public importance. No doubt church gatherings and poker games, as with any social activity, will take on different surface appearances with advancing globalization, but such involvements are likely to have little if any relevance to wider social or political trends even where these involvements might contribute to SC. Voting turnouts could indeed be undermined if globalization subverts—or is even perceived to subvert—the competence of national decision making and thereby leads to further alienation from politics. More than that: globalization endows capital with increased flexibility relative to labor, which means that unionization and labor protests always face obstacles—one key factor in union membership decline that Putnam bemoans as a sign of withering SC.

Amidst such telling distortions and omissions, any problems with Putnam's governing metaphor, "bowling alone," might seem trivial, for in reality bowling says little about either SC or civic disengagement. Yet there must be some kind of special meaning attached to the fate of bowling leagues, as the picture of a lone bowler on the book's cover clearly suggests. Putnam writes that roughly 8 percent of men and 5 percent of women participated in bowling leagues during their peak years of popularity spanning the late 1940s to mid-1960s. Over the past ten or fifteen years, he reports, league membership has declined by about 40 percent, corresponding to the overall downward trajectory in SC as indicated by the perpetual erosion of social and friendship networks; Americans continue to bowl but they are more likely to "bowl alone" (Putnam 2000, 112–15). The difficulty with this picture, however, is that bowling leagues were fashionable for only a short duration, mainly through the 1950s when the cultural atmosphere seemed more conducive to a middle-American sport like bowling. For the rest of the century the rates of participation were as low as if not lower than those of today. Leaving aside the issue of exactly how these leagues might have generated civic vitality, Putnam's statistics actually prove little: SC could have been re-channeled into an even more socially interactive sport like golf, which took off in popularity at the very time (mid-1960s) Putnam reports that bowling leagues began their descent. More to the point, there is nothing here proving that bowling leagues in fact gave way to *solo activity* at the lanes; people simply chose to bowl in more informal groups of friends or relatives rather than the formal leagues, as any close investigation of the lanes would quickly reveal. Of course more Americans have become spectators (thanks mainly to TV and the commercialization of sports), but many arenas of direct athletic involvement are on the upswing—not only golf but gym membership, aerobics, volleyball and handball, and self-defense classes; many others, such as basketball and softball, have at least matched their previous levels of activity. Preferences have no doubt changed, but there is no evidence that SC is down, in bowling or elsewhere. There is yet a deeper problem with Putnam's sloppy metaphor: why anyone concerned about the health of American politics should focus on bowling or golf—or Rotary clubs, choirs, dinner gatherings, and poker games, for that matter—remains a mystery.

Yet Putnam's agenda in *Bowling Alone* is far more high-minded than charting the intricate trends and nuances of social interaction as such: he wants to show how the vicissitudes of SC are historically and organically connected to the fate of "democracy" within a framework originally established by Tocqueville, whose attention was riveted on the different properties of civil society. He has set out to demonstrate how erosion of social life across all groups militates against civic virtue, citizenship, and popular decision making—and, by extension, against governmental stability and "performance." This book was inspired by an earlier study, *Making Democracy Work* (1993), where his goal was to analyze the strength of Italian democratic institutions by looking at variations in levels of social capital from region to region. He concluded there that democracy requires vibrant forms of "voluntary cooperation" which, as is well known, contrast markedly with the provincialism, isolation, and civic distrust that for many decades permeated most of Italian political culture. Such cooperation, he found, "is easier in a community that has inherited a substantial stock of social capital in the form of norms of reciprocity and networks of civic engagement" (Putnam 1993, 167).

SC involves complex systems of mutual trust and solidarity consonant with the requirements of economic dynamism and governmental efficiency, which Putnam looks to demonstrate by systematically comparing outcomes across the five large regional governments. While most of the South of Italy (including Sicily) exhibits civic disengagement associated with low SC, the central and northern regions are more often governed by stable, efficient, relatively democratic systems with much higher SC. Economically underdeveloped and politically volatile, the South has been paralyzed by such diminished expressions of SC as apathy, parochialism, distrust, and alienation from public life in general, whereas the Center and North have managed to sustain "dense networks of social exchange" grounded in civic activities like municipal clubs, sports associations, music ensembles, and cultural circles. Throughout the South, he writes, "everyone feels powerless, exploited, and unhappy." In the last sentence of his book, Putnam affirms that building social capital is the ultimate key to "making democracy work" (1993, 185).

All of this may sound reasonable enough—for Italy or indeed any country—except that it is profoundly misleading as an interpretation both of modern Italian history and of the general role social capital occupies in political development. It is well known that the North-South divide has deep origins in the Italian experience, sharpened by an incomplete capitalist revolution (the *Risorgimento)* in the late nineteenth century that led to sharply uneven development characterized by the ongoing domination of the South by the North. The logic of this history is that levels of SC can be expected to differ profoundly from South to North, owing above all to the unyielding force of economic relations: pre-industrial forms (the Church, landed estates, traditional peasantry, extended family, etc.) defined the South well into the modern period, contrasting with the predominantly industrial, urban, secular, "European" North and Center. There may have been abundant SC in the South, for example in activities revolving around the Church and extended family, but this particular SC shied away from distinctly common or *public* types of intervention; it remained local and provincial. Putnam hardly addresses these historical conditions, thus implicitly giving SC a developmental autonomy and conceptual primacy it does not merit. Moreover, the northern and central regions Putnam finds most laudable for governmental "performance" were deeply transformed by the great World War II anti-fascist Resistance movement that brought mass-based Socialist and Communist parties to local (and in some cases regional) power. These organizations worked strenuously to build a dynamic presence through (ideologically infused) networks of party units, unions, local councils, cooperatives, and auxiliary bodies, thoroughly revitalizing Italian politics during and after the war.

A democratizing outcome of this sort was unthinkable without sustained popular mobilization around a social bloc of forces, which in turn depended upon convergence of disparate grassroots struggles (with their new forms of SC) and cohesive national organization grounded in leftist ideological traditions which, following the *Risorgimento,* never fully penetrated the South. It is surely no secret that ideological and social cohesion was central to political success and, later, to far-reaching social reforms carried out within the political arena. It should be emphasized, however, that such cohesion was hardly the SC of sports leagues, choirs, and dinner gatherings but was instead the product of large historical trends and institutional forces that Putnam, as in *Bowling Alone,* seems at a loss to incorporate into his explanatory schema. Putnam argues that "politics without social capital is politics at a distance" (2000, 341), but he forgets to add that any viable—much less transformative—politics inevitably requires "distance" as the sine qua non of societal presence and institutional leverage.

For the United States, Putnam foresees a civic culture more vibrant and participatory, anticipating renewed formations of SC to fill the vacuum left by waning conventional SC he describes in the book. But SC in its virtually endless modalities is still there, visible for anyone to detect and perhaps even more cohesive and widespread than in the past: the problem is not only that so much contemporary SC departs radically from older forms Putnam seems to favor, but that it frequently leads *away* from generalized citizen activity within the public sphere. What Putnam refers to as the "dark side of social capital"—insular, provincial, antithetical to civic culture—has become more pervasive than he wants to concede. Meanwhile, the corporate economy and the corporatized political system it does so much to reproduce both militate *against* democratization based upon communal, egalitarian, participatory ideals. In such a milieu there can be no return to any Golden Age of civic participation where SC is the expression of largely genteel middle-class sensibilities—or where SC itself is somehow viewed as moving toward automatic political translation (i.e., toward "democracy"). It follows that Putnam's call for a strong national "agenda" to restore public spirit and civic engagement cannot hope to address the harsh dysfunctions and contradictions of a post-Fordist capitalist society in which civic privatism, possessive individualism, and political alienation are the norm; his concoctions for a remedy are predictably so mild as to be useless. At the end of *Bowling Alone,* Putnam calls for increased levels of volunteering and philanthropy, more community service

programs, improved education, a more accountable mass media, and religious awakening leading to a "spiritual community of meaning" (405–10).

As one might expect, none of these bromides requires any far-reaching
(i.e., effective) structural change or policy initiative that might finally confront the underlying *sources* of civic disengagement in American society.
Putnam writes: "To build bridging social capital requires that we transcend
our social and political and professional identities to connect with people
unlike ourselves. This is why team sports [bowling again?] provides good
venues for social-capital creation" (Putnam 2000, 411). The idea of connecting "with people unlike ourselves," for example volunteering and philanthropy, suggests yet another recycling of noblesse oblige which, in the
end, further illustrates just how impoverished and class-biased Putnam's
concept of SC turns out to be. As for Putnam's fantasy of revitalized team
sports: we have plenty of it today, and its "dark side" has become increasingly visible in the form of unbridled competition, worship of authority, violence, commercialism, and celebrity run amok—and not just in professional sports, as anyone familiar with Little League baseball can attest.

Putnam's single-minded focus on social networks as the foundation of
a revitalized politics makes superficial good sense, but it runs up against
an intractable problem: individuals in any society may want to experience
community and solidarity of one sort or another, but such impulses are
altogether separate—logically and historically—from the more general societal concerns of collective action and democratic participation. In much
of Putnam's discourse these two spheres collapse into one. In reality, the
struggle for community could serve to either enhance or *detract from* citizenship.

There are indeed powerful social and institutional forces at work in
American society which undermine citizenship so thoroughly that most
local manifestations of SC will be deflected or marginalized where they are
not actually crushed. The two-party system, referred to by Theodore Lowi
as a "duopoly," is so institutionalized within a rigid set of political, electoral, and legal norms that citizen participation seen as a matter of genuine choices and alternatives (presupposing real debates around issues) is
effectively ruled out (Lowi 2000). The duopoly has a vested interest in low
voter turnouts, dull campaigns, minimalist promises, and feeble democratic participation; even where SC is high, the political system thrives on
precisely the kind of depoliticized civic culture Putnam seems to bemoan.

Contemporary electoral politics follows above all a commercial marketing and advertising ethos, with the electoral reduced to the status of pas-

sive consumers. In the end, political communication within the legitimate public sphere lacks any clear narrative substance, which is perfectly consistent with the agendas of politicians and other opinion-makers who remain content with a duopoly that marginalizes the civic culture while giving elites more space to maneuver. The sad failure of American democracy runs much deeper than the popular influence of TV or decline of the bowling leagues.

Against this backdrop Putnam has launched what he calls a "great crusade" to turn back the tide of social and political alienation by getting American citizens to join groups again—or, more accurately, to join the familiar voluntary and community groups he would prefer they join. He wants more picnics, card games, dinner parties, club activities, and just plain outings among friends and relatives, hoping all the while for a reinvention of the kinds of local organizations that held sway in the United States through the 1950s. Interviewed at the time of his book's appearance, Putnam suggested that the country needs nothing short of a "dramatic revolution" over the next ten to fifteen years in the way public life is approached.[2] Yet, as even he would surely admit, getting more people to attend picnics (while possibly a nice idea) will never be considered much of a "revolutionary" act. Neither will it have much political relevance in any sense, for a recovery of political life depends upon a shared vision or project designed to transform or at least significantly influence the larger world. And until the corporate stranglehold over American social and political life is decisively broken, none of Putnam's outmoded, tepid prescriptions—and no rejuvenation of bowling leagues, choir ensembles, and reading groups—will make a dent in the process of civic disengagement.

Notes

1. On the evolution of mass media and its impact on popular consciousness, see Kellner (1995).
2. Putnam was interviewed in the *Los Angeles Times* (August 27, 2000).

References

Boggs Carl. 2000. *The End of Politics: Corporate Power and the Decline of the Public Sphere.* New York: Guilford Press.

Dionne, E. J., Jr. 1991. *Why Americans Hate Politics.* New York: Simon & Schuster.

Ehrenberg, John. 1999. *Civil Society*. New York: NYU Press.

Eliasoph, Nina. 1998. *Avoiding Politics*. New York: Cambridge University Press.

Greider, William. 1992. *Who Will Tell the People?* New York: Simon & Schuster.

Kellner, Douglas. 1995. *Media Culture*. New York: Routledge.

Lowi, Theodore. 2000. "Deregulate the Duopoly," *The Nation* (December 4).

Meyer, David S., and Tarrow, Sidney, eds. 1998. *The Social Movement Society*. Lanham: Rowman & Littlefield.

Ophuls, William. 1997. *Requiem for Modern Politics*. Boulder: Westview Press.

Putnam Robert D. 1993. *Making Democracy Work*. Princeton: Princeton University Press, 1993.

———. 2000. *Bowling Alone: The Collapse and Revival of American Community*. New York: Simon & Schuster.

Sandel, Michael. 1996. *Democracy's Discontent*. Cambridge: Harvard University Press.

Part III

Social Engagement in Practice
Local, National, and Global Contexts

Chapter Nine

Social Capital, Civic Engagement, and the Importance of Context

Yvette M. Alex-Assensoh

Active participation in civic and political life is a hallmark of American democracy. That is why, for Americans in general and racial minorities in particular, individuals' involvement in politics through conventional and unconventional means has gone a long way toward playing major roles in improving their societal conditions. Toward these ends, civic associations have provided Americans of all racial and ethnic backgrounds with the psychological tools, skills, and resources to participate meaningfully in the political process. It is no wonder, therefore, that many social scientists and journalists have chronicled the importance of participation in voluntary associations (Schlozman and Tierney 1986; Verba and Nie 1972; Verba, Schlozman, and Brady 1995), while also lamenting the gradual, but consistent, decline among Americans in various kinds of political activities (Putnam 1993; 1996). Most notable in the last decade—where scholarship has been concerned—is Robert Putnam's research on civic engagement and social capital, which has stimulated much discussion and debate about how participation in civic life enhances democratic institutions.

Noticeably absent from Putnam's work, however, is any viable attention to the ways in which structural factors affect access to organizational involvement, engagement, and social capital. Instead, Putnam and other scholars have focused primarily on individual factors that either facilitate or undermine social capital. Yet, the idea that social capital and civic engagement are primarily the result of individual factors is belied by mounting and convincing evidence, which shows that structural factors affect engagement in civic and political life.

With the foregoing nuances in mind and with Putnam's recent scholarship as a yardstick, this chapter utilizes a unique data set—which includes information on the social and political engagement of black and white inner-city residents—to demonstrate how the context or environment in which citizens live can profoundly influence their propensity to engage in civic and political participation above and beyond individual characteristics. Contrary to the traditional literature on the decline of civic engagement, which focuses on individual-level constraints to engagement, this study will also amply underscore that the civic engagement of inner-city residents is both inhibited and facilitated by contextual forces.

Civic Engagement, Context, and Race

As already pointed out above, recent research and debate on civic engagement and social capital have been animated largely by the work of Putnam, a political scientist who offers at least two different explanations for the relationship between engagement in civic associations and social capital. For example, in *Making Democracy Work*, Putnam contends that participation in civic associations facilitates collaboration, cooperation, and temperance among citizens which, in turn, leads to efficiency and a shared sense of purpose in democratic governance. Therefore, to him, social capital is the byproduct of civic engagement that includes trust, networks, and viable norms, which bring about a more enlightened and improved society. Most importantly, Putnam's conceptualization of social capital places emphasis on its collective and indivisible benefits, which suggest that social capital emerges from a structure of social engagement and interaction.

Furthermore, Putnam conceptualizes social capital in a different vein in some of his other writings. In "The Strange Disappearance of Civic America," for example, he defined social capital as " . . . the networks, norms and trust that enable participants to act more effectively to pursue shared objectives" (1996, 36). His definition of social capital places much more emphasis on how engagement in civic associations stimulates individual attributes among active citizens that is, in turn, useful for society. In contrast to Putnam's earlier conceptualization in *Making Democracy Work*, he presents social capital here as an attribute that is beneficial to individuals as well as society at large.

Emerging from these works are two subtly different conceptualizations of social capital, which emphasize the collective versus the individual benefits of social capital. Yet, what has remained constant in Putnam's writing about civic engagement and social capital is his absolute insistence that both are essential to the maintenance of American participatory democracy. Also, he clearly ascertains in his writings that, *inter alia*, most of the decline in civic engagement and social capital is due to such individual-level factors as too much television, occupational demands, and metropolitan sprawl. Lacking from the foregoing conceptualizations and discussions, indeed within the contexts of Putnam's works, is a serious discussion of how the contexts in which individuals live affect civic engagement and the production of social capital. Despite this focus on individual factors, there is ample evidence that contexts—especially within the ambiance of neighborhoods—go a long way to impact the manner and frequency of participation in social and political life.

Interestingly, other initial studies of context have shown how white racial attitudes and voting behavior have varied in accordance with the concentration of black populations (Bobo and Gilliam 1990; Carmines and Stimson 1989; Giles 1977; Key 1949; Walton 1985; Wright 1976). Subsequent research output has focused on the extent to which neighborhood context has had important political consequences as it influences partisan identification, satisfaction with neighborhood municipal services, political participation, and friendship networks (Huckfeldt 1986).

Also, contextual research has amply demonstrated that socially based activities like campaigning and petitioning, as opposed to individual actions like voting, are more likely to be affected by neighborhood context (Huckfeldt 1986). Additionally, other studies have demonstrated that neighborhood context is more important in explaining political participation than political orientations (Giles, Wright, and Dantico 1981), and still other studies have demonstrated the importance of context for public policy making (Carmines and Stimson 1989). Most importantly, there is a body of contextual research which effectively shows that social networks, coupled with voluntary and involuntary social interactions, serve as the mechanisms through which contextual effects impact political behavior (Huckfeldt 1986; Huckfeldt and Sprague 1987; 1995).

Until recently, contextual theories of political participation were limited by the empirical focus on middle- and working-class neighborhoods that are predominated by whites. Indeed, the current studies have focused on the effects of living in concentrated poverty neighborhoods. One line of research suggests that concentrated poverty neighborhoods have either very little impact on the civic engagement of poor residents (Berry, Portney, and Thompson 1991) or that the impact is positive, in that it compels citizens to work together in an effort to eradicate neighborhood problems (Crenson 1983).

A second body of research has shown that concentrated poverty neighborhoods have profoundly negative implications for educational attainment, organizational involvement, sociopolitical participation, and socioeconomic mobility (Alex-Assensoh 1993; Cohen and Dawson 1993; Wilson 1987). Most troubling about these research conclusions, however, is the finding that what separates today's inner-city communities from past disadvantaged neighborhoods is their limited connection with upwardly mobile individuals and mainstream institutions (Wilson 1987; Wilson and Wacquant 1989). Therefore, while current social capital research assumes that all citizens have an equal and unfettered opportunity to join civic associations and, thereby, benefit from social capital, there is mounting evidence on the undermining influences of inner-city environments which suggests that this is not the case (Wilson 1987; Wilson and Wacquant 1989).

With the foregoing stipulations in mind, this study further demonstrates that the neighborhood contexts in which black and white inner-city residents live affect their opportunities to join organizations, interact socially, and participate actively in as well as discuss politics. Consistent with several aspects of the previously delineated research literature, the impact of contextual influences is mixed. In some instances, it indeed undermines civic engagement; in other instances it facilitates it. The important thing, however, is that civic engagement and social capital are affected by more than just individual factors.

The Site of the Study

The data for this analysis come from a survey of black and white residents in Columbus, Ohio, a city noted for its strenuous efforts to engage citizens in local government decision making. Prior to 1983, civic associations were the major organizational vehicles that citizens utilized to influence local policy making. However, in the early 1980s, the number of civic organizations had grown to 300, making it virtually impossible for political officials to respond efficiently to citizens' needs and concerns. Consequently, the mayor's office established neighborhood area commissions, which were mandated in the Columbus city charter for the reorganization of the manner in which citizens of the city expressed their concerns to the mayor and the governing city council. Thus, citizens were given the organizational mechanism to effect policy changes through neighborhood area commissions, which served as facilitators of social activity as well.

The respondents selected for participation in the data survey came from four different neighborhoods in Columbus: they are Franklinton, a predominantly white, concentrated poverty neighborhood; South Linden, a predominantly black, concentrated poverty neighborhood; Hilltop, a predominantly white, low-poverty neighborhood; and North Central, a predominantly black, low-poverty neighborhood. All of these neighborhoods have active area commissions, although the commissions vary in age and the nature of its focus or activity.

Census tracts are utilized as proxies for neighborhood context. In the case of neighborhoods selected for this study, census boundaries generally conform with neighborhood boundaries set by the city of Columbus. Therefore, residents in each of the four neighborhoods were not merely assigned to a neighborhood context. Instead, their political orientations and behaviors were examined in light of perceived neighborhood boundaries.

The neighborhood-*cum*-census tracts earmarked for inclusion in the study were selected on the basis of three main criteria. The first criterion is that neighborhoods were selected on the basis of poverty rates, whereby concentrated poverty neighborhoods were characterized by poverty rates of 40 percent or more, while low-poverty neighborhoods were characterized by poverty rates of 20 percent. The second basis is that census tracts had to be contiguous, in keeping with the traditional notion of a neighborhood, while the third and final criterion is that census tracts had to be racially homogenous in order to ensure that racial differences would not confound the impact of contextual influence.

TABLE 9.1
Neighborhood and Citywide Statistics

Indicators	Citywide	Franklinton	Hilltop	South Linden	North Central
People below poverty	12%	49%	20%	49%	21%
People without high school degree	19	52	37	49	37
Percent black	23	16	4	91	90

As Table 9.1 shows, consistent with this chapter's theoretical underpinnings is the emphasis on the importance of context. Also, it has been necessary to demonstrate variations in terms of poverty level, educational attainment, and labor force participation among the four neighborhoods. Compared with 12 percent of citywide residents, who live below the poverty line, the poverty rates are alarming in the concentrated poverty neighborhoods of Franklinton and South Linden, where almost half of all neighborhood residents live below the poverty line. The poverty rates in the low-poverty neighborhoods of Hilltop and North Central are much lower (i.e., 20 percent) than those in concentrated poverty neighborhoods, but they are still considerably higher than the citywide average.

Additionally, while over 80 percent of Columbus residents, citywide, have earned high school diplomas or above, only about 50 percent of residents in the concentrated poverty neighborhoods reported having received high school diplomas. The disparities are even more alarming among residents with bachelor's degrees and above. Less than 5 percent of residents in concentrated poverty neighborhoods reported possessing a college degree, compared with almost 30 percent of the at-large Columbus residents.

Table 9.1 also provides some statistics on labor force participation. For example, unemployment among Columbus residents is relatively low. However, the unemployment rates among residents in concentrated poverty neighborhoods reveal that, compared with residents in low-poverty neighborhoods, such residents have serious problems in obtaining and keeping jobs that are commensurate with their skills. Finally, the statistics also illustrate the typically high levels of racial segregation in Columbus, whereby blacks and whites, respectively, live in neighborhoods predominated by members of their own race.

In using as a yardstick and, indeed, as a guide the recent literature on social capital, political participation, and the urban underclass (as spelled out in Table 9.2 below), it was both useful and necessary to select a total of seven variables, which include (i) electoral participation; (ii) nonelectoral participation; and (iii) political engagement. Some of the measures overlap with those used by Putnam and others in their discussion of social capital, while others are longstanding measures of political and civic involvement.

TABLE 9.2
Concepts and Operationalizations

Concepts	Operationalizations
Electoral Participation	Electoral registration, voting in local elections, voting in national elections.
Nonelectoral Participation	Working to solve community problems, contacting political officials, attending community meetings, discussing national and local politics.
Political Engagement	Interest in national politics, interest in local politics, political involvement of friends, discussion of politics in neighborhood at church.

Methodology

Analytically, it is part of the goal of this chapter to demonstrate how contexts affect the civic engagement of black and white citizens. Toward that end, it is necessary to control for individual factors like race and income that are normally associated with differences in civic engagement. Once these factors are controlled for, any differences in the political behavior of residents can be attributed to variations in the level of neighborhood poverty. Consequently, the first step in our analysis is to separate the poor residents from the nonpoor residents in all of the earmarked neighborhoods. Specifically, individuals who reported receiving less than $10,000 per year in income were characterized as being in the poor category, while individuals who received incomes above $10,000 were characterized as nonpoor. Thus, the individual impact of income/social status is controlled, while observing the impact of neighborhood context. Additionally, blacks who live in the predominantly white neighborhoods of Franklinton and Hilltop, as well as whites who live in the predominantly black neighborhoods of South Linden and North Central, were excluded from the analysis, basically to ensure that racial differences within neighborhoods did not interfere with the analytical goals of this study. Chi-square tests were utilized to assess the extent to which there were statistically significant differences in participation and attitudes in concentrated poverty and low-poverty neighborhoods.

Neighborhood Poverty and Civic Participation, in Black and White

Delineated in Tables 9.3–9.8 are the results of the bivariate analyses for electoral participation, involvement in community organizations, and

TABLE 9.3
*Electoral Activities among Blacks in Concentrated Poverty
and Low-Poverty Neighborhoods*

Responses	POOR BLACKS		NONPOOR BLACKS	
	Concentrated Poverty	Low Poverty	Concentrated Poverty	Low
Registered to vote				
Yes	85	94	88*	94
No	15	6	12	6
Voted in presidential election				
Hardly ever	22*	6	15*	9
Most of the time	78	94	85	91
Voted in local election				
Hardly ever	22*	7	16	13
Most of the time	78	93	84	87

SOURCE: 1991 Columbus Neighborhood Study Data Set.
*p ≤ .05.

TABLE 9.4
Electoral Activity among Whites in Concentrated and Low-Poverty Neighborhoods

Responses	POOR WHITES		NONPOOR WHITES	
	Concentrated Poverty	Low Poverty	Concentrated Poverty	Low
Registered to vote				
Yes	68	65	71	76
No	32	35	29	24
Voted in presidential election				
Hardly ever	31	23	30	25
Most of the time	69	77	70	75
Voted in local election				
Hardly ever	42	33	39**	30
Most of the time	58	67	61	70

SOURCE: 1991 Columbus Neighborhood Study Data Set.
**p ≤ .01

political communication. In terms of electoral participation, the majority of poor blacks—regardless of differences in neighborhood context—are registered to vote. However, there are significant differences in the electoral activities of blacks in concentrated poverty and low-poverty neighborhoods. As it became clear, blacks in low-poverty neighborhoods are considerably more likely to report that they voted in presidential and local elections than their counterparts in concentrated poverty neighborhoods.

Statistically, significant differences are evident in electoral activities of nonpoor blacks; a slightly higher percentage of residents in low-poverty neighborhoods are registered to vote. Also, nonpoor blacks in low-poverty neighborhoods are more likely to report that they voted in presidential elections than their counterparts in low-poverty neighborhoods. The differences in local electoral activity of nonpoor blacks are substantively small and statistically insignificant. Overall, these findings show that electoral participation, an important correlate of social capital, is greatly undermined by residence in concentrated poverty neighborhoods.

Among whites, the findings show similar levels of electoral registration and presidential voting across income levels and neighborhood contexts. Approximately 70 percent of all whites reported registering and voting in presidential elections. The major difference occurred among nonpoor whites in concentrated poverty and low-poverty neighborhoods, with whites in low-poverty neighborhoods more likely to report frequent participation in local elections than their counterparts in concentrated poverty neighborhoods.

Nonelectoral Civic Participation

While electoral participation is an important form of participation, citizens also impact the process of policy making by involving themselves in other forms of nonelectoral activity such as attending community meetings, working to solve community problems, and discussing political issues. Significant differences were evident across predominantly black neighborhood contexts, however, in attending community meetings. Poor blacks in concentrated poverty neighborhoods were more likely to report that they attended community meetings than their counterparts. Similarly, nonpoor blacks in concentrated poverty neighborhoods were more likely to attend community meetings.

A similar trend is evident among whites with respect to nonelectoral activity, whereby concentrated poverty tends to facilitate rather than undermine participation. Statistically significant differences among poor whites are noted in terms of contacting political officials. Compared with 15 percent of poor whites in low-poverty neighborhoods, 32 percent of poor whites in concentrated poverty neighborhoods reported contacting political officials in the last four years.

TABLE 9.5
Nonelectoral Activity among Blacks in Concentrated
Poverty and Low-Poverty Neighborhoods

Responses	POOR BLACKS		NONPOOR BLACKS	
	Concentrated Poverty Poverty	Low Poverty	Concentrated Poverty	Low Poverty
Worked to solve community problems				
Never	66	76	63	56
Once/more than once	34	24	37	44
Number of persons interviewed	178	178	492	492
Contacted political officials				
Never	85	85	77	70
Once/more than once	15	15	23	30
Number of persons interviewed	178	178	487	487
Attended community meetings				
Never	74*	90	68*	77
Once/more than once	26	10	32	23
Number of persons interviewed	177	177	490	490
Discussed local politics				
Never	49	47	35	32
Once/more than once	51	53	65	68
Number of persons interviewed	176	176	491	491
Discussed national politics				
Never	48	50	35*	28
Once/more than once	52	50	65	72
Number of persons interviewed	176	176	490	490

SOURCE: 1991 Columbus Neighborhood Study Data Set
*$p \leq .05$.

Additionally, whites in concentrated poverty neighborhoods were also more likely to report discussions of local and national politics.

Interest in and Discussion of Civic Affairs

Political interest and discussion of local and national politics are also important indicators of civic engagement and social capital. Among blacks, residence in concentrated poverty neighborhoods does not considerably affect interest in politics. Poor blacks in concentrated poverty neighborhoods and low-poverty neighborhoods report high levels of interest in local and national politics among people they know. However, a

TABLE 9.6
*Nonelectoral Activity among Whites in Concentrated Poverty and
Low-Poverty Neighborhoods*

Responses	POOR WHITES		NONPOOR WHITES	
	Concentrated Poverty Poverty	Low Poverty	Concentrated Poverty	Low
Worked to solve community problems				
Never	76	85	70	67
Once/more than once	24	15	30	33
Number of persons interviewed	133	133	482	482
Contacted political officials				
Never	68*	85	63*	72
Once/more than once	32	15	37	28
Number of persons interviewed	133	133	480	480
Attended community meetings				
Never	86	89	82	78
Once/more than once	14	11	18	22
Number of persons interviewed	129	129	475	475
Discussed local politics				
Never	60	67	50*	59
Once/more than once	40	33	50	41
Number of persons interviewed	132	132	481	481
Discussed national politics				
Never	49	52	64*	74
Once/more than once	51	48	36	26
Number of persons interviewed	132	132	480	480

SOURCE: 1991 Columbus Neighborhood Study Data Set.
*p ≤ .05.

substantively significant difference in discussions with neighbors indicates that poor blacks in concentrated poverty neighborhoods are significantly more likely to discuss politics with someone in the neighborhood than residents in low-poverty neighborhoods. In this instance, residence in a concentrated poverty neighborhood inspires and facilitates social capital.

Similar to blacks, political communication among whites does not appear to be impacted by residence in concentrated poverty neighborhoods. Most—or a majority of—poor whites, regardless of neighborhood context, reported that the people they know are interested in local and national politics. However, differences were evident among whites, with respect to discussions about politics. Poor whites in concentrated poverty

TABLE 9.7

*Political Communication among Blacks in Concentrated Poverty
and Low-Poverty Neighborhoods*

Responses	POOR BLACKS Concentrated Poverty Poverty	Low Poverty	NONPOOR BLACKS Concentrated Poverty	Low
People you know interested in national politics				
Interested	78	83	83	87
Not interested	22	17	17	13
Number of persons interviewed	153	153	460	460
People you know interested in local politics				
Interested	75	79	82	88
Not interested	25	21	18	12
Number of persons interviewed	156	156	463	463
Discuss politics with someone at church				
Yes	57	48	60	55
No	43	52	40	45
Number of persons interviewed	154	154	452	452
Discussed with someone in your neighborhood				
Yes	57*	37	58	56
No	43	63	42	44
Number of persons interviewed	155	155	454	454

SOURCE: 1991 Columbus Neighborhood Study Data Set
*p ≤ .05.

TABLE 9.8

*Political Communication among Whites in Concentrated Poverty
and Low-Poverty Neighborhoods*

Responses	POOR WHITES Concentrated Poverty Poverty	Low Poverty	NONPOOR WHITES Concentrated Poverty	Low
People you know interested in national politics				
Interested	64	79	63**	77
Not interested	36	21	37	23
Number of persons interviewed	109	109	447	447
People you know interested in local politics				
Interested	80	74	81*	88
Not interested	20	26	19	12
Number of persons interviewed	108	108	444	444
Discuss politics with someone at church				
Yes	28*	9	29	30
No	72	91	71	70
Number of persons interviewed	104	104	422	422
Discussed with someone in your neighborhood				
Yes	57*	38	55	51
No	43	62	45	49
Number of persons interviewed	104	104	422	422

SOURCE: 1991 Columbus Neighborhood Study Data Set
**p ≤ .01; *p ≤ .05.

neighborhoods were three times more likely to report that they discuss politics with someone at church than their counterparts in low-poverty neighborhoods. Also, compared with 57 percent of poor whites in concentrated poverty neighborhoods, 38 percent of poor whites in low-poverty neighborhoods reported talking to neighbors about politics.

Conclusion

Recent research on social capital has explained the decline of civic engagement and social capital primarily as a result of individual propensity and inclination. However, this research, which focused on the civic engagement and political participation among inner-city, black and white residents in Columbus, Ohio, has demonstrated that social capital and civic engagement are also impacted by the environments in which people live. In many instances, concentrated poverty neighborhoods inhibited civic engagement. For example, blacks and whites who lived in concentrated poverty neighborhoods were less likely to vote, discuss national politics, and express an interest in political affairs. Additionally, this study also showed that residence in concentrated poverty neighborhoods can facilitate social capital and civic engagement by spurring citizens to seek political redress for extant inequalities. Evidence in this sphere was found with respect to contacting political officials, attending community meetings, and discussing politics with neighborhood residents.

Theoretically, the foregoing findings suggest a need to integrate the variable role of context into any explanation of social capital and civic engagement. For it is only in doing so that social scientists can have a realistic understanding of wide-ranging factors that help in either facilitating or depressing social capital among all citizens in American democracy.

NOTE

Part of this essay was completed during Dr. Alex-Assensoh's nine-month Fulbright research and teaching assignment at the University of Zagreb, Croatia. Therefore, she wants to acknowledge the research/library resources she utilized at the institution.

216   YVETTE M. ALEX-ASSENSOH

REFERENCES

Alex-Assensoh, Yvette. 1993. *Neighborhoods, Family, and Political Behavior in Urban America*. New York: Garland.

Berry, Jeffrey, Kent Portney, and Ken Thomson. 1991. "The Political Behavior of Poor People," *The Urban Underclass*. Washington, D.C.: Brookings.

Bobo, Lawrence, and Franklin Gilliam. 1990. "Race, Socio-Economic Status, and Black Empowerment," *American Political Science Review* 84: 377–94.2.

Carmines, Edward, and James Stimson. 1989. *Issue Evolution: Race and the Transformation of American Politics*. Princeton: Princeton University Press.

Cohen, Cathy, and Michael Dawson. 1993. "Neighborhood Poverty and African American Politics," *American Political Science Review*. 87(2): 286–302.

Crenson, Matthew. 1983. *Neighborhood Politics*. Cambridge: Harvard University Press.

Giles, Michael. 1977. "Percent Black and Racial Hostility: An Old Assumption Reexamined," *Social Science Quarterly* 58: 412–17.

Giles, Michael, Gerald Wright, and Marilyn Dantico. 1981. "Social Status and Political Behavior: The Impact of Residential Context," *Social Science Quarterly* 62: 453–60.

Huckfeldt, Robert. 1986. *Politics in Context: Assimilation and Conflict in Urban Neighborhoods*. New York: Agathon.

Huckfeldt, Robert, and John Sprague. 1987. "Networks in Context: The Social Flow of Political Information," *American Political Science Review* 831: 1197–1216.

———. 1995. *Citizens, Politics, and Social Communication*. New York: Cambridge University Press.

Key, Vladimir O. 1949. *Southern Politics in State and Nation*. New York: Vintage Books.

Putnam, Robert. 1993. *Making Democracy Work*. Princeton: Princeton University Press.

———. 1996. "The Strange Disappearance of Civic America." *The American Prospect* (Winter), 35–49.

Schlozman, Kay Lehman, and John T. Tierney. 1986. *Organized Interests and American Democracy*. New York: Harper & Row.

Strate, John M., Charles J. Parrish, Charles D. Elder, and Coit Ford, III. 1989. "Life Span Civic Development and Voting Participation," *American Political Science Review* 83: 443–67.

Verba, Sidney, and Norman Nie. 1972. *Participation in America: Political Democracy and Social Equality*. New York: Harper & Row.

Verba, Sidney, and Norman Nie, Kay Lehman Schlozman, and Henry E. Brady. 1995. *Voice and Equality: Civic Voluntarism in American Politics*. Cambridge: Harvard University Press.

Walton, Hanes, Jr. 1985. *Invisible Politics*. Albany: SUNY Press.

Wilson, William J. 1987. *The Truly Disadvantaged*. Chicago: University of Chicago Press.

Wilson, William J., and Loic J. D. Wacquant. 1989. "The Cost of Racial and Class Exclusion in the Inner City," *The Annals* 501(22): 8–25.

Wright, Gerald. 1976. "Community Structure and Voting in the South," *Public Opinion Quarterly* 40: 200–15.

Chapter Ten

Building Social Capital on the Street
Leadership in Communities

Lane Crothers

As the other chapters in this volume make clear, Robert Putnam's *Bowling Alone* (2000) has shifted the apparent decline in social capital in the United States to a central position in discussions of contemporary politics. In large part as a result of his work, the relationships among social interaction, changed lifestyles, and the possibilities of democratic citizenship have become the topic of important and innovative research.

While the sources and meanings of a decline in social capital have drawn much attention, what, if anything, should be done about this decline has not received similar consideration. Put another way, Putnam expends a great deal of time and effort describing his assertion that the amount of social interaction among Americans has declined in recent decades (Putnam 2000, chapters 2–7). He also details the implications that this decline has for the amount of social trust and capacity for democratic self-governance in the United States (chapters 8, 17–21). And he focuses extensive attention on the factors that shape this decline in interaction and capacity (chapters 10–15). What he does not do—even, as will be discussed shortly, in the book's last two chapters grouped in a section entitled "What Is To Be Done?"—is actually lay out any means by which the apparent decline in social interaction can be reversed and its negative consequences overcome.

Putnam's failure to offer a positive program for addressing the decline in social capital in America is remarkable when one considers the significance he attributes to the concept and the promise offered in the section titled "What Is To Be Done?" It makes sense, for example, that if one despairs of a decline in a condition crucial to a nation's entire sociopolitical system that one would suggest a means of making things better. Unfortunately, the last two chapters of Putnam's book offer little in the way of positive suggestions for promoting social recapitalization. Chapter 23, "Lessons of History: The Gilded Age and the Progressive Era," is largely hortatory: it reminds readers that Americans suffered from low social capital in the latter years of the nineteenth century and holds the Progressive Movement up as an example of how combined social action can lead to a reinvigorated polity. (Interestingly, in recognizing the significance of the Progressives, Putnam still did not suggest that an actual movement or process of social recapitalization is necessary to overcome any contemporary malaise.) Chapter 24, "Toward an Agenda for Social Capitalists," lays out several core principles around which, Putnam argues, any campaign of social reinvigoration must be organized. Again, however, Putnam fails to imagine a process or strategy by which these principles might be realized in a meaningful campaign of social change. Despite the potential significance of such an effort, Putnam seems more concerned with describing the symptoms of a disease than promoting its treatment.

This chapter presents a model that can provide a foundation on which meaningful and effective programmatic responses to declining social capital can be built. Drawing on the literatures on leadership and community-oriented policing, this chapter argues that positive steps must be taken in order to achieve almost any social outcome, especially one as important as social recapitalization. Such action necessarily entails the intervention and action of leaders—people who can work to define and carry forward any agenda. However, imposing solutions for any decline of social capital from above is inherently flawed. Different communities—whether conceived of as contiguous geographic units or gatherings of like-minded individuals through social clubs or even the Internet—have varying needs and capacities for development. More, leaders who act in diverse communities to regenerate or reinvigorate social capital must be sensitive to the values, goals, and ideals of local populations if they are to act legitimately and serve as models of the kind of democratic action idealized in the concept of social capital. Finally, the concept of street-level leadership is articulated and explored as a means to understand the parameters of effective, pragmatic, and legitimate action for community change in local contexts.

The Centrality of Leadership in Politics

As Doig and Hargrove (1990) have noted, and Putnam manifests, the traditions of social science have tended to denigrate, or at least devalue, the roles that leaders play in political and social life. Focused, for example, on the influences that interest groups, bureaucratic routines, and external pressures place on public policy making, social scientists have tended to find that leaders are effective only at the margins of public life. As a consequence, there is some doubt about the roles that leaders may play in shaping policies in specific (Doig and Hargrove 1990).

Putnam's take on leadership in communities expresses this professional indifference. In chapter six, he reduces non-institutional social interaction to the behaviors of two groups of people. *Machers* are the elite of a given community: they are active in community service, follow community events, and participate in an array of formal events. (Who actually organizes these events is, interestingly, not discussed.) *Schmoozers*, by contrast, are less socially structured. Rather than participating in a large number of community events, such people are likely to engage in informal conversations with friends or participate in casual social events. Community life, Putnam seemingly argues, is constituted by the random actions of *machers* and *schmoozers* (Putnam 2000, chapter 6).

Yet in discussing neither group does Putnam acknowledge that in order to participate (or fail to participate) in structured events, someone has to organize the event in the first place. Indeed, even casual social interactions are almost never purely spontaneous: someone has to invite others to the backyard barbecue, someone has to buy food, someone has to organize utensils and bug-off spray. Put simply, in order to make social interaction possible, someone almost always acts as leader.

What is true for Putnam's focus on casual social interaction is equally true for his discussion of participation through formal organizations. Whether it is in voting (chapter 2), church attendance (chapter 4), workplace friendships (chapter 5), or any other kind of structured opportunity for social interaction, Putnam never discusses the role(s) leaders play in constructing the stage on which the interpersonal contact takes place. Such contexts are viewed as *a priori* and neutral—simply as places in which humans meet. The notion that prior effort and actions ground the nature, terms, and possibility of social interaction in these contexts seems to escape Putnam entirely.

Putnam's inattention to this point is unfortunate since, as Doig and Hargrove (1990) further note, there are exceptions to the pattern of professional skepticism to the significance of leaders in communities. In particular, there are at least two dimensions in which leadership can be anticipated to matter. The first lies in the arena of what has been called "situational leadership" (cf. Hersey and Blanchard 1988). Such leadership can have many components, and can perhaps best be illustrated by imagining a general outlining and then implementing a military campaign: in deciding when, how, and where to attack an enemy, a commanding general establishes the strategy and tactics that will shape the army's actions. Once in place such plans may, and almost inevitably will, change; but it can be seen that the leader's plans have shaped the all-around nature of the campaign. Analogously, political leaders can lobby fellow officials, develop popular support, and so on, in support for a particular action. Organizers of neighborhood watch associations similarly set the terms on which neighbors will meet. These leaders may or may not be fully successful, but their leadership can be seen to be situational in its relation to a specific goal.

A second area in which leaders can be expected to have significant influence is in defining the goals toward which the polity will or should aim. As Tucker (1981) has argued, the range of issues, topics, and concerns that might be part of the political system is much broader than the political system can handle. Much of what political leaders do, Tucker argues, is defining what can be and then actually becomes part of the political system. In presenting competing agendas and alternatives to citizens, leaders make politics real (Tucker 1981).

Leaders, then, are central to defining what groups and communities ought to do, and to influencing how chosen goals should be achieved. As Putnam's own example of the Progressive Movement suggests, it is naïve to believe that groups spontaneously form and sustain their actions over time in a leaderless fashion. While action may—or may not—begin spontaneously, leaders are almost always central to any political movement, including those promoting social change. Leaders—whether in government, organizations, or ordinary citizens—make choices and take actions to define and shape the opportunity for social participation. Accordingly, any work aimed at social reinvigoration must recognize and account for the roles leaders will play in this process.

Yet it is inadequate to say "let leaders lead" if one wants real social recapitalization. Democratic leadership must account for the varieties of needs, goals, and desires of the community if it is to be legitimate. Leaders might, after all, try to suppress political opponents in order to protect their positions of power, but this effort would not be democratic. In other words, the character of the leadership must promote and reinforce— "teach," in the language to be used below—the values of social engagement and trust on which the ideal of social capital rests. It is the task of the rest of this chapter to outline a model of leadership that builds on the dynamics of democratic politics to promote social recapitalization throughout the United States.

Building Communities: Lessons from Three Models of Policing

In order to ground a model of effective, legitimate social recapitalization, this chapter starts with a discussion of policing in America. At first glance, this may seem an odd place to begin: What, if anything, policing has to do with building a democratic community is not immediately clear. Yet the question of how and why police should do their jobs is, in some ways, a defining question of democracy. Police departments are, after all, the only agencies of government given legal sanction to detain, investigate, and even kill citizens. Police actions regularly straddle the line between society's demand for order and stability and citizens' fundamental rights. Police can be seen, then, to "teach" democracy by drawing explicit lines about appropriate behaviors and attitudes that are backed by extraordinary sanctions administered to citizens in direct, powerful ways. Accordingly, given the significance of policing in society, questions of what police ought to do and why they ought to do it have driven substantial research and commentary in the United States.

Social Capital and Patronage Policing

Historically, police, like most agents of government, were servants of political parties: patronage machines used the many positions available in police agencies as rewards for supporters. These patronage police then acted to enforce the party's control of the system by providing differential levels of service, protection, and enforcement for partisans and opponents of the party's leadership (Carte and Carte 1975; Monkkonen 1981; Walker 1977). Within the logic of the social capital and democratic education arguments developed in this chapter, "good" citizens were those who participated in and supported the party structure; "bad" citizens were those who either opposed the party or who, for various reasons, were deliberately excluded from the party organization.

As other government agencies professionalized, particularly after the creation of the civil service system in the 1880s and its expansion of scope during the New Deal, the model of patronage policing came under heavy attack. The practice of patronage policing ran counter to models of democracy that rested on values like universal rights and procedural equity: since laws are supposed to be applied to everyone equally, critics noted, and since the rights held by one American are held by every American, differential protection based on party or other affiliation was unconstitutional. Accordingly, in the post–World War II period a new model of policing was developed and implemented throughout much of the United States. Intended to balance concerns of procedural fairness and the geographic spread of the suburbs, this was the professional model of policing (Deakin 1988; Jordan 1972; Vila and Morris 1999).

Social Capital and Professional Policing

In the professional model, police generally are not expected to know the individuals with whom they are interacting. Instead, they are organized on a military strike force principle: problems arise, police are summoned (often from substantial distances, necessitating the use of cars as primary tools of policing), and then the police intervene to resolve the issue using a range of techniques from negotiation through arrest and finally force. Importantly, the anonymity of the police-citizen relationship is in part supposed to ensure that citizens are treated in full respect of their rights: police are trained to protect citizens' rights through departmentally and legally sanctioned procedures; police follow these rules in their interactions with anonymous citizens and so are likely to protect individual rights.

As far as it went, the professional model was a remarkable transition from patronage policing. The worst abuses of the political-police link were curbed, and increased attention to training and procedures promoted the formal protection of citizen rights. Further, as a pragmatic tool, the professional model provided a means to police suburban and rural communities encompassing large geographic areas and reflecting relative social, economic, and political homogeneity.

The model was not flawless, however. That it was only imperfectly implemented is an obvious point, and the many legal challenges to police procedure that have filled American courts in the last fifty years are testimony to the difficulties inherent in trying to establish real procedural fairness in complex social, legal, and political systems. A more important critique for the purposes of this chapter, however, is the version of democratic citizenship and social engagement it teaches its recipients. In the professional model, citizens are passive participants in government. External powers far beyond the boundaries of local communities set rules that unknown but powerful agents enforce by various means, including violence. Importantly, these policies may or may not take account of the particular needs of local communities: a department mandate may require a crackdown on speeding, for example, while a neighborhood is struggling with growth in the drug trade. In addition, the model does not admit a role for citizens in establishing order and stability in their own neighborhoods. Police serve as rule makers and rule enforcers; citizens play no part in making their communities strong and healthy. In the language of social capital, citizens are actively dissuaded from social and political action, and the police are organized to reinforce this message. The professional model is, then, ultimately a model of social decapitalization, not invigoration.

Indeed, by the 1970s and 1980s many analysts of policing in America came to see the structural disinvolvement of citizens in governing their own communities associated with the professional model as a cause of increasing crime rates, lack of social cooperation, and generalized patterns of community decay (Austin 1992; Kelling 1988). The professional model, according to this diagnosis, led citizens to avoid contact with police—police officers were often seen as rude, untrustworthy, out of the loop, and, perhaps most importantly, gone: once they handled a specific problem, officers left—leaving the root causes of crime, and often the neighborhood's worst criminal offenders, behind. On the reverse side of this relationship, police tended to view members of a given community as unreliable and untrustworthy. Put simply, citizens were unwilling to cooperate with police since once the officers left, the "bad guys" would still be in charge of the neighborhood. Likewise, police understood everything members of the community said to be lies and attempts to cover up crimes. Taken together, citizens were disempowered even as police proved structurally incapable of dealing with the complex problems of diverse communities.

Social Capital and Community-Oriented Policing

In response to such problems, a newer approach to police organization and philosophy of action emerged in the 1980s: community-oriented policing. Grounded on the idea that citizens should participate in shaping and implementing the policing they experience, community-oriented police strategies include forming neighborhood groups to assess community needs, creating different programs to address problems and issues in varying districts, and promoting police-citizen interaction through walking-the-beat, bicycle- or horse-borne officers, and establishing local stations throughout various communities. For example, while many neighborhoods suffer from the drug trade, different communities have variable levels of capacity to work against this problem: one district may be filled with younger families with many adults willing to volunteer in neighborhood watch programs, while another may be inhabited largely by elderly people who desire a more active police role in managing drug crimes. Community-oriented police programs work with residents to identify needs, shape policies that recognize the capacities of the neighborhood, and implement strategies that link needs, goals, and abilities in a localized context. Cumulatively, such programs are expected to both empower citizens and ensure that officers know the needs and problems inherent in different neighborhoods (Austin 1992; Friedmann 1992; Kelling 1988; Sparrow, Moore, and Kennedy 1990).

Contrasted with the professional model, community-oriented policing is an approach grounded in promoting and developing social capital. Citizens are viewed as active participants in governance. Their needs and abilities are central to the process. Through community-oriented policing, people are taught they are valuable members of the democratic system.

Discretion, Conflict, and the Problem of Legitimacy in Public Life

As outlined here, then, community-oriented policing might seem a perfect template for the development of programs aimed at expanding social capital in the United States. Be sensitive to neighborhood needs; design programs in light of citizen capacities; build agencies that link such schemes to worker training and evaluation—and social capital ensues. Indeed, as a first step in understanding how social capital might be reinvigorated in American communities, the model of community-oriented policing provides useful guidance. Rather than imposing top-down solutions through administrative sanctions and uniformity, a more participatory model is to be preferred. Unless citizens are engaged, social capital cannot be taught.

This is at best a first step, however, for as outlined above the model of community-oriented policing has yet to address two structural conditions that shape political life and problematize any campaign for social recapitalization. The first of these is conflict about means and ends of various programs and actions. The second is the discretion that many workers and leaders enjoy in translating program principles into empirical practice.

The idea that programs framed as community-oriented policing policies will inevitably lead to social recapitalization begins to break down in two types of conflicts about what to do: first, when a community has deep internal conflicts about what ought to be done; and second, when a neighborhood's preferences run counter to the laws and norms of the broader society. For example, if police-sponsored neighborhood meetings identify competitive priorities for police service, or stimulate divisions about the participation of the district in the development of programs, police agencies (or any group engaged in social reconstruction) have to make choices about what to do and why. Given that community-oriented policing programs are justified in terms of community needs and demands, such conflicts problematize the legitimacy of the chosen alternative: no matter what is done, someone or some group is likely to feel disempowered, left out, or even angry and bitter—in short, to be taught that their participation is not valued. Mediation and other types of programs may ameliorate these tensions, but it is nonetheless often the case that the actual implementation of programs will leave some citizens' preferences unsatisfied. Accordingly, there is always a potential to promote social decapitalization in conditions of conflict.

Alternatively, it may be that a neighborhood's norms, preferences, and values run substantially counter to the goals and ideals of the broader community. One example would be areas in which area residents substantially support organized crime groups. Neighborhood preferences, then, might urge police to establish policies that ignore types of crimes that are considered serious elsewhere, and indeed that challenge the legal mandates on which police functions rest. Little in the logic of community-oriented policing provides a means by which policies that challenge neighborhood preferences might be legitimated.

The problem of conflict within and among neighborhoods is exacerbated when one considers the level of discretion that some individuals and leaders have as they do their jobs. For example, even if the agent in question is a low-ranking bureaucrat working in a government agency, it is nonetheless inevitably the case that regardless of the care, attention, and effort put into the process of designing rules and procedures to encompass the work that such people do, that they will sometimes have the opportunity—and need—to exercise discretion. When dealing with leaders, whether in an organization or as a private citizen, discretion is likely to be even greater given the absence of formal institutional rules limiting their choices.

Consider the following example:[1] At 2:30 A.M., a police officer on patrol stops a vehicle for speeding and weaving on the road. He says it is his intent to examine the driver for a driving under the influence violation. On approaching the car, he sees it is fully loaded with several males and one female who appears to be much younger than the other passengers in the car. He asks everyone to exit the vehicle, examines the driver for DWI/DUI (finding no violation has occurred), and then questions the female passenger about her age, whether her parents knew she was out, and how well she knew the other passengers. Discovering that she was several years younger than the other passengers, that her parents did not know she was out so late, and that she had just moved to the area and did not know the other passengers very well, he decides to release the other passengers but to drive the female to her home. Once there, he questions a family member about how the girl was likely to be treated once her parents came home (her parents were out at the time). On being told that the girl would be punished but not abused, he releases the female into her sister's custody and returns to his patrol.

Clearly, discretion was exercised in this case. The law allowed the officer to stop a vehicle for speeding and weaving in a lane, but did not require it. It is not a crime to ride around in a car late at night, and the area where this incident was observed did not have a curfew requirement for young people. Thus, the decision to remove the female from the car and drive her home was a discretionary one. Finally, the officer was under no legal obligation to check on the family's disciplinary routines once he had delivered the female to her house. At each stage, discretion was at the center of the officer's actions.

Moreover, this officer exercised two types of discretion: outcome and process. Outcome discretion refers to the worker's ability or power to

28 LANE CROTHERS

choose what the end point of an intervention should be. In the example
just cited, the officer exercised outcome discretion by deciding to take the
female home while releasing the other passengers. Process discretion refers
to the worker's ability or power to decide what means to use to achieve a
given goal: interviewing the girl's older sister about their parents' punishment styles constitutes process discretion.

Importantly, even in a case like this, in which a patrol officer is working
for a formal bureaucratic agency that is heavily rule-bound, there is little
that any agency can—and should—do to limit discretion. As Lipsky
(1980) explains, some bureaucratic agents inevitably enjoy substantial discretion in the daily performance of their jobs. This occurs for several reasons. First, some circumstances are immensely complicated. Discretion is
required to apply rules in specific cases: "street-level bureaucrats often
work in situations too complicated to reduce to programmatic formats"
(Lipsky 1980, 15). Second, situations require bureaucratic agents to make
judgment actions: "street level bureaucrats work in situations that often
require responses to the human dimensions of situations" (15). Third,
"street-level discretion promotes workers' self-regard and encourages
clients to believe that workers hold the key to their well-being." Thus, the
practice of discretion is reinforced (15). Finally, many workers do their
jobs outside supervisory control (Lipsky 1980). Discretion, then, is inevitable in certain contexts, and is unlikely to simply "go away."

It is noteworthy that the officer himself was well aware of the discretion
he was exercising. He admitted that he was unsure of what to do since the
passengers and driver had committed no crime—yet he expressed the
opinion that were he the female's parent, "I'd want her brought home."
Further, he directly stated that he needed to balance the desire to inform
the girl's parents of her activities with his commitments to patrol his zone:
had it not been a "slow" night, he said, he probably would not have decided
to return the girl to her home. Finally, he indicated that he would leave the
female at home only if an adult were present and he was satisfied that she
would not be harmed. Each of these decisions was discretionary, and in
Lipsky's terms, were ungovernable by administrative rules and policies.

It is also important to note that the officer exercised his discretion in
conditions of conflict—over values, goals, duties and preferences. The officer engaged in a debate with himself about what his obligations were on
multiple fronts—to himself, his organization, his community, the girl's
parents, and so on. The female herself certainly did not want to go home
and face punishment; indeed, it was her claim that she might be abused

that led the officer to question the adult in the home about the punishment styles of the girl's parents. His actions, then, were not based on a sense that a consensus of opinions required him to make the choices he did. Instead, they embodied discretionary choices in a contested context.

Accordingly, it is not sufficient to build a model of social recapitalization that assumes unanimity of interests, goals, and values, or that popularly held ideas in one area are inevitably the proper foundation for promoting political regeneration. There may be a vast variety of choices available to leaders, especially those not bound by institutional roles and rules. Moreover, discretionary choices in specific contexts will often be made in conditions of conflict and disagreement over both means and ends. To properly understand what will be necessary for the effective creation of social capital, then, it is important to address how the legitimacy of specific policies, programs, and actions can be established in real world circumstances.

Leadership, Conflict, and Discretion on the Street

This chapter argues that leadership provides the conceptual frame through which the twin issues of discretion and legitimacy can be integrated effectively and then mated to a real process of social recapitalization. Leadership theory directly embodies dimensions of values, goals, and means. These concepts can be seen to be central to the legitimate, discretionary implementation of public policy. In integrating the concept of leadership to discretionary action, a model of legitimate, democratic discretion can be developed. In fact, two models of leadership, transactional/situational leadership and transformational leadership, are held to be particularly useful for the analysis and evaluation of legitimate discretionary action.

James MacGregor Burns, in his seminal text *Leadership* (1978), uses two models of leadership—transactional and transformational—to frame the interaction of discretion, conflict, and democratic citizenship. For Burns, values are central to leadership. Thus, in conditions of conflict and discretion, it is values that provide the means by which the legitimacy of leadership acts in a democratic context can be distinguished from totalitarianism or corruption. For example, Burns insists that authoritarian rulers are not leaders at all: instead, they are power-wielders. This means that while their acts *may* correspond with the preferences and values of the citizens they govern, this correspondence is coincidental, not deliberate. Ultimately, authoritarian leaders serve their own interests, and if this happens to serve the goals of the broader community, so much the better. It is not a requirement of authoritarian rule, however. By contrast, democratic leadership must serve the interests of the community as a whole. Leaders are leaders precisely because they derive their legitimacy from the root ideals, goals, and values that shape particular communities.

Importantly, Burns shows that it is possible to develop values-based models of legitimacy even in conditions of conflict within a community about what ought to be done. He does this by building two types of models of legitimate democratic leadership—one in which there is little conflict about social goals, and one in which there is substantial conflict: transactional leadership and transformational leadership. Transactional leadership is a process-oriented model of leader action and legitimacy. It occurs, Burns argues, when community goals and preferences are relatively clear. While there may be disagreements about how to achieve certain goals, the ends themselves are relatively shared. Accordingly, leaders should serve as transactional figures: they balance competing interests, link goals and means, and provide the conduits through which community ends can be realized. Indeed, it would be inappropriate for the leader to do more. It is only in helping the group achieve its goals that the transactional leader's legitimacy is established (Burns 1978).

Transactional leadership is similar to concepts of situational leadership, as expressed in Table 10.1 below. The model developed in this table was grounded in Hersey and Blanchard's 1988 work on situational leadership. Similar to Burns' model, the Hersey and Blanchard model derives the legitimacy of leader actions from the goals and values inherent to the group being led. In particular, Hersey and Blanchard argue that leaders should provide only enough direction to help the group achieve its goals. Any more effort on the leader's part, even if it is effective, is not seen as legitimate.

By contrast, transformational leaders are individuals who act to change the established order of things; who try to shift the purposes and ends of the organizations, groups, or communities they lead to some other set of goals and values. They can use power, rhetoric, moral suasion, or any other appropriate technique to move the community in a new direction. Importantly, while the exercise of power may be a component of changing a group's course, that use of power is legitimated by the underlying goals, values, and desires *inherent to the group, organization, or community itself.* Thus, even though transformational leaders are making discretionary choices in the context of conflict, they choose goals that, while latent, are nonetheless native to the community under treatment. In contrast with power-wielders, who impose their will on the group independent of its values, transformational leaders are legitimate because they help the community, group, or organization achieve ends it desired but was not able to achieve without the leader's assistance (Burns 1978). They then act within means and practices that are appropriate with democratic politics.

Model of Street-Level Leadership

The outlines of the concepts of transactional/situational and transformational leadership given above suggest two basic principles through which discretionary action can be evaluated. First, as a practical matter, those who enjoy broad discretion to carry out their tasks act, in effect, as situational (transactional) or transformational leaders, or both. Second, the actions such people take can and ought to be legitimated (or challenged) in terms of models of leadership. It is to this end that the model of street-level leadership was developed. (The model's relevance to the question of social recapitalization will be addressed after the model is described.)

The model of street-level leadership discussed here is presented in Table 10.1 below. Developed in over 1,500 hours of observational research with patrol officers in the Huntsville, Alabama, Police Department, the Spokane County, Washington, Sheriff's Department, the Phoenix, Arizona, Department of Economic Security, and the McLean County, Illinois, Department of Children and Family Services, the model arrays specific leadership models on the two dimensions of discretion discussed above: process discretion and outcome discretion.

TABLE 10.1
Street-Level Leadership

OUTCOME DISCRETION	
Substantial Discretion	
(3)	(4)
Transformational Leadership	*Transformational and Situational Leadership*
Discretion over results but not process	Discretion over process and results
(1)	(2)
Administrative Procedure	*Situational Leadership*
Little discretion	Discretion over process but not results
Minimal Discretion	Substantial Discretion

PROCESS DISCRETION

Quadrant one describes conditions in which very little, if any, discretion—and thus opportunity for leadership—is exercised. There is consensus about what ought to be done and about the appropriate steps to be taken to achieve the expected goal. Accordingly, this is not a particularly relevant category for this chapter, and so draws no more discussion here.

Not all situations can be reduced to such programmed responses, however. Quadrant two, for example, describes cases in which individuals enjoy some discretion over how to resolve a situation, but the specific goal they are to attain is relatively clear. Such situations might occur when a police officer is serving a warrant or when a social welfare worker has to visit a family to do a follow-up report on a complaint. The worker's outcome discretion is proscribed; however, the person typically has choices over how to achieve the goal. Thus, a police officer might use force to quell a suspect who is resisting a court's order, or might simply serve the warrant if the subject is relatively compliant.

Importantly, the legitimacy of the worker's discretion can be established (or challenged) in terms similar to those suggested by the concepts of transactional or situational leadership. For example, however *effective* the use of force might be if a suspect is compliant, the use of force against a nonresisting person can be seen as illegitimate since it is unnecessary. The legitimacy of the officer's actions (or challenges to such legitimacy) is derived from the means they use to achieve relatively agreed-upon ends. Quadrant three draws attention to circumstances in which agents have discretion over what outcome ought to be achieved, but little discretion over the process by which the goal is to be achieved once it has been chosen. Social welfare workers, for example, exercise this type of discretion when they decide to remove a child from a home after an allegation of abuse. They are legally required to remove children if they find conditions to meet established standards—but it is up to them to determine whether the criteria have been met. Once this outcome decision has been made, however, their discretion becomes circumscribed: typically, workers are required to fill out numerous forms, transport the child to a care facility, and take other steps once they have decided certain criteria for removal have been met.

As was the case in the discussion of quadrant two, quadrant three suggests criteria through which such a controversial decision as removing a child from a home can be legitimated (or challenged). Essentially, the removal decision would be legitimate *assuming that the underlying values, norms, and ideals which inform the decision are themselves inherent to the group, community, or society being led.* That is, while the parents of the child being removed may not desire the outcome, if larger social goals of order and safety can be seen to supercede the individual's desires, then the decision can be seen as legitimate. In contrast, if the decision to remove is not made based on larger and broadly shared social values, but instead on ones like race hatred or personal enmity, that decision can be seen as illegitimate. As in the concept of transformational leadership, it is the relationship between individual actions and the values of the broader community that can legitimate specific choices.

Finally, quadrant four describes situations in which individuals must make discretionary choices about both the goals to be achieved and the means chosen to reach them. Police officers deciding what level of force to use in breaking up a fight, and then whether to arrest its participants, operate in this quadrant. So do social welfare workers who are called to a scene of apparent child abuse to make a determination of whether or not a child should be removed from a home and then whether or not such a removal, if desired, should be handled immediately or would require court action. Importantly, both decisions—the one to remove a child and the means by which to effect the removal—can be explained and evaluated through reference to models of transformational and situational leadership. The decision to remove the child (or not) can be defended or criticized through reference to social, organizational or moral standards, and the means by which a removal (if chosen) is effected can be interpreted through a model of situational leadership. The legitimacy of both the goals and the means can be considered within the model of street-level leadership.

Leadership and Building Social Capital on the Street

The model of street-level leadership contains several core ideas that must be acknowledged if any project of social recapitalization is to be undertaken. In particular, it emphasizes the realities of discretion, conflict, and legitimacy in public action. Moreover, it places individuals—whether public bureaucratic workers, as discussed in the model, or people taking steps to reinvigorate communities, as implied in Putnam's work—in the center of the matrix: individuals will make choices about what needs to be done, why this is the case, and how it ought to be done; and individuals will need to take steps to ensure the legitimacy of their discretionary choices, often in conditions of conflict. Additionally, the concept embodies models of leadership that contain standards by which the legitimacy of individual choices can be established even if there is conflict over means, or ends, or both. Accordingly, the model provides a useful frame through which we can imagine ways to rebuild social capital in the United States—ways that are empirical, pragmatic, and not, *contra* Putnam, largely hortatory.

While not every dimension of the street-level leadership model applies to the process of social recapitalization, eventually leaders and followers will need to take concrete steps in real world conditions to actually impact social life. It is likely that such actions will be taken in multiple conditions ranging from substantial agreement about means and ends through profound disagreements about what to do and how to do it. More, the process by which goals are defined and programs are implemented will inevitably "teach" citizens whether their participation is actively sought (as in the model of community-oriented policing) or opposed (as in the professional model of policing). Actions aimed at social regeneration in such circumstances will require democratic legitimation.

This section lays out several principles around which effective values- and capacities-based programs for social recapitalization can be built. Rather than prescribing a one-size-fits-all model of the ideal community, this section builds on the insights that conflict about what and why things ought to be done will vary, that leaders will have to make discretionary choices about what to do and how to do it, that these choices will need to teach the value of democratic participation, and that diverse communities will have different needs and varying levels of capabilities for achieving their goals. Accordingly, real social recapitalization will need to be built from the street up, not imposed from the penthouse down.

1. *Leaders, whether holding formal positions in organizations or individuals serving as organizers, facilitators, or visionaries in extra-institutional settings, are central to any project of social recapitalization.* In contrast with Putnam's neglect of the factors that shape the contexts in which human interaction occurs, leaders are crucial to the process of initiating and maintaining social discourse. Someone has to conceive of the possibility that a given moment can support effective participation and citizenship, and the interactions of the individuals present in the specific relationship must be facilitated in ways that promote the values of democratic citizenship and social trust on which the concept of social capital rests. It is not adequate to hope, as Putnam seems to, that people will again interact in multiple spheres of life. The contexts and mechanisms of interaction

must be constructed and maintained. Leaders are at the heart of this process.

2. *Leaders must recognize whether the community, however conceived, is in a transactional or a transformational context regarding social recapitalization.* It may be that a given community has a general consensus about what it wants or needs. Alternatively, the community may be conflicted about what needs to be done, or its preferences may run counter to the legal and moral standards of the broader society. In conditions of consensus, transactional leadership will be the key to achieving specific program goals *and* to effectively teaching democratic citizenship. Alternatively, if conflict within or among groups and communities is present, resolutions to this disagreement must come through the explicit and open discussion of values, including an explanation of why some choices were made instead of others. This does not mean that decisions cannot be made without consensus; rather, it is a reminder that if we are going to try to teach democratic citizenship, we have a responsibility to explain to people why their preferences have been rejected in favor of others.

3. *Recognize the significance of community norms and values in shaping programs that are effective and legitimate.* Community ideals must be admitted to the debate if the programs and policies that are developed for social recapitalization are to be legitimate. It may be, of course, that specific groups and communities have such problems that new solutions must be imposed from the outside, but this imposition must be legitimated in terms that are meaningful in a broader context. Unless programs are grounded in these kinds of values, they run the risk of teaching the same lesson of citizenship that the professional model of policing taught: nonparticipation and hostility. By building on community values and goals, programs can model the kind of democratic citizenship that the concept of social capital embodies.

4. *Don't miss the trees for the forest.* In many ways, Putnam's *Bowling Alone* is a macro-level analysis of decline. Yet, as the experience of community-oriented policing demonstrates, there are meaningful resources "on the street" that can serve as a resource for political redevelopment. Some communities may have large numbers of committed individuals who can serve as program resources, while others may have only a few experienced community volunteers; some groups may have traditions of regular interaction, while others may lack such histories. Actions aimed at resolving macro-level problems may fall flat if they fail to account for the different needs, contexts, and capacities various communities hold.

5. *Train leaders of community programs to be aware of the interplay of values, goals, and interests as they do their work.* The people who actually enter communities to try to promote social recapitalization need to do so with an awareness of the values, norms, and conflicts that shape their work. Rather than blindly following pre-established routines, then, such leaders need to engage in a process of constant reevaluation, critique, and grounding. Legitimacy is a key to teaching democracy; sensitivity to the terms by which the legitimacy of specific programs can be established is a requirement of effective community service.

Conclusion

The question of social capital is an important one. Building a community of engaged, capable citizens is a crucial component of the democratic project. Robert Putnam is to be commended for drawing our attention to these issues in a new and dramatic way. Now it is time to move to a new plane, and make democracy real where people actually live: in their homes, their communities, and on the street.

Note

1. This case was observed by the author while doing research for a separate project. It, and the findings this research reported, were published in: Vinzant and Crothers (1998). See also, for discussion of the street-level leadership model, Crothers and Vinzant (1996), and Vinzant and Crothers (1996; 1995; 1994). The analysis that follows in this chapter is drawn from this body of work, and due credit must be offered to Janet Vinzant of Arizona State University for her contributions.

References

Austin, David. 1992. "Community Policing: The Critical Partnership." *Public Management* 74: 3–9.
Burns, James M. 1978. *Leadership.* New York: Harper & Row.
Carte, Gene, and Elaine Carte. 1975. *Police Reform in the United States: The Era of August Vollmer, 1905–1932.* Berkeley: University of California Press.
Crothers, Lane, and Janet Vinzant. 1996. "Cops and Community: Street Level

Leadership in Community Based Policing." *International Journal of Public Administration* 19 (7): 1167–91.

Deakin, Thomas. 1988. *Police Professionalism: The Renaissance of American Law Enforcement*. Springfield, Ill.: C. C. Thomas.

Doig, Jameson, and Erwin C. Hargrove. 1990. *Leadership and Innovation*. Abr. ed. Baltimore: Johns Hopkins University Press.

Friedmann, Robert. 1992. *Community Policing: Comparative Perspectives and Prospects*. New York: St. Martin's.

Hersey, Paul, and Kenneth Blanchard. 1988. *Management of Organizational Behavior*. Englewood Cliffs, N.J.: Prentice-Hall.

Jordan, Kevin. 1972. *Ideology and the Coming of Professionalism*. Unpublished thesis, Rutgers University.

Kelling, George. 1988. "Police and Communities: The Quiet Revolution." *Perspectives on Policing* 1 (June).

Lipsky, Michael. 1980. *Street Level Bureaucracy: Dilemmas of the Individual in Public Service*. New York: Russell Sage.

Monkkenen, Eric H. 1981. *Police in Urban America, 1860–1290*. Cambridge: Cambridge University Press.

Putnam, Robert. 2000. *Bowling Alone: The Collapse and Revival of American Community*. New York: Simon & Schuster.

Sparrow, Malcolm, Mark Moore, and David Kennedy. 1990. *Beyond 911: A New Era for Policing*. New York: Basic Books.

Tucker, Robert C. 1981. *Politics as Leadership*. Columbia: University of Missouri Press.

Vila, Bryan, and Cynthia Morris, eds. 1999. *The Role of Police in American Society*. Westport, Conn.: Greenwood.

Vinzant, Janet, and Lane Crothers. 1998. *Street Level Leadership: Discretion and Legitimacy in Front Line Public Service*. Washington, D.C.: Georgetown University Press.

———. 1996. "Street Level Leadership: Rethinking the Role of Public Servants in Contemporary Governance." *The American Review of Public Administration* 26(4): 457–76.

———. 1995. "A Model of Street Level Leadership." In *Leadership and Ethics*. Washington, D.C.: American Society for Public Administration.

———. 1994. "Street Level Leadership: The Role of Patrol Officers in Community Policing." *Criminal Justice Review* 19(2): 189–211.

Walker, Samuel. 1977. *A Critical History of Police Reform*. Lexington, Mass.: Lexington Books.

Chapter Eleven

Social Rights or Social Capital?
The Labor Movement and the Language of Capital

Michael Forman

As I sit to write this, I am getting ready for yet another social event at Local 23. It will be a gathering of dockers, Steelworkers, Teamsters, and "tree-huggers" at the hall of the International Longshore and Warehouse Workers Union (ILWU) in Tacoma, Washington. These groups first met each other in the Puget Sound area in 1999, as they prepared to greet the World Trade Organization (WTO) that November. The early meetings were straight business: human rights and environmental activists, union bureaucrats, some rank-and-file members, and a smattering of leftist professors attended to search for a common language and strategy. The discussion was about bringing various groups together so the voices of the excluded would be heard over the loud murmur of finance ministers and representatives of international capital. Some of those present early on, mostly environmental activists and a handful of the more militant longshore rank and filers, boasted they would "shut down the WTO"; hardly anyone took them seriously. Today, everyone knows they did. Tonight's fundraiser for Jobs with Justice was made possible by the relationships that emerged from of those discussions and the solidarity that grew out of chanting through pepper gas on the streets of Seattle.

The rallies and marches of the week of November 30, 1999 (N30), the civil disobedience and the uncivil window breaking, the police violence and the abrogation of democratic rights that made up "the Battle in Seattle" together revealed common interests and interpretations and strengthened links among activists from new and old social movements. Whereas the cameras of local television mostly covered the events from behind the police lines, while the television screens mostly repeated footage of a handful of masked people breaking windows at a Starbucks, something unheard of in decades was happening in Seattle. Indeed, for the first time in recent memory, the mainstream of the U.S. labor movement had taken to the streets alongside environmentalist, human rights, and feminist activists. The oldest of social movements appeared ready to join with the newest. Ever since, "Turtles and Teamsters" have protested and partied together—often inviting the troubadours (people like "Desert Rat" and Anne Finney) they met amid the chemical clouds and pepper spray on the streets of Seattle. The event I will attend tonight is one of those gatherings, a concert and a party, a common person's fundraiser with beer, barbecue, and song.

The question, for this essay, is whether "social capital" is an adequate tool for the construction of a theoretical account of these developments—an account that also has a practical intent that makes it available to the labor movement. An adequate account of the potential new role of labor in politics must locate its object within the larger social and historical context while revealing its distinctiveness. From the point of view of labor and politics, this larger context, or, if you will, conjuncture, is characterized by that cluster of phenomena usually referred to as globalization. These include the ideological triumph of neo-liberalism, the emergence of "network society" (Castells 1997), and the ascent of the new or restructured transnational institutions and regimes (e.g., the WTO) which serve as conduits for the exercise of international system-integrating power. Related to these phenomena are the nearly complete abandonment by the traditional reformist left (European Social Democrats, Labourites, and Socialists, not to mention U.S. Democrats) of their labor constituency and social welfare programs in favor of a "third way" (see Howell 2000; Mair 2000; Petras 2000; and, of course, Giddens 1998). Finally, the restructuring of industrial processes into extended chains of production along with measures such as the increasing casualization of labor forces and the deployment of techniques of lean production and management by stress have materially affected the immediate context in which labor movement activity occurs (Moody 1997). The question, then, is whether social capital provides an adequate account of the conflicts of interests, power, and values the labor movement must face in capitalist democracies at the dawn of the twenty-first century. Does it contribute to an explanation and interpretation of contemporary politics which will further the course of democracy and, one hopes, human emancipation?

While, on the surface, it may appear inappropriate to apply such an obviously normative standard to a social scientific category, there are two good reasons to do so. One is that social action is best understood as "the combined result of reactive compulsions and meaningful interactions" (Habermas 1989, 88). Social theory, if it is not to act simply as legitimator of the status quo, must take the standpoint of freedom to grasp human interactions not only as products of causal chains, but also as processes where people interpret their own actions and choose among alternatives. But it is not only the standards of critical theory that call for subjecting social capital to normative criteria. More immediately, a normative criterion is appropriate because Robert Putnam, one of the main proponents of the social capital approach, has *consistently and rightly* taken up this category in normative terms. Putnam has embraced the notion of social capital both as (1) a tool to explain the generally acknowledged decline in political participation and civic orientation that has afflicted the United States for some time now, and (2) a programmatic item to guide action aimed at the revitalization of democracy. Social capital would not only help to account for the quandary in which we find ourselves, it would also name the key resources for its solution. As Putnam puts it in the concluding chapter of *Bowling Alone*, "[t]he challenge for us . . . is not to grieve over social change, but to guide it" (2000, 402). If we take his conclusion seriously, as it deserves to be taken, we must consider not only whether social capital is effective in disclosing causes and consequences, but also whether it is suitable as a theoretical category of action oriented toward human emancipation. An examination of the category from the standpoint of labor will validate some of the concerns that inform the social capital approach and disclose the deeply ideological sources of its limitations.

Social Capital and Labor

As other essays in this volume detail, the notion of social capital has a long history. Here my focus is primarily on the concept in Putnam's extensive work with it, and especially on its usefulness in constructing an account of contemporary labor politics. Yet, to get there, it will be helpful to examine the rhetorical implications of social capital as well as the theoretical concerns this category aims to resolve. Drawing on Coleman (1990, 300–21), Putnam applies social capital to the task of theorizing the societies and associations de Tocqueville thought crucial to the life democracy in the United States. "Social capital," Putnam says, "refers to features of social organization, such as trust, norms, and networks, that can improve the efficiency of society by facilitating coordinated actions" (1993a, 167). Conceptually then, Putnam aims to frame the otherwise intangible qualities of de Tocqueville's narrative in the empiricist terms of a concept of modern economics. Capital is, by most accounts, a discernible set of resources employed to enhance the ability to produce some good; thus, social capital would be the productive use of trust, norms, and social networks. The term suggests that we should think of trust, norms, and social attachments as assets to be cultivated, increased, and, of course, exploited; it also promises that, if we employ these resources carefully and if we continually replenish them, other aspects of social life will also benefit. The metaphor deserves careful consideration.

The metaphor of social capital evokes the qualities of physical capital to suggest the kind of social scientific analysis associated with economics rather than the soft philosophical ambiguity associated with the discourse of "civic virtue." Unlike civic virtue, which would suggest a principled attachment to the larger community as well as a discourse about justice and other such qualities, social capital introduces the language of measurement and quantity, of resources, private interests, function, and accumulation. Like other forms of capital, "social capital is productive, making possible the achievement of certain ends . . . Like physical capital and human capital, social capital is not completely fungible but is fungible with respect to specific activities" (Coleman 1990, 302). Capital, of any form, is a resource that exists only in a given application. Money, for example, is financial capital only when it is put to use in investments with the purpose of yielding a profit. Similarly, it would seem, social capital is trust, norms, and networks that are *treated* as assets and put to productive use. The term social capital, then, asks us to draw analogies between some set of more or less intangible resources located in civil society and the lifeworld, on the one hand, and the productive assets of the economic realm. Putnam makes this clear and aims to highlight it when he introduces the category in *Bowling Alone*: "Just as a screwdriver (physical capital) or a college education (human capital) can increase productivity (both individual and collective), so too social contacts affect the productivity of individuals and groups." This is not to say that social capital is exactly the same as physical capital for, as he continues, "[w]hereas physical capital refers to physical objects and human capital to properties of individuals, social capital refers to connections among individuals" (Putnam 2000, 19). Putnam then explores the analogy further, suggesting that, like physical capital, social capital can have positive and negative externalities and that it can take more than one form. It is, however, James Coleman who identifies the key distinction between capital in its social and other forms.

Coleman argues that social capital is a way of conceiving of social-structural resources as assets for individuals. Social capital, he says, "is not a single entity, but a variety of different entities having two characteristics in common: They all consist of some aspect of a social structure and they facilitate certain actions of individuals who are within the structure" (1990, 302). Units of social capital, then, are fungible, but not infinitely so; they are also useful in certain contexts but not in others. In this, it would be like other forms of capital: private assets functioning to increase the supply of some good or commodity. Yet, social capital does exhibit four principal characteristics that distinguish it from the objects of purely economic analysis (Coleman 1990, 314–18). First of all, it is not strictly speaking a private good. Rather, it behaves like a public good benefitting both those who provide it and those who do not. Second, social capital cannot be readily exchanged, and, third, it cannot be readily divided. But the biggest difference for present purposes would be, as Coleman puts it, that "[u]nlike other forms of capital, social capital inheres in the structure of relations between persons and among persons. It is lodged neither in individuals not in physical implements of production" (1990, 302).

There is a contradiction in Coleman's claims that is worth noting in passing because it bears upon the obfuscation inherent in the category of social capital. He says that all capital is conceivable only in social-structural terms, yet he suggests that only social capital resides in the structure that emerges from social relations. Still, if capital, in general, is a function in a social structure, it too can exist only in the structure of social relations. This is so because, as classical political economy from Smith and Ricardo to Marx points out, the social structure is, from the point of view of production, an extended social division of labor where some provide or manage or accumulate capital, others sell their labor or labor power, and so on. Thus, capital is itself a social function or relation, even if, to borrow from Marx's words, in the "inverted world" the "relation of the producers to the sum total of their own labour is presented to them as a social relation . . . between the products of their labour" (1978, 320). The point here is that either all capital is indeed a social relation, so there is nothing especially social about social capital, or all capital is in principle privatizable, in which case social capital is not capital at all and calling it so becomes another way for the ideology of markets and value to enter consciousness and colonize the lifeworld. The conceptual power of capital, then, would reflect its economic and political position and make the social capital approach particularly detrimental for a critical understanding of the labor movement and its politics. In simpler terms, the discourse of social capital, concerned as it is about the burgeoning of atomistic individualism, replicates the problem by appealing to the normative structure of greed.

This has serious consequences for the theory and the program of the "social capitalists." Putnam is concerned about the pervasiveness of asocial attitudes; still, his language puzzlingly suggests an effort to appropriate that of neoclassical economics: "the core idea of social capital is that social networks have value" (2000, 18–19). In effect, Putnam looks to economics for the nomothetic categories with which to think all social action. Conceptually, this opens the door to an instrumental evaluation of those qualities associated with civic virtue. In Putnam's hands, these qualities take on renewed importance and de Tocqueville's insights finally can be appropriated for social scientific research to resolve game theoretical paradoxes such as the tragedy of the commons, the problem of public goods, and the related "dismal logic of collective action," as well as the various versions of prisoners' dilemmas (Putnam 1993b, 163–64). Unfortunately, much of the civic quality of social action that de Tocqueville highlights will be lost in the process.

Putnam and Social Capital

Social capital has been a central category in Putnam's work for some time. His most significant early engagement with the concept came in a study of democracy in Italy where (along with Leonardi and Nanetti) he concludes that social capital is the most significant determinant of the "conditions for creating strong, responsive, effective representative institutions" (1993a, 6). This volume, *Making Democracy Work*, examines the impact of a series of institutional reforms in Italy over a period of twenty years (1970–1989) by comparing the performance of a set of regional governments constructed along the same pattern. Putnam and his collaborators measure differences in the performance of these institutions and conclude that none of the other variables (e.g., institutional design, ideology, income levels, industrialization, etc.) is as strong a predictor of effective government as the three factors associated with social capital: trust, networks of civic engagement, and norms of reciprocity. Each in its own way, these elements reduce transaction costs, frame expectations, and, generally, provide the resources that fuel further civic engagement and, so, the articulation of the expectations of citizens and public officials. In his later work, Putnam returns to these findings to argue, for example, that the solution for the lack of prosperity in the inner cities of the United States lies at least in part in the realization that social capital is "a vital ingredient in economic development" (1993b, 38), and, even, to suggest that "[s]ocial capital, symbolized by the Joy Luck Club . . . is an underappreciated element in East Asia's economic miracles" (1995, 200).

The key point Putnam advances in these works is that social capital is a necessary condition for democratic governance, for prosperity, for social order, and for any other number of social goods. Given these conclusions, it would seem that social capital would be an especially useful concept for the study of labor movements and their role in politics. After all, American unions, as organizations, appear as vehicles for instrumental action which seek to provide benefits for their members. They are much like the road-building associations de Tocqueville observes in early nineteenth-century New England or the fictional mahjong clubs turned into investment groups that Putnam touts.[1] Indeed, in his recent global diagnosis of the ailments of the United States, *Bowling Alone*, Putnam describes unions in these terms. They are "networks of reciprocity" which both depend upon and generate social capital to address the problems associated with the logic of collective action (Putnam 2000, 81). Before turning to Putnam's analysis of the labor movement, it would be useful to review how unions and social capital appear in the terms of microeconomics-based rational actor theory.

As a conceptual solution to the game theoretical problem of public goods, social capital seems custom tailored for the examination of labor organization. After all, Mancur Olson (1971; 1982) identifies unions as one of the two paradigmatic cases of the dilemma of collective action (the other is national defense). The paradox is familiar, but it bears brief restatement. Even if rational actors (i.e., cost-benefit calculators) agree that all employees in a given firm will benefit from collective bargaining (the public good), they are unlikely to provide themselves with it because the benefits are universal and can be enjoyed even by free-riders while the costs are discernible and borne by particular individuals. Following this logic, every rational actor will seek to avoid the costs and the public good will not be provided.

When it comes to union organizing, this logic is apparently implacable. As anyone who has been in such a situation will testify, many workers who otherwise agree that union representation would be beneficial fear taking the necessary steps because they may lose income, lose their jobs, and otherwise suffer serious consequences. Others are concerned over paying union dues, particularly in open shop situations where they know that co-workers who do not pay will still reap the rewards. Still others are faced with problems of uncertainty: if I show up for the picket line, will I be alone? Employers also know this, as their support for open shop laws and other measures that aim to disaggregate the costs of unionization suggest. The point is that the logic of collective action clearly indicates that what needs explaining is not why workers do not join unions but, rather, why there are any unions at all. Social capital would provide a way of disentangling this dilemma.

Economists and other advocates of rational actor models propose that the provision of public goods is explained by the exercise of authority (say, closed shop arrangements and apprenticeship requirements) and arrangements for discernible individuated benefits such as consumer discounts for union members (i.e., "side-payments"). This is a well-established game theoretical solution but one that is not fully satisfactory because it may explain how certain unions act, but it does not provide theoretical guidance for general statements about why unions exist and what their political significance might be. Explanations of this tend to be ad hoc, such as the suggestion that in certain settings (e.g., rural mining towns) thuggery is the way the costs of free riding are allocated. Proponents of social capital advance a different way of taking on this theoretical issue while still remaining on empiricist ground. In their account, workers who would organize can tap into existing resources embodied in shared norms, in habits of reciprocity, and in other social networks to reduce the uncertainties and costs of forming labor organizations. Once established, the unions themselves would become social capital, available to foster further accumulation of social capital which can be used to enhance the collective and private benefits members can expect.

The social capital solution is theoretically elegant, but it fails to resolve the interpretive problems that face rational choice reasoning. To see the weaknesses of the approach, it is necessary to review why Putnam examines unions and to give a bit more background on the ideological concerns that lie behind social capital and Putnam's retreat from politics. First, there is the matter of how Putnam conceptualizes the labor movement in the United States: he is less concerned with studying labor organizations than with using their slow decline as yet another example of the disappearance of long established community bonds. He is certainly right on both counts. Indeed, and despite my earlier account of the Battle in Seattle and the following bridge building, membership in labor unions is clearly one of the types of social engagement that are declining most seriously in the United States.

While Putnam misses much when he claims that "[t]he solidarity of the union halls is now mostly a fading memory of aging men" (2000, 81), it is undoubtedly true that union membership has been dropping for almost half a century and that the fall has been precipitous since the mid-1970s. What is even more worrisome is that union membership and density continue to drop despite the very serious campaign to turn back the tide that the AFL-CIO has undertaken since 1995. Of course, the Federation's efforts have not been totally in vain. As it proudly announces, union membership rose by more than 265,000 in 1999, the largest increase in twenty years. Yet, this increase was due in good measure to a handful of major organizing victories, including the 75,000 California home health aide workers, the 65,000 Puerto Rican public employees, and the 5,000 Pillowtex/Cannon textile workers in North Carolina who signed on that year (AFL-CIO 2001). Since then, many more workers have joined in both traditional and nontraditional areas, in the rust belt and in Silicon Valley, in warehouses, in bookstores, and even on college campuses as teaching assistants from New York to California and Washington have sought and won recognition. These efforts, however, have only managed to slow the decline of the labor movement in the United States. Data from the Bureau of Labor Statistics' *Current Survey of Population*, for example, confirm the continuing drop in union strength: whereas, on average, 13.9 percent of U.S. workers were union members in 1999, the proportion has declined to an average of 13.5 percent in 2000, and the actual number of members has also fallen slightly (BLS 2001).

Putnam's account of this decline is largely descriptive and abstract. He does consider some of the more commonly advanced explanations such as the decline of blue-collar employment and the changes in the legal and political climate since the Reagan administration, but he suggests that they tell only a small part of the story. Mostly, the problem would be that there is little demand for labor unions. This declining demand for unions could not be simply due to "public resentment of union power" for, as Putnam acknowledges, union power has also been eroded and potential members are aware of this. The real problem, he says, is "not so much skepticism about the idea of 'union' as skepticism about the idea of 'membership' particularly among younger workers" (Putnam 2000, 82). This position, of course, is consistent with his overall finding that the main reason for civic disengagement in the United States is generational change (2000, 283). However, a great deal is missing here because the category of social capital reproduces the kind of orientation that is at the root of most of the troubles of worker organizations in the United States.

Moody (1997) has described the traditional U.S. model of labor activism as "business unionism." This model became established in the post–World War II era as the unions came to accept that their role was only to negotiate with capitalists over wages, hours, and benefits. Unlike their European counterparts, U.S. unions officially disengaged from political activity and from concerted efforts to extend social rights to organize or to government-provided benefits beyond those acquired during the New Deal. While unions, since the Roosevelt era, have been seen as partners in the Democratic party, the fact is that they rarely acted even to influence the Party's choice of standard-bearer. For example, it was only in 2000 that the AFL-CIO openly endorsed a candidate in the presidential primary. Also, and particularly at the local level, unions have maintained links to Republican officials while generally presenting themselves as somehow apolitical. Furthermore, many unions have developed close connections with their industries, acting as its surrogates on those occasions when they have become openly involved in politics: the main example here is the long history of collaboration between unions and firms in search of protectionist trade policies.[2] Yet, when all of this is said, the most seriously problematic aspect of U.S. business unionism has been the presentation of unions as bargaining agents for their members.

With few exceptions, it is the official labor movement itself that has fostered the image of worker associations as service providers. In their letters to their members, unions may still address them as "union brothers and sisters," and they may still sign "in solidarity," but, in between, the members hear a great deal about how the union is an asset to them. The fact that most unions in the United States do not choose their officials democratically and do not encourage active involvement on their part only helps to aggravate the problem. Thus, when organizers approach workers at a site, they should not be surprised to hear these potential members ask: what will the union do for me? It is, indeed, as if union membership were like membership in the Automobile Association. Surely, the aging unionists of

Putnam's account do not think of unions in these terms, but their younger brothers and sisters do precisely because business unionism encourages them to think of membership as an asset rather than as an activity. And the discourse of social capital does little to remedy this condition because it too uses the language of value and the commodity. A more appropriate language would emphasize what the more democratic and militant labor organizations do: the values of solidarity among workers and between them and the oppressed of the world, as well as the language of empowerment, of political engagement within the union and in the broader world. The revitalization of labor calls for the restoration of the old language of freedom, dignity, democracy, and rights.

This, however, seems very much to be the kind of discourse from which the social capital school is retreating. The discussion of the labor movement in *Bowling Alone* comes in the context of a chapter about "Connections in the Workplace" (Putnam 2000, 80–92). There, Putnam considers unions alongside professional organizations such as the American Medical Association and the American Bar Association and even suggests their similarity to business associations. From the point of view of a purely rational purposive account, it is as if there were no differences between the structural location of professional associations and that of unions; it is also as if there were no difference in how the hegemonic ideology valuates these groups. In short, the account ignores politics at the level of the shop floor and at that of the society at large. Of course, Putnam recognizes that many "bemoan the economic consequences of teachers' unions or bar associations," but he insists that even their detractors must acknowledge "the social capital they represent" (2000, 80). This is true, but it is also part of the problem. By placing all of these organizations in the same category, Putnam provides an abstract and anti-political account of how the labor movement fits into the overall scheme of contemporary politics. Conceding that there is some controversy associated with the public's view of the institutions of the labor movement does little to highlight the broader issues and much to reaffirm the claim that politics does not count.

Again, Putnam is right in his assessment that labor unions are important factors in the life of a democratic society. However, much is lost when he looks at them through the lens of social capital. The fact is that labor unions are *not* much like bowling clubs, Boy Scouts, Jaycees, or the AMA. Of course, all of these groups do represent social engagement, but none of the latter can be said to represent a challenge to the dominant interests embedded in the relations of production or to have had to confront the hostility of state institutions as the labor movement historically has. Unions tend to encounter this hostility because, at the level of the economic structure, the establishment of even the most moderate of them represents a shift in power relations in the workplace. This is one of the reasons managements regularly resist efforts to organize and often attempt to undermine existing worker associations.

The labor movement simply does not enjoy the same rights or the same status of respectability that professional and business associations do, or the same acceptability as that accorded to most of the societies Putnam discusses. In fact, as a recent report by Human Rights Watch highlights (2000), the legal and political climate of the United States is particularly unfavorable to workers' freedom of association: the laws, as they exist, are openly in conflict with even some of the minimal provisions of the International Labor Organization's principles of which this country is a signatory.[3] Furthermore, the enforcement of the laws that do spell out the rights of workers is often so minimal and ineffective that it is easy to get around.[4] The reality is that few other legal organizations in the United States encounter the same kind of hurdles. Nor does any other legal organization in the United State have to contend with the coercive power of the state in quite the same way. The police do not infiltrate meetings of the Girl Scouts or routinely investigate the backgrounds of leaders of the National Association of Manufacturers. Participation in events sponsored by labor organizations differs from involvement in the activities of a bridge club and brings along with it a distinct official reaction: police are often present at strikes to protect property, yet they seldom appear at meetings of the AMA. Furthermore, labor unions never enjoy the kind of official delegation of authority that certain professional associations do. The law, at best, recognizes the existence of labor unions and grants them the power to represent workers in contractual bargaining. On the other hand, professional associations such as the AMA and ABA actually set the standards of practice that the state enforces. Finally, soccer leagues have never been illegal as labor unions were before the enactment of the Wagner Act. My point here is that classifying labor unions as bearers of social capital alongside professional and business associations, let alone bowling leagues, simply serves to obfuscate the distinctively political quality of labor movement activities and to direct our attention away from a politics that should be oriented to enhancing social rights. This is a mistake.

Putnam might reply that his concern is not studying unions as such. Rather, he would claim that his concern is with how the workplace has become less community friendly, less of a site where social capital is created. Yet, even in this case, a more political understanding might have stretched his analytical reach. For example, after a discussion highlighting longer work hours and the emergence of teamwork in the form of "quality circles" and related strategies, Putnam wonders why the work experience does not result in closer social ties: "[t]he modern workplace thus encourages regular collaborative contacts among peers—ideal connections, one might think, for social capital creation" (2000, 87). What Putnam misses here is that the reorganization of workplaces was never meant as a way to encourage social capital formation but, rather, as a means of increasing managerial control over labor, intensifying the labor process, and, not incidentally, making the establishment and maintenance of autonomous worker organizations that much more difficult. Quality circles, for example, serve to increase competition among groups of workers by pitting them against each other. They also serve to make employees internalize the values of management so they can prod each other to work harder and longer. Finally, quality circles actually facilitate the process of supervision. All of these goals are very much contrary to the goals and values of the labor movement. The notion of social capital, then, serves to conceal rather than explain politics because it does not address the structural conflict of interest between labor and management, the differentials in their access to institutional power, or, ultimately, their conflicting values.

Nor are my observations anything new. Putnam seems fond of quoting David Hume's famous observation about the two farmers who should find it in their interest to cooperate (1993b, 35; 2000, 135) and of offering social capital as a shortcut to neighborly behavior. However, when discussing the question of associations of working people he would have been better served by turning to Hume's compatriot, Adam Smith. Indeed, Smith recognizes both that there is a fundamental conflict of interest between wage earners and owners of capital and that the latter tend to have the upper hand. In the normal course of events, they have the upper hand because they control access to employment so they are more necessary in the short term to the workers than the workers are to them. Furthermore, since the wealth of the "masters" can be transformed into consumption items, a confrontation is likely to have less dire consequences for them. Also, business organizations and "combinations" are so common that they are generally accepted and rarely even noticed. Finally, the laws tend to reflect these disparities in power and to favor business organizing while restricting labor union activities. Thus, Smith argues that when there is a strike "[t]he workmen . . . very seldom derive any advantage from the violence of those tumultuous combinations which, partly from the interposition of the civil magistrate, partly from the superior steadiness of the masters, partly from the necessity which the greater part of the workmen are under . . . generally end in nothing" (1993 [1776], 66).

More than two centuries ago then, Smith recognized something that seems to escape the social capital school: the politics of labor are distinctively and directly rooted in conflict in the relations of production and the allocation of social wealth, and they are mediated through the state. Of course, a great deal has changed since the days of Adam Smith. In his day "combinations of workmen," despite their obvious provenance from the guilds of old, were actually something new and anomalous. Today, they remain rare and largely unfamiliar, at least in the United States, but they are no longer new. In his day unions were legally banned while they are now sanctioned (which does not mean that labor organizations have the same standing or freedom as Chambers of Commerce). Most importantly, however, the main difference is that the England of the late eighteenth century may have been a liberal society, but it was not democratic. Today, democracy has spread not only in terms of the expansion of the franchise but, more importantly, in terms of the widespread legitimacy that popular rule enjoys the world over. This has made the state into a potential avenue for the exercise of labor's power. The labor movement the world over has, in fact, made this power felt again and again, achieving more or less significant social rights in various countries. But this has only happened when labor organizations oriented their activities toward the state rather than toward civil society and its economic structure.

Such considerations are important when we take into account that Putnam's claim is that there is a link between social engagement and democracy. The problem here is that the category of social capital tends to suggest that social engagement is a private good, albeit one that only exists in the sphere of social relations, in civil society if you will. In doing so, social capital systematically accepts existing limits on the scope of state action while, at the same time, proposing to turn social action away from political practice and toward private interactions among self-interested individuals engaged in processes that reduce the costs of providing public goods. Such an attitude is consistent with the recent orientation toward civil society understood as a "market-organized network of mutual dependence" that has taken hold of political science and political theory (Ehrenberg 1999, 99). This attitude suggests that democracy is best served not so much by intense public engagement as by apolitical attitudes in community settings. Thus, rather than demand the extension of social rights, social capital proposes a retreat from politics and activism in the name of enhancing governmental performance. This concern is not new and it forms some of the theoretical ancestry to the social capital approach.

In a recent essay, Pharr, Putnam, and Dalton have recalled some of this background by referring to the literature on the crisis of governability of the mid-1970s. In particular, they discuss the work of Crozier, Huntington, and Watanuki (1975). Then, as Pharr, Putnam, and Dalton recapitulate, the claim was that "the Trilateral democracies were becoming overloaded by increasingly insistent demands from an ever-expanding array of participants, raising fundamental issues of governability" (2000, 5). As this happened, confidence in governmental and nongovernmental institutions also declined, leading to what Huntington, in particular, referred to as a "democratic distemper" that justified fears for the viability of capitalist democracies. In those days, the concern was that the social and political order was confronting a problem of critical proportions which became manifest in disrespect for established authority, an instrumental attitude toward the state, and the resulting incapacity of states to carry out macro-economic management, as revealed in what would be called "stagflation." But, what was the source of the problem?

In an article where he summarized the findings of the American part of the Trilateral study, Huntington presented his answer quite succinctly: "The immediate causes of the simultaneous expansion of governmental activity and the decline of governmental authority are to be found in the democratic surge of the 1960's" (1975, 32). At least in the United States, the government was simultaneously doing more and losing its claim to citizen allegiance *because* its citizens had become overly engaged. The real problem was, simply, that a broader segment of citizens had come to expect greater access to the institutions of power. In short, the citizens were overly involved in politics. This problem had its roots in two facts. First, the public had lost sight of the fact that democracy, understood as a "way of constituting authority . . . [was] not universally applicable." In some issues, the claims of expertise ought to have carried more weight. More importantly, both the public and their leaders had lost sight of another reality: "the effective operation of a democratic political system usually requires apathy and noninvolvement on the part of some individuals and groups" (Huntington 1975, 36–37). This became especially problematic once formerly marginalized groups (Huntington referred specifically to

African Americans, but labor organizations and new social movements clearly also had a role) were integrated and raised demands for civil, political, and social rights. Under such circumstances, demand would be added upon demand and overload was a necessary consequence.

Huntington's claim was that the problem of capitalist democracy was that it was overly democratic. As it became more inclusive and its citizens became more demanding, capitalist democracy became less able to govern. The citizens, it seems, no longer were willing or able to maintain that level of moderating political apathy required to manage what Almond and Verba had termed the "balance between consensus and cleavage" (1989, 358). Quite the contrary, in the 1960s and 1970s citizens demanded, and often achieved, extensions of rights—of civil, political, and eventually social rights. In the United States, this encompassed significant steps toward the inclusion of marginalized groups (ethnic and racial minorities, women, etc.), along with pro-labor measures broadening social welfare programs and expanding the scope of public authority in workplace safety (on OSHA, see Noble, 1986). In Europe, similar demands in many cases achieved even greater success. Yet, the fulfilment of such demands, the overload theorists suggested, only encouraged more political activism which lead to more ineffective government. The solution involved reducing the scope of state action and otherwise promoting a retreat from politics on the part of citizens. And this is precisely what happened. The OECD countries have since pursued policies congruent with these conclusions. Particularly in the United States and in Great Britain, the state has limited its activities in the areas of social welfare and the regulation of working conditions. Meanwhile, alternating parties in government have taken up neo-liberal positions and a rhetoric that denigrates public activity and promotes increasing commodification. Not surprisingly, the main survivor from the activism of the 1960s has been a distrust of established authorities which has transmogrified into a broad-based decline in confidence in public institutions and political action.

This decline in confidence is the main concern of Pharr, Putnam, and Dalton. Of course, they do not share all of the concerns of their predecessors for, even after N30, a sense of imminent social disintegration, if not revolution, is hardly widespread at the opening of the third millennium. Rather, what Pharr, Putnam, and Dalton recognize is a widely shared sense of political and social estrangement. Like most observers of the American political scene, they see a public which holds its leaders in low regard and has little sense of responsibility toward its fellow citizens. Thus, no one would argue that there is a democratic surge. At the same time, Pharr, Putnam, and Dalton have inherited from their predecessors the worry that the citizens of the advanced capitalist democracies no longer trust their political and social institutions, along with a sense that the reason is partly an earlier orientation toward rights and entitlements. This informed a new generation and resulted in disappointment as governmental capacities declined and leaders came to be seen as unfaithful to their constituencies (Pharr, Putnam, and Dalton 2000). Social capitalists have also inherited a discourse that advances a retreat from politics into the purported havens of civil society as a way to revive democracy without extending its reach. This will not serve the interests or the institutional position of workers and their associations.

Conclusion

Putnam's "agenda for social capitalists" aims "to reweave the fabric of our communities" (2000, 403). In a context where the very concept of society is challenged and the idea of community is increasingly denigrated, Putnam's goal is a good thing. The question, however, is who will do the reweaving, whose interest will be served, whose institutional location will be enhanced, and what set of norms will guide the participants. Surely, the structure of the loom has some bearing upon the cloth it produces. Putnam, however, seeks to reconstruct the community by leading us away from politics to the realm of civil society, where private interests weigh most heavily.

Implementing Putnam's social capitalist agenda would involve improvements in civics education and, generally, in the form and content of school activities in order to breed greater attachment to the society. It would also entail voluntary efforts to make the workplace more community oriented, along with a commitment to guarantee that people spend less time going to and from work. In addition, Putnam would want to channel the energies of the currently on-going religious revival toward greater tolerance. Finally, he proposes that the electronic media foster greater rather than lesser connection among citizens (Putnam 2000, 404–11). All of these recommendations are praiseworthy, yet, if the discussion of the changes in the workplace is any indication, they are woefully oblivious to political considerations and, consequently, likely to lead to further political disengagement.

Looking at the workplace, Putnam says: "*Let us find ways to ensure that by 2010 America's workplace will be substantially more family-friendly and community congenial, so that American workers will be enabled to replenish our stocks of social capital both inside and outside the workplace*" (2000, 406; italics in the original). Further, he recognizes that "[c]ivic engagement and social connectedness can be found inside the workplace" and he even exhorts "[e]mployers, labor unions, labor relations experts, and employees themselves . . . to be more creative in meeting the social connectivity needs of temps" (2000, 407). Certainly, from the point of view of labor, these recommendations are not objectionable. However, they do not seem especially practical because they do not take into account either the current status of institutional power relations in the workplace and in society at large or in history. The increasing use of part-timers and "independent contractors," for example, is partly a response to broad changes in markets and international capitalism, but it is also part of a managerial strategy to promote lower costs through "flexible labor" practices which, among other things, undermine labor associations. Clearly, unions do themselves a disservice if, having lost the battle to retain in-house labor, they are hostile to contingent employees. However, bringing these workers into the fold of labor associations is likely to be resisted by employers and to require changes in the labor laws. Such changes will only occur as a result of political activism.

It is precisely a commitment, however timid, to political activism and social militancy that has unevenly informed "big labor's" actions in recent times. The involvement of the AFL-CIO in the week of protests of November 1999 is very much an example of this attitude. The AFL-CIO's participation actually came from a request on the part of the International Confederation of Free Trade Unions (ICFTU), the most important international association of national labor federations. The ICFTU, prompted primarily by its German, French, Swedish, and Brazilian members, has long advocated the inclusion of a Social Democratic–inspired "social clause" in the agreements that shape the World Trade Organization. In months preceding the Seattle ministerial meeting, the AFL-CIO embraced this position and called for a social clause that would include the enforcement of core labor rights as part of the WTO's mission. This was essentially a reformist position, but one that was a clear break from traditional American business unionism. The albeit timid, drift away became more apparent once the AFL-CIO began to explore the terms of its solidarity with environmental, feminist, and especially human rights[5] activists at the national, regional, and local levels. There was, of course, an exchange of resources (after all, by the standards of most social movements, labor is rich). However, the participants did not frame it and could not have framed it in the language of social capital. Rather, the common language of old and new social movements was the old progressive labor movement discourse of justice, of freedom, of equality, of solidarity, of rights, and, yes, of democracy.

The fact is that while Putnam recognizes the importance of labor organizations for the health of democracy, an examination of labor and its position in society highlights the key weaknesses of the category of social capital as a diagnostic and therapeutic tool to identify and heal the illnesses of democracy. This is so because the proponents of social capital, much like their predecessors—the advocates of the civic culture and the physicians of governmental overload—seek not so much to ground democratic politics in a participatory culture, but to displace the energies of political dissidents to the realm of civil society. More importantly, the notion of social capital seems to assume that harmony is the normal or natural condition of civil society—an untenable proposition in a capitalist society, particularly when it comes to the role of organized labor which always involves the intersection between class interests and the institutions of powers. Finally, the very notion of social capital reveals its contradictions precisely when it confronts labor: for labor the key goals are freedom, dignity, and solidarity, not accumulation.

Postscript

The party at Local 23 was both disappointing and inspiring. There was no beer, and salad with grains had replaced the barbecue—was it a concession to the vegetarians in the crowd or was it the influence of the women dockers? More to the point, attendance was small and no one had a fully satisfactory explanation. Despite this, the group was quite mixed. Present were, of course, the president of the local and many rank-and-file longshoreworkers (they no longer use the old "longshoremen"). There were also steelworkers, musicians, and teachers. No Teamsters seemed to be there, but some "Turtles" were. There was much conversation about struggles, about past and ongoing organizing campaigns, and about old and new friends. Of course, there were the obligatory speeches. And there was much talk of "union power," of freedom, and rights for workers and poor people, but there was no mention of social capital. Interestingly, given Putnam's observations, most of the crowd did not consist of nostalgic old men. Rather, those present were mostly young enough that many did not even know the old organizing songs. This was quickly remedied: as midnight approached and we left the ILWU hall, everyone could sing "Solidarity Forever," and, even, a few bars of the "Internationale" could be heard in the parking lot.

Notes

1. The "Joy Luck Club" Putnam refers to is a novel of that title by Amy Tan (1989).

2. This practice has become less common as traditionally organized industrial firms have restructured to take advantage of liberalized trade and investment legislation.

3. For example, many categories of workers (farm workers, domestic employees, many public employees, the growing ranks of low-level supervisors, etc.) are explicitly denied the protection of the National Labor Relations Act.

4. For an interesting first-hand account of how businesses sidestep the law or take advantage of its provisions and loopholes to restrict workers' freedom of association, see Levitt (1993). For a scholarly account of some successful strategies to counteract union busting, see Juravich and Bronfenbrenner (1999).

5. The alliance was a natural one. Human rights groups have become ever more concerned with workers' freedom of association, with workplace issues, the continuing prevalence of coerced labor abroad and even among certain immigrants in the United States. Labor rights are now, clearly, human rights.

References

Almond, Gabriel, and Sidney Verba. 1989. *The Civic Culture: Political Attitudes and Democracy in Five Nations.* Newbury Park, Calif.: Sage Publications. [Reprint]

American Federation of Labor-Congress of Industrial Organizations. 2001. "More Join." http://www.aflcio.org/voiceatwork/morejoin.htm. 16 Feb 2001.

Bureau of Labor Statistics. 2001. News release. http://stats.bls.gov:80/news.release/union2.nr0.htm. 16 Feb 2001.

Castells, Manuel. 1997. *The Information Age: Economy, Society, and Culture,* 3 vols. Oxford, UK: Blackwell.

Coleman, James. 1990. *Foundations of Social Theory.* Cambridge: Harvard University Press.

Crozier, Michel, Samuel P. Huntington, and Joji Watanuki. 1975. *The Crisis of Democracy: Report on the Governability of Democracies to the Trilateral Commission*. New York: NYU Press.

Ehrenberg, John. 1999. *Civil Society: The Critical History of an Idea*. New York: NYU Press.

Giddens, Anthony. 1998. *The Third Way: The Renewal of Social Democracy*. Malden, Mass.: Polity Press.

Habermas, Jürgen. 1989. *On the Logic of the Social Sciences*. Translated by S. W. Nicholsen and J. A. Stark. Cambridge: MIT Press.

Howell, Christopher. 2000. "From New Labour to No Labour? The Industrial Relations Project of the Blair Government," *New Political Science* 22 (June): 201–30.

Human Rights Watch. 2000. "Unfair Advantage: Workers' Freedom of Association in the United States under International Human Rights Standards." http://www.hrw.org/reports/2000/uslabor/.

Huntington, Samuel P. 1975. "The Democratic Distemper," *Public Interest* 41 (Fall 1975): 3–38.

Juravich, Tom, and Kate Bronfenbrenner. 1999. *Ravenswood: The Steelworkers' Victory and the Revival of American Labor*. Ithaca: Cornell University Press.

Levitt, Martin Jay. 1993. *Confessions of a Union Buster*. New York: Crown.

Mair, Peter. 2000. "Partyless Democracy," *New Left Review* 2 (March/April): 21–36.

Marx, Karl. 1978. *Capital* [Selections], pp. 294–439. In *The Marx-Engels Reader*, 2d. ed. Ed. by Robert C. Tucker. New York: Norton.

Moody, Kim. 1997. *Workers in a Lean World: Unions in the International Economy*. London: Verso.

Noble, Charles. 1986. *Liberalism at Work: The Rise and Fall of OSHA*. Philadelphia: Temple University Press.

Olson, Mancur. 1971. *The Logic of Collective Action: Public Goods and the Theory of Groups*. Cambridge: Harvard University Press.

———. 1982. *The Rise and Decline of Nations: Economic Growth, Stagflation, and Social Rigidities*. New Haven: Yale University Press.

Petras, James. 2000. "The Third Way: Myth and Reality," *Monthly Review* 51 (March): 19–35.

Pharr, Susan J., Robert D. Putnam, and Russell J. Dalton. 2000. "Trouble in Advanced Democracies? A Quarter Century of Declining Confidence," *Journal of Democracy* 11 (April): 5–25.

Putnam, Robert D., with Robert Leonardi and Raffaella Y. Nanetti. 1993a. *Making Democracy Work: Civic Traditions in Modern Italy*. Princeton: Princeton University Press.

———. 1993b. "The Prosperous Community: Social Capital and Public Life," *The American Prospect* 13 (Spring): 35–42.

———. 1995. "Comment on 'The Institutions of Governance of Economic Development and Reform,' by [Oliver] Williamson," pp. 198–200. *Proceedings of the World Bank Annual Conference on Development Economics, 1994.* Washington, D.C.: World Bank.

————. 2000. *Bowling Alone: The Collapse and Revival of American Community.* New York: Simon & Schuster.

Smith, Adam. 1993 [1776]. *An Inquiry into the Nature and Causes of the Wealth of Nations.* Ed. by Kathryn Sutherland. Oxford: Oxford University Press.

Tan, Amy. 1989. *The Joy Luck Club.* Putnam.

Chapter Twelve

Robert Putnam, Social Capital, and a Suspect Named Globalization

Manfred B. Steger

The five hundred and forty-one pages of *Bowling Alone: The Collapse and Revival of American Community* (2000) constitute the culmination of Robert Putnam's longstanding reflections on the purported decline of civic engagement in the United States. Advertised on the jacket cover as a "groundbreaking work" that "shows how social bonds are the most powerful predictor of life satisfaction," Putnam's study has received high ratings from prominent commentators on American politics and society. As is evident on the back flap of the book, such enthusiastic evaluations cut across the mainstream ideological spectrum in the United States. Liberals like former Labor Secretary Robert Reich and Harvard urban sociologist William Julius Wilson praise the study's "original and provocative thesis," and conservatives like William Kristol, the editor and publisher of the *Weekly Standard*, suggest that "Putnam's argument deserves to be seriously considered by everyone interested in our social well-being." Evidently, the communitarian message of the book enticed leading advisers of George W. Bush to consult with Robert Putnam on the incoming President's inaugural address (Milbank 2001, A1). To some extent, I agree with these positive assessments of Putnam's work. Indeed, fairness demands that a critical evaluation of *Bowling Alone* start out with an explicit acknowledgment of the study's considerable virtues. First, the author manages to encapsulate the spirit of his thesis in a two-word title that resonates with core themes in American culture. Bowling has long been a national pastime, and the image of the lone individual is deeply anchored in our collective psyche. Yet, by establishing a counterintuitive link between the social activity of bowling and the painful condition of loneliness, the phrase "Bowling

Alone" suggests the existence of a serious problem in contemporary America—a fundamental tear in the social fabric of the nation. Indeed, the study's catchy title has the potential to get even the casual bookstore browser to pick up the book and proceed to the cash register.

Second, even those academics (like this author) who favor normative approaches to the study of politics and society over more quantitative methods cannot help but be impressed with the ability of Putnam and his research assistants to utilize empirical evidence in support of his thesis. Methodologically more sophisticated than his three original essays on the subject (Putnam 1995a; 1995b; 1996), *Bowling Alone* draws on data extracted from several independent social surveys that have chronicled American's changing behavior over the past twenty-five years.

Third, Putnam proves himself to be an excellent writer. Interweaving his lively narrative with the clear presentation of important information, he embroils the specialist and the general reader alike in a riveting account of civic disengagement that resembles more closely a detective story than the rather dry, long-winded prose of most scholarly writing. Indeed, Putnam consciously evokes the aura of a mystery novel to make his case to a skeptical audience (184–88). The crime to be investigated is murder—the "killing of civic engagement"—alleged to have taken place over the last three decades. The crime scene is civil society in the United States of America. And, of course, the central question is: Whodunit? Who, or what, has committed this heinous crime? Like any good mystery novel, the early chapters of *Bowling Alone* lure the reader into entertaining a number of false leads. Finally, the author introduces his line-up of eleven plausible suspects, ranging from increased time pressure and urban sprawl to television watching and the impact of the 1960s—including Vietnam, Watergate, and the cultural revolt against sexual repression and authority (187). However, as in Agatha Christie's *Murder on the Orient Express*, Putnam's mystery suggests that the crime has more than a single perpetrator. Proceeding to sort out ringleaders from accomplices, the Harvard political scientist analyzes and interprets in some detail the clues left behind by each of the eleven suspects. Eventually, he identifies the four main perpetrators of the crime.

Pressures of time and money, including the special pressures on two-career families, account for about 10 percent of the decline of civic engagement and social capital. Commuting and suburban sprawl are responsible for an additional 10 percent. The privatizing effects of electronic entertainment—above all, television—account for about 25 percent of the problem. Fourth, and most important, generational change—the slow, steady, and ineluctable replacement of the older "civic generation" of people born between 1910 and 1940 by their less involved children and grandchildren—is responsible for about half of the overall decline in social capital (283–84). The mystery appears to be solved. Inspector Putnam is now prepared to deal with his two remaining intellectual tasks: substantiating his claim that social capital has salutary effects on individuals and communities, and making suggestions for how sagging civic engagement in the United States might be reversed (288–414).

Putnam's confident tone notwithstanding, however, this author remains skeptical. In fact, I do not consider the mystery solved. This chapter argues that *Bowling Alone* neglects what I believe to be the most important cause of this country's declining civic vitality: neoliberal globalization. Ironically, Putnam's initial line-up of suspects does include what he calls "changes in the structure and scale of the American economy, such as the rise of chain stores, branch firms, and the service sector, or globalization" (187). Given the intensification of economic, political, and cultural interdependencies on a global scale that occurred precisely during the last three decades, it makes good sense to suspect that the liberalization of markets and their global integration has played a central role in declining civic engagement. Yet, after a superficial discussion of the subject, Putnam hastily dismisses the possibility that globalization processes such as the changing nature of capitalism might be significant contributors to the depletion of social capital (282–83).

Fearing that I might have missed a more substantial discussion of globalization in a different section of *Bowling Alone*, I reread the entire book again—to no avail. Still skeptical, I turned to the massive, 26-page index of the study (515–41). To my surprise, I could find no entry for "globalization" (although the word appears a few times in the study). The only substantial discussion of "global economy" occurs in the above-mentioned, brief passage (282–83). In addition, there are no entries for "deregulation," "privatization," "marketization," "market(s)," or "neoliberalism." I could not locate any references to "Thatcher" or "Thatcherism," but there does exist an entry for "Diana, Princess of Wales."

By remaining almost completely silent on those profound social changes of our time that go by the name of globalization, the analysis contained in *Bowling Alone* retreats from a critical discussion of profound political and economic issues. When placed within the academic framework of mainstream political science in the United States, however, Putnam's reluctance to grapple with pressing political and ideological matters is not at all extraordinary. Even a casual perusal of articles published in the discipline's leading journals, such as *American Political Science Review*, the *American Journal of Political Science*, or *Political Theory*, reveals a striking reluctance on the part of the authors to discuss what is perhaps the most dramatic political event of our time.[1]

Turning its attention to the phenomenon of neoliberal globalization, this chapter insists on the relevance of politics for any theory of social capital. I posit a direct relationship between the waning stocks of social capital and the politics of neoliberal globalization, thus implicitly accepting Putnam's claim that civic disengagement in the United States has indeed been taking place in the last three decades. Other contributors to this volume might be less willing to cede so easily such contested terrain to Putnam. Here is my response: I wish to subject the arguments presented in *Bowling Alone* to an immanent critique that explores how and why Putnam prematurely dismisses the obvious suspect named "neoliberal globalization." Consequently, I also examine why he fails to situate his four main "ringleaders" within the dominant material and ideational framework of our time.

My exposition proceeds in three stages. First, I discuss the origin and meaning of neoliberal globalization. Next, I establish the relevance of my discussion for Putnam's thesis of the decline of social capital in the United States. Third, I offer a review and a critical analysis of Putnam's sparse comments on the subject of globalization. I conclude that a critical consideration of the relationship between neoliberal globalization and civic disengagement brings politics back into the social capital debate. Ultimately, I hope to persuade the American participants in this debate to broaden their geographical and methodological perspectives and pay more attention to the dynamics of globalization.

Neoliberal Globalization: Origin and Meaning

What is globalization? Academics often respond to this question by attempting to take conceptual possession of globalization as though it were something "out there" to be captured by the "correct" analytical framework. As Stephen J. Rosow (2000, 31) points out, many researchers approach the topic as if they were dealing with a process or an object without a meaning of its own prior to its constitution as a conceptual "territory."

Often sharing the same methodological approach, social scientists have nonetheless invoked the concept of globalization to describe a variety of changing economic, political, and cultural processes that are alleged to have accelerated since the early 1970s. No generally accepted characterizations of globalization have emerged, except for such broad definitions as "increasing global interconnectedness," "the rapid intensification of worldwide social relations," "the compression of time and space," "a complex range of processes, driven by a mixture of political and economic influences," and "the swift and relatively unimpeded flow of capital, people, and ideas across national borders."[2] A number of researchers even object to those general descriptions, a few going so far as to deny the existence of globalization altogether.

Consequently, the principal academic approaches to the subject range from the suggestion that globalization is little more than "globaloney" to more affirmative interpretations of globalization as significant economic, political, or cultural processes. Most scholars consider globalization a real phenomenon that signals an epochal transformation in world affairs as the flow of large quantities of trade, investment, and technologies across national borders has expanded from a trickle to a flood (Gilpin 2000, 19). Suggesting that the study of globalization be moved to the center of social scientific research, scholars working in the burgeoning field of "globalization studies" examine the evolving structure of global economic markets, global governance, and growing cultural interdependencies (Scholte 2000, 39–40).

Such studies are frequently embedded in thick historical narratives that trace the gradual emergence of globalization to the 1944 Bretton Woods Conference (Schaeffer 1997). Under the leadership of the United States and Great Britain, the major economic powers of the West reversed the protectionist policies of the interwar period (1918–1939) by committing themselves to the expansion of international trade. The major outcomes of the Bretton Woods Conference include the limited liberalization of trade, the creation of a stable currency system, and the establishment of binding rules on international economic activities. However, within these prescribed limits, individual nations remained free to control the permeability of their borders, which allowed them to set their own economic agendas, including the implementation of extensive social welfare policies. The Bretton Woods Conference also set the institutional foundations for the establishment of three new international economic organizations, the International Monetary Fund (IMF), the World Bank, and, four years later, the General Agreement on Tariffs and Trade (GATT), which in 1995 turned into the World Trade Organization (WTO).

During its thirty-year operation, the Bretton Woods system contributed greatly to the establishment of what some observers have called the "golden age of controlled capitalism" (Luttwak 1999, xii, 27). Mechanisms of state control over international capital movements were put into place in the wealthy countries of the global North to achieve the goal of full employment and to expand social policies. Rising wages and increased social services secured in those countries a solid welfare state system based on a temporary "class compromise" (Esping-Anderson 1990). Yet, the rise of "neoliberal" ideas and the emergence of serious economic problems contributed to the collapse of the Bretton Woods regime in the early 1970s. High inflation, low economic growth, high unemployment, public sector deficits, and two major oil crises within a decade fueled the spectacular election victories of conservative parties in the United States and the United Kingdom. Under the leadership of Ronald Reagan and Margaret Thatcher, these parties guided the neoliberal movement toward the expansion of international markets—a dynamic supported by concrete political decisions such as the deregulation of domestic financial systems, the gradual removal of capital controls, and an enormous increase in global financial transactions (Gilpin 2000, 65–75).

During the 1980s and 1990s, Anglo-American efforts to establish a single global market were further strengthened through comprehensive trade-liberalization agreements that increased the flow of economic resources across national borders. The rising neoliberal paradigm received further legitimation with the 1989–1991 collapse of command-type economies in Eastern Europe. Shattering the postwar economic consensus on Keynesian interventionist principles, neoliberal free-market theories pioneered by Friedrich Hayek and Milton Friedman established themselves as the new economic orthodoxy (Yergin and Stanislaw 1998). The central tenets of neoliberalism include the primacy of economic growth, the reduction of the welfare state, the downsizing of government, the deregulation of the economy, and an evolutionary model of social development anchored in the Western experience and applicable to the whole world (Friedman 1982). The dramatic political shift from the state-dominated paradigm of the 1950s and 1960s to the market-dominated world of the 1980s and 1990s was accompanied by technological innovations that lowered the costs of transportation and communication. As a result, the value of world trade increased from $57 billion in 1947 to an astonishing

$6 trillion in the late 1990s (Gilpin 2000, 20). Most importantly, however, the interpretation of the meaning of globalization for the general public has fallen disproportionately to a powerful phalanx of social forces that has arrayed itself around a neoliberal market ideology which I have called "globalism" (Steger 2001). Anglo-American proponents of globalism have found in the concept of "globalization" a new guiding metaphor for their neoliberal message. Although recent editions of the United Nations' *Human Development Report* suggest that neoliberal globalization has led to a worldwide rise of social inequality, globalists seek to cultivate in the popular mind the uncritical association of "globalization" with what they claim to be the universal benefits of market liberalization. Asserting that societies have no choice but to adapt to the irresistable free-market logic of globalization, globalists claim that the liberalization and integration of markets not only raises the living standard of people worldwide but also furthers the spread of democratic principles in the world. By portraying neoliberal globalization as a "natural stage" in the process of social evolution, globalists seek to naturalize and thus depoliticize an ostensibly political project that serves primarily the interests of transnational capital. Yet, it is not the inevitable evolution of "the global economy" that dictates to politicians an agenda of unrestricted laissez-faire, but rather a politics of neoliberal globalization that unfetters global market forces. Although globalism has encountered considerable resistance in the streets of Seattle and other cities, neoliberals have responded to this challenge with a powerful arsenal of media-disseminated ideological representations, political co-option, and economic coercion. For the time being, it seems that globalists have managed to solidify their political project of market liberalization and economic integration.

The Relevance of Neoliberal Globalization to Putnam's Thesis

Since the rise of industrial society in the early part of the nineteenth century, progressive voices have been warning against the dire social consequences that might arise from liberal efforts to "free" markets from all forms of social control. In his seminal study of modern British economic history, Hungarian-Canadian political economist Karl Polanyi (1944) examines the attempt of nineteenth-century liberals to realize their utopia of a self-regulating market system. Contesting their views, Polanyi argues that free markets never arise in spontaneous fashion from people's "natural" tendencies to act on the basis of self-interest. Rather, the modern market system represents the outcome of conscious political actions and governmental decisions. As he puts it, "While *laissez-faire* economy was the product of deliberate state action, subsequent restrictions on *laissez-faire* started in a spontaneous way. *Laissez-faire* was planned; planning was not" (Polanyi 1944, 141).

After pointing to the political forces behind laissez-faire capitalism, Polanyi makes a crucial point that is highly relevant to Robert Putnam's theory of social capital. Polanyi shows in convincing fashion how efforts to liberalize markets and remove social controls *destroyed complex social relations of civic obligation*. The nineteenth-century market revolution in England undermined existing communal values such as civic participation, reciprocity, and redistribution, not to speak of human dignity and self-respect. Laissez-faire capitalism left ever-larger segments of the British population without an adequate system of social security and communal support. Most people caught in these powerful free-market dynamics experienced a strong sense of alienation and loneliness that contributed to a decline of civic engagement and the weakening of social bonds.

Eventually, however, workers and farmers organized themselves politically, sometimes even resorting to radical measures to protect themselves against the market forces imposed on them by the owning and trading classes. Anti-liberal social movements gave birth to new political parties that worked for the passage of social legislation on the national level as well as the imposition of protective tariffs on imported goods. After a prolonged period of severe economic dislocations following the end of World War I, the nationalist-protectionist impulse contained in these anti–free-market sentiments experienced its most extreme manifestation in Italian fascism and German National Socialism. In the end, the classical liberal dream of subordinating society's institutions to the requirements of the free market had generated an equally extreme backlash that turned markets into mere appendices of the fascist state (Polanyi 1944, 237). To use Robert Putnam's terminology, the disintegration of positive "bridging social capital" brought on by laissez-faire capitalism was followed by the generation of negative "bonding social capital" responsible for extreme forms of exclusivism (Putnam 2000, 22–23).

Thus, the relevance of Polanyi's analysis to Putnam's theory of social capital seems obvious. As neoliberal globalization tendencies strengthen, societies become more and more dominated by unbridled market forces that damage people's social relations and discourage civic engagement. In a world organized around the notion of individual liberty understood primarily as unrestrained economic entrepreneurship, traditional communal values of cooperation, solidarity, and civic participation are trumped by competitive market norms. Like its nineteenth-century predecessor, today's era of neoliberal globalization represents an experiment in unleashing the utopia of the self-regulating market on society. After a successful start in its respective countries in the 1970s, the phalanx of dominant Anglo-American globalist forces has been turning the entire world into its laboratory. Following Polanyi's analysis, one would expect the social costs of this free-market experiment, that is, declining social capital worldwide, to be staggering.

Putnam on Globalization: Review and Critique

Putnam's remarks (2000) regarding the potential correlation between neoliberal globalization and declining civic engagement in the United States are limited to a one-page discussion of the role of "big business, capitalism, and the market" (282–83). While grossly inadequate in scope and depth, his musings on globalization are nonetheless sufficiently revealing to offer the reader a glimpse of his overall rationale for recommending a swift dismissal of this particular "suspect." To begin with, Putnam acknowledges that social critics have long emphasized the tendency of capitalism to erode interpersonal ties and social trust by devaluing human ties to the status of mere commodities. But, for Putnam, the problem with such "generic theories of social disconnectedness" is that they "explain too much." As he emphasizes, "America has epitomized market capitalism for several centuries, during which our stocks of social capital and civic engagement have been through great swings. A constant can't explain a variable" (282).

But is American market capitalism really a "constant"? I submit that the answer to this question is, "No." The list of academic authors who have documented the passing of qualitatively distinct phases of capitalism in the United States is far too long to be reproduced here in its entirety.[3] Few, if any, political economists dispute the assertion that, for example, the "welfare capitalism" of the 1950s and 1960s represents a very different constellation from the "laissez-faire capitalism" of the 1920s or the "turbo-capitalism" of the 1990s. Indeed, acknowledgments of the changing face of American capitalism appear as matter-of-fact statements in introductory textbooks on American politics. It is hard to imagine reasons other than those intended to avoid a critical discussion of contemporary neoliberalism that would prompt Putnam to turn distinct phases of capitalism into an easily dismissable "constant." By admitting that capitalism is not a constant but a variable, Putnam would have to concede that changing economic dynamics are potential causes for the rise and fall of social capital in the United States.

Titled "Lessons of History: The Gilded Age and the Progressive Era," Putnam's sole sustained attempt to offer a critical reading of American capitalism can be found in chapter 23 of *Bowling Alone* (367–401). It is precisely in this section of the book that the author suddenly engages in a critique of political economy that contradicts his previous assertion that capitalism is a constant and therefore incapable of explaining the declining stocks of social capital. Putnam starts with the observation that the decades at the end of the nineteenth century and beginning of the twentieth were a period "uncannily like our own." He emphasizes that the Gilded Age saw the flourishing of new technologies that revolutionized virtually everything, from communication to agriculture. Between 1871 and 1913, the expansion of the American economy averaged an astonishing 4.3 percent annually. In spite of this economic expansion, however, the gap between rich and poor widened, putting more than half of the national wealth into the pockets of the top 1 percent of the population. America's cities turned into crime-ridden "industrial wastelands; centers of vice, poverty, and rampant disease" (373). It was a time of unbridled individualism, corporate mergers, urban growth, and massive migration. The dominant philosophy of laissez-faire celebrated individual gain and competitive self-interest. The widespread belief in the "natural laws of the marketplace" found its public expression in social Darwinism. As Putnam aptly observes, "in important respects this philosophy [of social Darwinism] foreshadowed the libertarian worship of the unconstrained market that has once again become popular in contemporary America" (378).

Putnam's reflections on the Gilded Age culminate in the realization that "older strands of social connection were being abraded—even destroyed—by technological and economic and social change" (382). Thus, he suddenly affirms what he had rejected only a few chapters earlier, namely, the strong possibility of a correlation between unregulated capitalism and civic disengagement. As he puts it, "Almost exactly a century ago America had also just experienced a period of dramatic technological, economic, and social change that rendered obsolete a significant stock of social capital" (367–68). Thus, Putnam concedes that concrete policy decisions such as the deregulation of markets are, after all, capable of depleting existing stocks of social capital.

But why does Putnam deny the central role of neoliberal politics in a similar epochal shift one hundred years later? Perhaps he is reluctant to embrace a position that would put him at odds with the powerful globalist forces of today. After all, judging from his own analysis of the Gilded Age, he should have arrived at an obvious hypothesis. If periods of marketization, commodification, and unconstrained market worship have led to episodes of civic disengagement in the past, then the emergence of similar marketization tendencies in our time is likely to bring about the same result, namely, the depletion of social capital.

In his brief discussion of globalization (282–83), Putnam presents his readers with an extremely narrow understanding of globalization as pertaining to the "replacement of local business structures in the United States." In other words, Putnam reduces the topic of globalization to a brief inquiry into the possible "decline in civic commitment on the part of business leaders." Contemplating the possibility that economic globalization might have some negative impact on the philanthropic activities of American business leaders, he ultimately finds that "it is less clear why corporate delocalization should affect, for example, our readiness to attend a church social, or to have friends over for poker, or even to vote for president" (283).

Having thus absolved business interests from any significant involvement in the "killing of civic engagement," Putnam returns to a consideration of the "ringleaders" responsible for the killing of civic engagement and social capital: increased work-related pressures of time and money (including longer commutes to suburbs), television, and generational change. But Putnam's discussion of these factors occurs in a political vacuum. Limiting his discussion of globalization to relatively unimportant themes of philanthropy and the declining civic business activities, Putnam disregards more substantive developments suggesting a link between globalization and disappearing social capital. For example, neoliberal globalization has contributed to growing social inequalities, the need to work longer to stay afloat, and a shrinking middle class. This, in turn, leads people to report "financial worries" and what Putnam calls "time pressures." The widening gap between the rich and poor is also a prime candidate responsible for the growth of insular neighborhoods as well as the breakdown of associations linking social groups. Finally, Putnam fails to mention that the connection between globalization and disappearing social connections is based on not just the time spent watching TV but also the content of TV and its intrusion into leisure time. In sum, I argue that much of what Putnam identifies as "declining social capital" is the result of concrete political decisions of globalist forces. Let me elaborate on these points in more detail.

First, let us examine Putnam's arguments with regard to mounting work pressures. He admits that the "economic climate in America from the middle 1970s to the middle 1990s was one of increasing anxiety" (189). Here, he explicitly refers to the financial worries experienced by Americans of all walks of life in the last three decades (192). While conceding that financial anxieties and economic troubles can have a profoundly depressing effect on people's social involvement, he nonetheless refuses to make neoliberal politics responsible for declining social capital. As he puts it, "The economy went up and down [since the 1970s], but social capital only went down" (193).

No doubt, during the last three decades, the U.S. economy has gone through several cycles of boom and recession. Still, there is overwhelming evidence for the existence of a constant that corresponds to the falling levels of social capital: widening inequalities of income and wealth. Since the early 1970s, the average wages for middle-income earners have barely kept pace with inflation, and those incomes at the bottom of the scale actually have fallen in real terms. Inequality of wealth also widened, with gaps between haves and have-nots escalating to levels last experienced during the Great Depression (Galbraith 2000, xix). At the same time, corporate and business profits have risen to new heights, as did the incomes of corporate managers. From 1989 to 1999, CEOs enjoyed a 62.7 percent pay raise, while 90th percentile earners gained only a meager 12.9 percent. In 1999, the typical CEO earned 107 times more than the typical worker, up from the 1989 ratio of 56:1. At the close of the 1990s, the top 1 percent of stock owners in the United States held almost half of all stocks, while the bottom 80 percent owned just 4.1 percent of total stock holdings (Mishel et al. 2001). As most economic models show, the existence of pronounced inequalities of income and wealth poses a significant threat to the health of democracy, because rising social inequalities correlate strongly with declining civic participation (Galbraith 2000; Mishel et al. 2001).

Yet, Putnam barely mentions rising levels of inequality in America, and he also fails to offer the reader important historical comparisons of social and economic policy. For example, during the period of welfare capitalism from 1945 to 1970, the U.S. government as a whole was committed to the pursuit of full employment, price stability, steady economic growth, and social protection for low-income workers. During the neoliberal turn beginning in the 1970s, however, Keynesian policies and welfare provisions were gradually withdrawn as U.S. corporate profit margins fell significantly as a result of the greater international competitiveness of East Asian and European industry (Gowan 1999). American corporations responded by cutting workers' wages and benefits and through an increasing eagerness to move their production sites to cheap-labor regions. The state accommodated the desire of U.S. corporations to increase their leverage vis-à-vis workers by pushing the expansion of a neoliberal trade regime. This led to the strengthening of the global trend toward corporate buyouts and mergers rather than investment in workers' training. The neoliberal withdrawal of the U.S. industry's long-term commitment to the work force sounded the death knell to Putnam's Golden Age of company-sponsored bowling leagues. The capitalist logic of enhancing the profitability of corporations trumped the ethical imperative to protect and enhance social cohesion. Government policies reinforced this dynamic by opting for the classical liberal twin strategy of maintaining a tight money supply and tolerating high levels of unemployment. Thus, declining levels of social capital undermined the middle-class character of American society (Galbraith 2000, 10).

By failing to criticize the negative impact of neoliberal policies on social equality, Putnam closes his eyes to the strong possibility that *particular political decisions* might be responsible for chronic financial anxiety, increased time pressure, and enhanced working hours—factors that, according to his own analysis, partly account for declining social capital in America.[4]

The necessary critique of neoliberal politics is also missing from Putnam's discussion of television and other forms of electronic entertainment. He argues forcefully that increased television watching can be linked empirically to the rise of civic disengagement in this country. Connecting this argument to his claim that generations born after 1940 are socially less engaged than their parents and grandparents, Putnam identifies younger people as members of an intensely private, socially disconnected, and passive "TV generation." He summarizes his findings on this topic in the following way: "Americans at the end of the twentieth century are watching more TV, watching it more habitually, more pervasively, and more often alone, and watching more programs that were associated with civic disengagement (entertainment, as distinct from news). The onset of these trends coincided exactly with the national decline in social connect- edness, and the trends were most marked among the younger generation . . ." (246).

Putnam is surely right on the first point. There is little doubt that Americans have become more hooked on televised entertainment than ever before. The daily average viewing time spent per TV home has in- creased from 5 hours and 56 minutes in 1970 to 7 hours and 26 minutes in 1999. In 1999, TV household penetration stood at 98.3 percent, with 73.9 percent of TV households owning two or more sets. In the same year, cable TV penetration climbed to a record 67.2 percent and VCR penetra- tion reached an astonishing 84.6 percent (Television Bureau of Advertising 2000). Putnam also correctly points to a steep increase of shallow "enter- tainment shows" at the expense of more informational and educational programs. Perhaps he is even right in his controversial claims that exces- sive television watching is mildly addictive, causes anxiety, irritation, and depression, undermines physical health, encourages lethargy and passivity, steals valuable family and community time, obstructs civic enlightenment, provides merely pseudo-personal connections, and replaces social aware- ness and neighborly concern with asocial entertainment values (238–46).

Yet, nowhere in *Bowling Alone* can one find a critical analysis of the *pol- itics of television placed within the context of neoliberal globalization.* What are the social and political forces that have fueled the expansion of what political theorist Benjamin Barber (1996, 60) has called the "infotainment telesector"? What are the political and economic interests that are driving the proliferation of entertainment programs on television? Putnam (2000, 245) correctly refers to "the encouragement of materialist values" as "an- other probable effect of television." But he remains silent on the principal *causes* of the commercialization of television, thus failing to explore the political forces and shifting social conditions behind these developments. In fact, Putnam speaks of "the rise of electronic communications and en- tertainment as one of the most powerful social trends in the twentieth century" (245)—as if the commercialization of television was a natural phenomenon that "just happens," like bad weather or an earthquake.

Communications scholars Edward Herman and Robert McChesney (1997) have pointed out that the same powerful phalanx of social forces behind neoliberal globalization are also responsible for the creation of a global commercial media system. The dissemination of TV images around the world is controlled by a small number of super-powerful, mostly

U.S.–based transnational media corporations that also dominate global markets for other types of entertainment such as radio, publishing, music, theme parks, and cinema. According to communications expert David De-mers (1999, 4), twelve media corporations accounted in 1999 for more than half of the $250 billion in yearly worldwide revenues generated by the communications industry. In the first half of 2000, the volume of merger deals in global media, Internet, and telecommunications totaled $300 bil-lion, triple the figure for the first six months of 1999, and exponentially higher than the figure ten years earlier (McChesney 2001). AOL-Time Warner, Disney, Sony, Viacom, Vivendi, Bertelsmann, and the News Cor-poration did not exist in their present form as media companies as re-cently as fifteen years ago. In 2001, nearly all of these corporations ranked among the largest 300 nonfinancial firms in the world. Even some defend-ers of globalism like Christopher Dixon, media analyst for the investment firm Paine Webber, concede that the recent emergence of a global com-mercial-media market amounts to the "creation of a global oligopoly. It happened to the oil and automotive industries earlier this century; now it is happening to the entertainment industry" (cited in McChesney 2001, 2).

Only tangentially committed to the promotion of democratic values, critical thinking, and robust public debates about social inequalities and injustices, the global media system "works to advance the cause of the global market and promote commercial values, while denigrating journal-ism and culture not conducive to the immediate bottom line or long-run corporate interest" (McChesney 1997, 11). Not necessarily linked by a conspiratorial intent but by the pursuit of profits, the mainstream media in the United States nonetheless share a neoliberal worldview that results in the creation of remarkably similar TV programs. In this regard, one of the most glaring developments of the last two decades is the transforma-tion of informational broadcasts and educational programs into shallow entertainment shows filled with endless commercials and trivial "human interest stories." The commercialization of news makes sense in the con-text of the "new economy" and its deregulatory neoliberal policies. Given that news is less than half as profitable as entertainment, media firms are increasingly tempted to pursue higher profits by ignoring journalism's much vaunted separation of newsroom practices and business decisions. Partnerships and alliances between news and entertainment companies are fast becoming the norm, making it more common for publishing exec-utives to press journalists to cooperate with their newspapers' business op-erations. As communications scholar William Solomon (2000) emphasizes, the attack on the professional autonomy of journalism is part of the neoliberal transformation of media and communication.

The consumerist values disseminated by transnational media enterprises contribute not only to the cultural hegemony of American culture, but also to the global depoliticization of social reality and the weakening of civic bonds. A ceaseless barrage of TV and radio advertisements facilitates the formation of consumerist self-images that structure people's wants and desires from the time they learn to speak. Unfortunately, Putnam has no comment on the explosive growth of advertisement "clutter" on television and radio. As media specialist Matthew P. McAllister (1996, 24–25) points out, TV clutter has increased since the early 1970s in a number of ways. First, today there exist more television outlets that carry ads. Second, the major networks try to squeeze in more commercials, especially in popular entertainment and sports shows. The TV advertisement volume in the United States has increased from $3.60 billion in 1970 to $50.44 billion in 1999 (Television Bureau of Advertising 2000). Accordingly, advertisement clutter on radio and network television reached new record levels in 2000. ABC and NBC averaged over 15 minutes of commercials per prime time TV hour, not including cutaways for local ads (Mass Media News 2000). The daytime level of advertising on major TV networks increased to 20:53 minutes per hour. These remarkable figures indicate that today's TV stations and advertisers have more power than ever to transmit consumerist images and values to the viewing public (Kaufman 2000).

Third, TV clutter increased as a result of the shift to neoliberal deregulation. In the area of communications, this means that the barriers to commercial exploitation of media and to concentrated media ownership have been relaxed or eliminated (McChesney 2001). The 1996 deregulation of the telecommunications industry fundamentally weakened public control over the dissemination of sounds and images in the United States. Yet, Putnam is content to discuss only the final *effects* of this chain of political developments leading back to the rise of neoliberal globalization in the 1970s. In order to present the reader with a comprehensive genealogy of these "uncivic" effects of television—as measured in the depletion of social capital—Putnam would have to offer a critical analysis of the political forces behind these commercial interests. In addition, the link between the growth of the global media system and the loss of social capital with regard to the younger generations must be properly politicized. For example, recent studies show that American children at age 12 watch an average of 20,000 TV commercials a year, and that 2-year-old toddlers can already develop brand loyalties (Real Vision 2000). It seems obvious that the increasing ability of commercialized television to reach young people contributes to the formation of less communitarian generations.

The political causes of growing TV clutter are hardly a mystery. But a number of recent political initiatives show that it is possible to contest the marketization of society that underlies the decline of social capital. For example, when Sweden assumed the rotating chair of the European Union in 2001, Swedish representatives in Brussels pushed to have their domestic ban on TV advertising to children made into a law binding to all EU nations (McChesney 2001). Based on a clear understanding of the political causes of excessive commercialism and the socially destructive effects unleashed by neoliberal globalization, the Swedish initiative represents what Karl Polanyi would expect to see in response to the global imposition of the free market: transnational social forces seeking increasingly to limit the power of the corporate media giants that dominate commercial children's television. Except for a historical chapter on the rise of progressivism in response to the Gilded Age, *Bowling Alone* contains neither the critical analysis nor the political engagement required to identify and counteract a neoliberal dynamic that fuels the decline of civic engagement in America.

Concluding Remarks

In this chapter, I have argued that Robert Putnam's *magnus opus* contains impressive evidence for the book's central thesis: civic engagement in American communities is on the wane. Yet, Putnam fails to engage in a political discussion that focuses on the relationship between the decline of social capital and the rise of neoliberal globalization—even though both phenomena emerged at roughly the same time. As demonstrated by his critical analysis of political and economic developments during the Gilded Age and the Progressive Era, however, Putnam seems to be keenly aware of the correlation between periods of unconstrained market worship and the weakening of social bonds. And yet, he retreats from a similar analysis with regard to the politics of neoliberal globalization.

This chapter ends by offering two constructive suggestions for future research on social capital. First, the American participants in this debate ought to make a special effort to bring politics back into their discussion.

We need to open ourselves up to the dramatic political developments of our time, particularly to the unprecedented compression of time and space reflected in the tremendous intensification of social, political, economic, and cultural interconnections and interdependencies on a global scale. To be sure, globalization is an incipient process, slowly giving rise to a new condition of globality whose eventual qualities and properties are far from being determined. We do know from past experience, however, that such periods of rapid social transformation represent mixed blessings by threatening existing forms of solidarity as well as offering new forms of solidarity and new ways of rebuilding human community.

This leads me to my second suggestion. No serious scholar of social capital can afford to discuss the changing patterns of social structures in relative isolation, that is, within the increasingly anachronistic framework of the nation-state. Putnam (1993) has written extensively on Italian civil society; perhaps his next study of social capital will incorporate cross-cultural findings. In the age of globalization, social trends in the United States are profoundly influenced by events around the globe. If I am correct in postulating a significant cause-effect relationship between neoliberal globalization and declining social capital, then civic disengagement ought to be evident not only in the United States of America, but in virtually all countries of the world. Hence my hope that the social capital debate will become more comparative in method and more internationalist in character. The time has come to expand the parochial horizon that still defines mainstream "American political science." As social thinkers embedded in our historical context, we need to reconceptualize the dimensions and boundaries of our discipline in innovative and serious ways that allow us to see the bigger, global picture. If we fail in this endeavor, we may continue to cultivate a sense of detachment within our ivory towers, but such academic serenity most often bears the price of political irrelevance.

NOTES

1. For example, already six years ago, Indiana University political theorist Jeffrey Isaac (1995) noted the "strange silence of political theory" with respect to the momentous 1989 revolutions in Eastern Europe. As Isaac points out, between 1989 and 1993, the *American Political Science Review* and *Political Theory* published a grand total of one article that dealt with these "dramatic current events of earth-shattering importance" (637).

2. See, for example, Giddens (1990); Holton (1998); Lechner and Boli (2000); Mittelman (2000); Robertson (1992); Waters (1995).

3. See, for example, Brandes (1976); Eisner (1998); Faulkner (1989); Fite (1973); Galbraith (1980); Luttwak (1999); Munkirs (1985); Norton (1985); O'-Toole (1990); Shaffer, 1999 ; Soule (1968); Stein (1988); and Tufte (1998).

4. As Mishel et al. (2001) point out, in the late 1990s, the average family worked 83 weeks a year, up from 68 weeks in 1969.

References

Barber, Benjamin. 1996. *Jihad vs. McWorld: How Globalism and Tribalism Are Reshaping the World*. New York: Ballantine Books.

Brandes, Stuart. 1976. *American Welfare Capitalism, 1880–1940*. Chicago: University of Chicago Press.

Demers, David. 1999. *Global Media: Menace or Messiah?* Cresskill, N.J.: Hampton Press.

Eisner, Robert. 1998. *The Keynesian Revolution: Then and Now*. Northhampton, Mass.: E. Elgar.

Esping-Anderson, Gosta. 1990. *The Three Worlds of Welfare Capitalism*. Princeton: Princeton University Press.

Faulkner, Harold. 1989 [1951]. *The Decline of Laissez Faire, 1897–1917*. Armonk, N.Y.: M. E. Sharpe.

Fite, Gilbert. 1973. *An Economic History of the United States*. 3d ed. Boston: Houghton Mifflin.

Friedman, Milton. 1982 [1962]. *Capitalism and Freedom*. Chicago: University of Chicago Press.

Galbraith, James K. 2000 [1998]. *Created Unequal: The Crisis in American Pay*. Chicago: University of Chicago Press.

Galbraith, John Kenneth. 1980. *American Capitalism: The Concept of Countervailing Power*. Armonk, N.Y.: M. E. Sharpe.

Giddens, Anthony. 1990. *The Consequences of Modernity*. Stanford: Stanford University Press.

Gilpin, Robert. 2000. *The Challenge of Global Capitalism: The World Economy in the 21st Century*. Princeton: Princeton University Press.

Gowan, Peter. 1999. *The Global Gamble: Washington's Faustian Bid for World Dominance*. London: Verso.

Herman, Edward S., and Robert W. McChesney. 1997. *The Global Media: The New Missionaries of Corporate Capitalism*. London: Cassell.

Holton, Robert J. 1998. *Globalization and the Nation-State*. New York: St. Martin's Press.

Isaac, Jeffrey C. 1995. "The Strange Silence of Political Theory," *Political Theory* 23.4: 636–52.

Kaufman, Ron. 2000. "Ratings and Advertising: What Are Americans *Really* Watching?" http://www.netreach.net/~kaufman/ratingsAds.html.

Lechner, Frank J., and John Boli, eds. 2000. *The Globalization Reader.* Malden, Mass.: Blackwell.

Luttwak, Edward. 1999. *Turbo-Capitalism: Winners and Losers in the Global Economy.* New York: HarperCollins.

Mass Media News. 2000. "Two TV Networks Running 15 Minutes of Ads." http://taa.winona.msus.edu/mediaupdate/00/11nov.html.

McAllister, Matthew P. 1996. *The Commercialization of American Culture: New Advertising, Control, and Democracy.* Thousand Oaks, Calif.: Sage.

McChesney, Robert W. 2001. "Global Media, Neoliberalism, and Imperialism," *Monthly Review* 52.10 (March): http://www.monthlyreview.org/301rwm.html.

———. 1997. "The Global Media Giants: The Nine Firms that Dominate the World," *Extra* 10.6 (November/December). http://www.fair.org/extra/9711/gmg.html.

Milbank, Dana. 2001. "Needed: Catchword for Bush Ideology," *Washington Post* (February 1): A1.

Mishel, Lawrence, Jared Bernstein, and John Schmitt. 2001. *The State of Working America 2000–2001.* Ithaca: Cornell University Press.

Mittelman, James H. 2000. *The Globalization Syndrome: Transformation and Resistance.* Princeton: Princeton University Press.

Munkirs, John. 1985. *The Transformation of American Capitalism.* Armonk, N.Y.: M. E. Sharpe.

Norton, Hugh S. 1985. *The Quest for Economic Stability: Roosevelt to Reagan.* Columbia: University of South Carolina Press.

O'Toole, Thomas. 1990. *The Economic History of the United States.* Minneapolis: Lerner Publications.

Polanyi, Karl. 1944. *The Great Transformation.* Boston: Beacon Press.

Putnam, Robert D. 2000. *Bowling Alone: The Collapse and Revival of American Community.* New York: Simon & Schuster.

———. 1996. "The Strange Disappearance of Civic America." *The American Prospect* (Winter): 34–49.

———. 1995a. "Bowling Alone: America's Declining Social Capital," *Journal of Democracy* 6: 65–78.

———. 1995b. "Tuning In, Turning Out: The Strange Disappearance of Social Capital in America," *PS: Political Science and Politics* 28: 664–83.

———. 1993. *Making Democracy Work.* Princeton: Princeton University Press.

Real Vision. 2000. "Facts and Figures about our TV Habit." http://www.tv-turnoff.org.

Robertson, Roland. 1992. *Globalization: Social Theory and Global Culture*. London: Sage.

Rosow, Stephen J. 2000. "Globalization as Democratic Theory," *Millennium* 29.1: 27–45.

Schaeffer, Robert K. 1997. *Understanding Globalization: The Social Consequences of Political, Economic, and Environmental Change*. Lanham: Rowman & Littlefield.

Scholte, Jan Aart. 2000. *Globalization: A Critical Introduction*. New York: St. Martin's Press.

Shaffer, Harry G. 1999. *American Capitalism and the Changing Role of Government*. Westport, Conn.: Praeger.

Solomon, William S. 2000. "More Form than Substance: Press Coverage of the WTO Protests in Seattle," *Monthly Review* 52.1 (May). http://www.monthlyreview.org/500solo.html.

Soule, George. 1968. *Prosperity Decade: From War to Depression*. New York: Harper & Row.

Steger, Manfred B. 2001. *Globalism: The New Market Ideology*. Lanham: Rowman & Littlefield.

Stein, Herbert. 1988. *Presidential Economics: The Making of Economic Policy from Roosevelt to Reagan*. 2d. rev. ed. Washington, D.C.: American Enterprise Institute.

Television Bureau of Advertising. 2000. "Advertising Volume in the United States." http://www.tvb.org.

Tufte, Edward R. 1998. *Political Control of the Economy*. Princeton: Princeton University Press.

Waters, Malcolm. 1995. *Globalization*. London: Routledge.

Yergin, Daniel, and Joseph Stanislaw. 1998. *The Commanding Heights: The Battle Between Government and the Market Place That Is Remaking the Modern World*. New York: Simon & Schuster.

Afterword

Scott L. McLean

This book began by lamenting the civic disappointments in the election of 2000; it ought to end with a critical postscript on the hopes for civic revival after the horrific terrorist attacks of September 11, 2001. As Robert Putnam put the question in a February 2002 article: Is September 11 "a period that puts a full stop to one era and opens a new, more community-minded chapter in our history? Or is it merely a comma, a brief pause during which we looked up for a moment and then returned to our solitary pursuits" (Putnam 2002, 20)?

In 1776, Thomas Paine stated that the shock, grief, and rage at seeing fellow citizens murdered by invaders is a "seedtime" for a new republic (Paine 1976 [1776], 107). But in an old republic, such moments may offer only fleeting reminders of the theoretical foundations of the regime. It is rare and profoundly difficult, as Abraham Lincoln knew, for citizens to refound their republic, and rededicate themselves to "the public thing." Still, there were signs of hope in the smoldering wreckage of the twin towers. So many Americans reacted admirably; volunteering, emergency blood donations, and even enlistment in Americorps all increased dramatically just after the attacks (Copeland 2001).

An ocean of American flags signified a powerful sense of unity and pride of country, as well as a sorrowful tribute to fallen innocents and rescue workers. Major League baseball instituted the singing of "God Bless America" during every seventh-inning stretch. Surveys revealed a myriad of spontaneous displays of patriotism. Gallup found in the week after the attack that over 80 percent of Americans displayed an American flag, 60 percent attended memorial services, almost three-quarters prayed, and an equal number said they were showing greater affection than usual for loved ones (Gallup 2001a). The *Washington Post*/ABC News poll found that nearly three-quarters of the public described themselves as "strongly patriotic"—a level not matched since the middle of the 1991 Gulf War (1991; 2001).

Hoping to probe more deeply into these trends, Putnam and his colleagues, in the fall of 2001, reinterviewed people he had talked to the previous summer. His surveys revealed Americans quickly returning to the routines of their private lives. But what of public life? "We found unmistakable evidence of change," said Putnam (Putnam 2002, 20). He reported that trust in government, trust in the police, and interest in politics were all significantly higher than they were before September 11. More Americans reported cooperating with neighbors to solve problems. Volunteering and donations of money or blood all increased, slightly. Even church attendance saw a 7 percent spike, though it has returned to its previous level (Gallup 2001c; Gallup 2001d).

Putnam also found that television viewing was up and having friends over to visit was down (Putnam 2002, 21). Gallup found in the days after the attacks about half of Americans favored the idea that Arabs, even those who are U.S. citizens, should be required to carry special identification papers (Gallup 2001a). There was an outbreak of hate crimes against Muslims, and on the September 13 airing of *The 700 Club*, Reverend Jerry Falwell blamed the attacks on abortionists, feminists, gays, lesbians, and the ACLU—all "who have tried to secularize America" and turn the nation away from God. (People for the American Way 2001).

Despite these danger signs, the American people should be credited for resisting these immediate reactions of hatred better than "the greatest generation" did in 1942. President George W. Bush rightly struck a public image of religious toleration and bipartisanship. And though the attorney general rounded up a few hundred suspicious Arab immigrants, nothing on the scale of Franklin Delano Roosevelt's internment of Japanese-Americans is likely to occur. Even the President's plan to hold secret military trials for suspected enemies was limited significantly because of public pressure.

Putnam himself has correctly given a stronger governmental prescription for consolidating the post-9/11 improvements in civic life than he did in *Bowling Alone*. Shocking pictures of terrorism and destruction can shake us out of our isolation and our familiar existence, but symbols of patriotism and images of solidarity are not a sturdy foundation for a civic revival. As Putnam put it, "though the crisis replenished the wells of solidarity in American communities, those wells so far remain untapped" (Putnam 2002, 22). Putnam appears now to recognize that civic change requires more than simply boosting the number of volunteers, picnics, or sporting leagues. The revival will be more a matter of reorganizing the structure of civil society. The state can play a necessary role here in channeling people's energy into public-regarding activities, as it did during World Wars I and II (Putnam 2001; Skocpol et al. 2000).

What are the political and social limitations for the American state to repeat the mobilization efforts of previous eras? Certainly leaders have the capital to expend on such a project. In a tremendous demonstration of the "rally 'round the flag" effect, the job approval ratings of the chief flag bearer, President Bush, went from 51 percent just before the attacks to 86 percent in a record-breaking overnight leap (Gallup 2001b). The public is rallying behind the President but it is still waiting for a clear signal about what burdens and sacrifices citizens must bear in the war on terrorism. One signal has been to remain calm, return to a normal routine, and continue consumer spending. In his speech to Congress and the nation on September 20, the President said, "Americans are asking: What is expected of us? I ask you to live your lives and hug your children" (Bush 2001).

President Bush may be correct that a return to a tolerant and calm (if self-absorbed) civil society today is preferable to the dangers of unleashing xenophobia and extreme nationalism. Still, it is interesting to note the contrast between Bush's message, and President Roosevelt's 1942 call to sacrifice. "Here at home everyone will have the privilege of making whatever self-denial is necessary," Roosevelt said (1942). Roosevelt called for the deferment of personal consumption and higher taxes and said that sacrifice is "not the proper word for this program of denial ... The price is not too high" (1942).

President Bush gave a different call to sacrifice: "In the sacrifice of soldiers, the fierce brotherhood of firefighters, and the bravery and generosity of ordinary citizens, we have glimpsed what a new culture of responsibility could look like. We want to be a nation that serves goals larger than self" (Bush 2002). States would be required to get even more welfare clients into the workforce or lose federal support. To pick up the slack in social services, the President called every American to volunteer a minimum of 4,000 hours (two years) in community service. Faith-based organizations would be allowed grants to shoulder the social service burden. Government-sponsored service organizations like the Peace Corps and Americorps would be expanded. Colleges would be required to place more students in community organizations in order to get federal funds. Finally, Bush also created USA Freedom Corps that will assist with homeland security and emergency efforts.

The rhetoric of community service is reminiscent of an older republican vision of the amateur citizen, but it conceals the modern state's need for experts and technicians. A day after President Bush called for greater volunteerism, Tom Ridge, the director of the Office of Homeland Security, seemed at a loss to explain what to do with volunteers. Ridge called for retired engineers, police officers, and health care professionals as the prime targets for volunteer recruitment, not ordinary citizens (Mitchell 2001).

Why? Voluntary labor is not free. Whether they volunteer for government or for community organizations, screening, training, and monitoring volunteers, especially for the technical tasks of wartime mobilization and security, is costly. Ordinary citizens volunteer not only from a general desire to serve but also because they are personally invited to serve by someone they know. Hence, generalized calls for volunteers from the bully pulpit are not as effective as direct recruiting efforts at the grassroots (Krueger 2002). A study by Jean Baldwin Grossman estimated that the additional 100 million Americans called for volunteer service would require management costs of around $30 billion (Krueger 2002). To pay for volunteers, government would have to ask multi-millionaires and corporations to fund service organizations, or raise taxes. Given Washington's desire to cut taxes for the wealthy, the latter is unlikely. But either way, it seems that the government will attempt to promote volunteerism on the cheap and focus most on recruiting highly skilled volunteers.

In closing, we should look once again at the connection between democracy and trust in government. Trust that the government does the right thing may very well indicate unity, patriotism, or acceptance of executive leadership. A rally in trust was reflected in higher confidence in the President, Congress, the media, state and local government, and even religious institutions. It was as if immediately after September 11 virtually every national institution became more "trustworthy." Are these rally effects caused more by surges of patriotism during crisis? Or do they only cause temporary suspension of criticism from media and opposition political leaders (Brody 1991, 77; Parker 1995, 540)? If it is the latter, we can expect a fading trust in government and passionate patriotism as news of the Middle East conflict and the fiercely contested battle for control of Congress heats up. Indeed, by January 2002, trust in government had dropped almost halfway back to its pre-9/11 level (CBS/New York Times Poll 2002).

Nevertheless, it remains unclear why increased trust in government should matter for democracy, at least as it is measured in the standard survey question (Moore 2002, 9). A person who answers in a survey that he or she trusts the government to do the right thing only "some of the time" may be a better citizen than the one who answers that he or she trusts government "just about always." The "trust government sometimes" group is just as likely to be well informed and vote as those who say they trust government "always" or "most of the time" (Institute for Social Research 1998)

America after the terrorist attacks still echoes Tocqueville's view that "An American attends to his private concerns as if he were alone in the world, and the next minute he gives himself up to the common weal as if he had forgotten them" (Tocqueville 1990, 142). Community sentiments or allegiance to the values of American institutions are necessary for democratic revival, but they are not sufficient to the task. Consumerism, television, declining cities, economic inequalities, globalization, and the role of corporate America in politics are persistent realities that cannot be wished away with good community feelings. Ironically, after September 11, 2001, the gap between community sentiments and civic engagement seems wider than ever.

References

Brody, Richard A. 1991. *Assessing the President: The Media, Elite Opinion, and Public Support.* Stanford: Stanford University Press.

Bush, George W. 2001. "Address to a Joint Session of Congress and the American People." September 20. http://www.whitehouse.gov/news/releases/2001/09/20010920-8.html.

———. 2002. "State of the Union Address." January 29. http://www.whitehouse.gov/news/releases/2002/01/20020129-11.html.

CBS/*New York Times* Poll. 2002. Telephone survey of 1,034 randomly selected U.S. adults, January 21–24. Question: "How much of the time can you trust the government in Washington to do what is right—just about always, most of the time, only some of the time, or never?" Results: just about always, 5 percent; most of the time, 41 percent; some of the time, 51 percent; never, 1 percent.

Copeland, Larry. 2001. "Volunteering Up since September 11." *USA Today*, November 23–25: 1A.

Gallup Poll. 2001a. Telephone survey of 1,032 randomly selected U.S. adults, September 14–15. Question: "(I'd like to ask you a few questions about the events (terrorist attacks) that occurred this past Tuesday (September 11, 2001) in New York City and Washington, D.C.). . . . Please tell me if you would favor or oppose . . . the following as a means of preventing terrorist attacks in the United States. How about . . . requiring Arabs, including those who are U.S. citizens, to carry a special ID?" Results: favor, 49 percent; oppose, 49 percent; no opinion, 2 percent.

Gallup Poll. 2001b. Telephone survey of 1,032 randomly selected U.S. adults. September 14–15. Question: "As a result of the terrorist attacks this past Tuesday, have you, personally, done or plan to do any of the following?" Display American flag: 82 percent yes, 18 percent no; attend memorial service: 60 percent yes, 39 percent no; pray more than you usually do: 74 percent yes, 25 percent no; show more affection for loved ones than you usually do: 77 percent yes, 22 percent no.

Gallup Poll. 2001c. Telephone survey of 1,005 randomly selected U.S. adults, September 21–22. Question: "Did you yourself, happen to attend church or synagogue in the last seven days, or not?" Results: yes, 47 percent; no, 53 percent.

Gallup Poll. 2001d. Telephone survey of 1,019 randomly selected U.S. adults, December 14–16. Question: "Did you yourself, happen to attend church or synagogue in the last seven days, or not?" Result: yes, 41 percent; no, 59 percent.

Institute for Social Research. 1998. *American National Election Study.* Belleview, Wash.: MicroCase Corporation.

Krueger, Alan B. 2002. "Economic Scene: The President Wants Americans to Volunteer to Pick up the Slack in Social Services. But Will That Be Enough?" *New York Times,* February 7: C2.

Mitchell, Alison. 2001. "After Asking for Volunteers, Government Tries to Determine What They Will Do." *New York Times,* November 10: B7.

Moore, David W. 2002. "Just One Question." *Public Perspective,* January/February: 7–11.

Paine, Thomas 1976 [1776]. *Common Sense.* New York: Penguin Books.

Parker, Suzanne L. 1995. "Toward an Understanding of 'Rally' Effects: Public Opinion in the Persian Gulf War." *Public Opinion Quarterly* 59.4 (Winter): 526–546.

People for the American Way 2001. Transcript of Pat Robertson's Interview with Jerry Falwell. http://www.pfaw.org/911/robertson_falwell.html.

Putnam, Robert 2001. "A Better Society in a Time of War." *New York Times,* October 19: A19.

———. 2002. "Bowling Together: The United State of America." *American Prospect,* February 11, 2002: 20–22.

Roosevelt, Franklin D. 1942. "A Call to Sacrifice" April 28. http://fordham.edu/halsall/mod/1942roosevelt-sacrifice.html.

Skocpol, Theda, Marshall Ganz, and Ziad Munson. 2000. "A Nation of Organizers:

The Institutional Origins of Civic Voluntarism in the United States. *American Political Science Review* 94.3: 527–546.

Tocqueville, Alexis. 1990. *Democracy in America.* Volume 2. New York: Random House.

Washington Post/ABC News Poll 2001. Telephone survey of 1,215 randomly selected U.S. adults, September 25–27. Question: "Do you consider yourself strongly patriotic, somewhat patriotic, or not very patriotic at all?" Results: strongly patriotic, 73 percent; somewhat patriotic, 24 percent; not very patriotic, 2 percent.

Washington Post/ABC News Poll 1991. Telephone survey of 778 randomly selected U.S. adults, February 27. Question: "Do you consider yourself strongly patriotic, somewhat patriotic, or not very patriotic at all?" Results: strongly patriotic, 70 percent; somewhat patriotic, 26 percent; not very patriotic, 4 percent.

About the Contributors

Yvette M. Alex-Assensoh is Associate Professor of Political Science at Indiana University, where she teaches and conducts research in the areas of urban politics, political behavior, and minority politics. She is the author of *Neighborhoods, Family and Political Behavior in Urban America* (Garland, 1998); the co-editor of *Black and Multiracial Politics in America* (NYU Press, 2000); and the co-author of *African Politics and History: Ideological and Military Incursions, 1900–Present* (St. Martin's Press, 2001). Her research has been funded by the National Science Foundation, Social Science Research Council, the Ford Foundation, the National Academy of Education, and the Spencer Foundation. Her current research projects focus on the political consequences of racial school segregation in America, and a comparative analysis of minority political incorporation in Croatia and the United States.

Carl Boggs is Professor of Social Sciences at National University in Los Angeles. He is the author of numerous books in political and social theory, European politics, and mass movements. His most recent works include *The End of Politics* (Guilford Press, 2000), *The Socialist Tradition* (Routledge, 1996), and *Intellectuals and the Crisis of Modernity* (SUNY Press, 1993).

Lane Crothers is Associate Professor of Political Science at Illinois State University. His fields of expertise are political culture and political leadership. He is the author or editor of two books: *Street Level Leadership: Discretion and Legitimacy in Frontline Public Service* (Georgetown University Press), coauthored with Janet Vinzant of Arizona State University; and *Culture and Politics: A Reader* (St. Martin's Press), co-edited with Charles Lockhart of Texas Christian University. He is currently involved in two more book-length projects, one on the Reagan, Bush, and Clinton presidencies, and another on the modern American militia movement.

John Ehrenberg is Professor and Chair of Political Science at the Brooklyn Campus of Long Island University. He has published extensively on socialist and democratic political theory and has been presenting the results of his scholarly work at professional meetings for many years. His latest book, *Civil Society: The Critical History of an Idea*, was published by NYU Press in 1999 and was awarded the Michael Harrington Award by the Caucus for a New Political Science for the best book of that year. He is also a member of the editorial board of *Science and Society*.

Michael Forman is Assistant Professor of Social and Political Theory at the University of Washington in Tacoma, and also a member of the Tri-Campus Center for Labor Studies of the University of Washington. He is author of numerous articles and of *Nationalism and the International Labor Movement: The Idea of the Nation in Anarchist and Socialist Theory* (Penn State University Press, 1998), which won the 1999 Michael Harrington Award. He has also acted as a consultant for the Washington State AFL-CIO, for the Central Labor Council of King County, Washington, and for the International Longshore and Warehouse Workers Union (ILWU).

Amy Fried is Associate Professor of Political Science at the University of Maine. She teaches courses on American public opinion, American political thought, political participation, women and politics, and media and politics. She is the author of *Muffled Echoes: Oliver North and the Politics of Public Opinion* (Columbia University Press, 1997) and numerous articles and chapters on citizen values and participation, gender politics, political movements, and public opinion. Fried's 1999 paper on Tocqueville and the social capital debate was awarded the John C. Donovan Prize for the best paper presented at the New England Political Science Association Annual Meeting.

Jessica Kulynych was Assistant Professor of Political Theory at Winthrop University, and is now an independent scholar. She has published articles on the impact of postmodern and feminist theory on contemporary understandings of political participation and public deliberation. She is also working on a book exploring the incorporation of children's voices into the democratic public sphere. She is currently on leave from academia to advocate for children and care for her daughter.

Scott L. McLean is Associate Professor of Political Science at Quinnipiac University, Political Analyst in the Quinnipiac University Polling Institute, and Chair of Service Learning at Quinnipiac University. He is frequently featured as a political commentator on elections and voters in regional and national media. He is a frequent contributor to *The Public Perspective* and C-SPAN's Website. He serves on the Connecticut Secretary of the State's Youth Democracy Advisory Board and is a member of the Advisory Board of the Albert Schweitzer Institute. His scholarly research focuses on political theory, civic attitudes, civic education, urban politics, and the history of American patriotism. His current research focuses on the intellectual impact of imperialism in the late nineteenth century.

Douglas Rae is the Richard S. Ely Professor of Management and Political Science at Yale University. He is a specialist in the political economy of cities, electoral politics, political ideology, and power relations. He took leave from the Yale faculty in 1990 and 1991 to serve as Chief Administrative Officer of the City of New Haven. He currently is codirector of the federal government's Community Renaissance Fellowship Program. He is author of numerous books and articles including *Equalities* (Harvard University Press, 1981), *Political Consequences of Electoral Law* (Yale University Press, 1967), and editor (with Theodore J. Eismeier) of *Public Policy and Public Choice* (Sage Publications, 1979).

David A. Schultz is Director of the Doctoral Program in Public Administration and professor in the Graduate School of Public Administration and Management at Hamline University, where he teaches classes including ethics in government, legislative process, research methods, housing and economic policy, and public policy. Professor Schultz is also holds appointments at the University of Minnesota Law School and at Hamline University in the Criminal Justice Studies Program. He is the author of over sixteen books and over forty articles on topics that include civil service reform, campaign finance reform, land use, constitutional law, and the media and politics. His most recent publications include *Leveraging the Law: Using the Courts to Achieve Social Change* (1998), *The Politics of Civil Service Reform* (1998), *Inventors of Ideas: An Introduction to Western Political Philosophy* (1998), *The Encyclopedia of American Law* (Facts on File, 2002), and *Money, Politics, and Campaign Finance Reform Law in the States* (2002).

Michael J. Shapiro is Professor of Political Science at the University of Hawaii, Monoa, where he teaches classes in political theory, global politics, media, and culture. He received his Ph.D. in political science from Northwestern University. His most recent publications include *Violent Cartographies: Mapping Cultures of War* (University of Minnesota Press, 1997); *Cinematic Political Thought: Narratives of Race, Nation, and Gender* (NYU Press, 1999); and *For Moral Ambiguity: Theory, Genre, and the Politics of the Family* (University of Minnesota Press, 2001).

Stephen Samuel Smith is Associate Professor of Political Science at Winthrop University in Rock Hill, South Carolina. He conducts research on education policy and urban politics, and his publications have appeared in the *Journal of Urban Affairs* and *Educational Evaluation and Policy Analysis*. He is currently completing a book entitled *Boom for Whom? Education, Desegregation, and Development in Charlotte* to be published by SUNY Press in 2003. He recently served as an expert witness for the black plaintiffs in the reopened *Swann* case, the original litigation of which gave rise to the 1971 landmark Supreme Court decision allowing intra-district busing for school desegregation.

R. Claire Snyder is Associate Professor of Government and Politics in the Department of Public and International Affairs at George Mason University where she teaches the history of political thought, women and politics, American political theory, and democratic theory. She is the author of *Citizen-Soldiers and Manly Warriors: Military Service and Gender in the Civic Republican Tradition* (Rowman and Littlefield, 1999). Her current research interests include social conservatism, radical republicanism in the United States and France, and youth civic engagement. Snyder is a longtime associate of the Kettering Foundation, the former director of their projects on the History of Higher Education and the Evolution of Public Life, and a member of their Public-Scholars working group.

Manfred B. Steger is Associate Professor of Politics and Government at Illinois State University, and affiliated faculty member at the Globalization Research Center at the University of Hawaii, Monoa. He specializes in comparative political theory and globalization studies. His many publications include, most recently, *Gandhi's Dilemma: Nonviolent Principles and Nationalist Power* (St. Martin's Press, 2000), *Globalism: The New Market Ideology* (Rowman & Littlefield, 2001), and *Globalization: A Very Short Introduction* (Oxford University Press, forthcoming).

Index

Putnam, Robert, xiii, 1, 4, 45, 164, 183–184, 218; *Bowling Alone*, 1–3, 8, 9, 75, 91–92, 93, 101, 144, 183, 240, 244, 260–262; on leadership, 152, 220, 234–236, 240; *Making Democracy Work*, 6–7, 21, 75, 79, 91, 195–197, 204, 243–244; on race and gender, 179–180; on September 11 attacks, 282–283; as sleuth, 101, 261, 270; social capital concept, 35–36, 128, 61, 70–71, 94, 203–204, 239–242; and Tocqueville, 26, 28–41, 51–52

Ranciere, Jacques, 116–117
Rap music, 113–115. *See also* Media; Television
Rational choice theory, 9–11, 243, 244–245, 265. *See also* Free rider problem
Reagan, Ronald, 159, 177, 246, 265. *See also* Conservatism
Reciprocity, 71. *See also* "Prisoner's dilemma"
Religion, 10–11, 36, 147, 186, 282
Ridge, Tom, 284
Riesman, David, 92–93
Roosevelt, Franklin D., 161, 282, 283
Rosenblum, Nancy, 78

Sandel, Michael, 172, 193
September 11 attacks, 281–282, 283–285
Skocpol, Theda, 135–136
Smith, Adam, 6, 133, 250–251
Social capital: bonding social capital, 7, 80, 267; bridging social capital, 7, 80, 198, 267; definitions, xi, 1, 5–6, 79–80, 128, 140–141, 142, 195, 204, 241–242; and government, 31, 58, 69, 195; *machers*, 220; Putnam's use of, 35, 80, 183, 185, 195, 203–204, 239–240, 267; *schmoozers*, 152, 220
Students for a Democratic Society, 178. *See also* New social movements

Television, 1–2, 121, 272–276. *See also* Media
Tocqueville, Alexis de: on African Americans, 105–106, 120; on aristocracy, 60; on associations, 56–58, 76–78, 88; capitalism, 77; on colonialism, 106–107; on Islam, 103–104; on Native Americans, 102–103, 104–105, 119; political thought, 21–42, 50–60, 99–100, 102–109, 285; Robert Putnam and, 26, 28–41, 51–52, 83, 100–101
Tradition, 8–9, 10, 82. *See also* Political culture
Truman, David, 88–90
Trust, xiii, 81, 168, 169, 170, 191, 195, 218, 241, 244, 284–285

Vietnam War, 2, 156, 158–159, 160, 178, 190
Volunteerism, 40, 51, 71, 149, 162, 174, 175, 185, 197–198, 211–212, 225, 235, 282, 283–284
Voting, xiii, xiv, 2, 37, 159, 198, 285. *See also* Political parties
Voting Rights Act, 1965, 174. *See also* African Americans

Wallace, George, 172
Walzer, Michael, 163
Warren, Mark, 78, 92
Watergate scandal, 2, 156, 190
Welfare, 179,180
Women, 154–155, 178–179, 180. *See also* Feminism
World Bank, 264
World Trade Organization (WTO), 14,193, 238, 255. *See also* Globalization
World War II, 147, 148, 151,159, 160–161, 196, 264, 282–283

X, Malcolm, 176